About This Book

Why is blended learning important?

Developing effective e-learning programs is difficult and complex. There are a dizzying number of tools, technologies, and approaches. "Blended Learning," the integration of e-learning and instructor-led approaches into a seamless program, has become a critical paradigm for training professionals. This book will help training managers, program managers, executives, and developers understand the principles, best practices, and proven methodologies for blended learning.

What can you achieve with this book?

This book walks you through the entire process of blended learning in detail. It defines blended learning, fits blended learning into today's training environment, and describes each step in defining, budgeting, building, managing, and measuring blended learning programs.

How is this book organized?

The book is built on six years of research into successful, innovative, and challenging blended learning programs. It walks the reader through the design, budgeting, development, and management process and is filled with real-world examples and case studies to give the reader specific best practices. Every chapter has a set of "lessons learned," which can be applied directly to the job.

About Pfeiffer

Pfeiffer serves the professional development and hands-on resource needs of training and human resource practitioners and gives them products to do their jobs better. We deliver proven ideas and solutions from experts in HR development and HR management, and we offer effective and customizable tools to improve workplace performance. From novice to seasoned professional, Pfeiffer is the source you can trust to make yourself and your organization more successful.

Essential Knowledge Pfeiffer produces insightful, practical, and comprehensive materials on topics that matter the most to training and HR professionals. Our Essential Knowledge resources translate the expertise of seasoned professionals into practical, how-to guidance on critical workplace issues and problems. These resources are supported by case studies, worksheets, and job aids and are frequently supplemented with CD-ROMs, websites, and other means of making the content easier to read, understand, and use.

Essential Tools Pfeiffer's Essential Tools resources save time and expense by offering proven, ready-to-use materials—including exercises, activities, games, instruments, and assessments—for use during a training or team-learning event. These resources are frequently offered in looseleaf or CD-ROM format to facilitate copying and customization of the material.

Pfeiffer also recognizes the remarkable power of new technologies in expanding the reach and effectiveness of training. While e-hype has often created whizbang solutions in search of a problem, we are dedicated to bringing convenience and enhancements to proven training solutions. All our e-tools comply with rigorous functionality standards. The most appropriate technology wrapped around essential content yields the perfect solution for today's on-the-go trainers and human resource professionals.

www.pfeiffer.com

Essential resources for training and HR professionals

I would like to dedicate this book to my wife, Heidi, who put up with the long nights and early mornings I spent researching, writing, and editing this manuscript. Her continual support made it possible to complete a work of this magnitude.

The Blended Learning Book

Best Practices, Proven Methodologies, and Lessons Learned

Josh Bersin

Pfeiffer

A Wiley Imprint

www.pfeiffer.com

Published by Pfeiffer
An Imprint of Wiley
989 Market Street, San Francisco, CA 94103-1741   www.pfeiffer.com

For additional copies/bulk purchases of this book in the U.S. please contact 800-274-4434.

Pfeiffer books and products are available through most bookstores. To contact Pfeiffer directly call our Customer Care Department within the U.S. at 800-274-4434, outside the U.S. at 317-572-3985 or fax 317-572-4002 or www.pfeiffer.com.

Pfeiffer also publishes its books in a variety of electronic formats. Some content that appears in print may not be available in electronic books.

ISBN: 0-7879-7296-7

Library of Congress Cataloging-in-Publication Data
Bersin, Josh
  The blended learning book:best practices, proven methodologies, and lessons learned / Josh Bersin.
     p. cm.
  Includes bibliographical references and index.
  ISBN 0-7879-7296-7 (alk. paper)
1. Employees—Training of.   2. Employees—Training of—Computer-assisted instruction.
3. Internet in education.   4. Computer-assisted instruction.   I. Title.
  HF5549.5.T7B4815 2004
  658.3'124—dc22   2004006426

Acquiring Editor: *Lisa Shannon*
Director of Development: *Kathleen Dolan Davies*
Editor: *Rebecca Taff*
Senior Production Editor: *Dawn Kilgore*
Manufacturing Supervisor: *Bill Matherly*

Printed in the United States of America

Printing   10 9 8 7 6 5 4 3

Contents

Introduction   xiii

**Chapter One : How Did We Get Here?
The History of Blended Learning**   1

The Evolution of Technology-Based Training   2

Instructor-Led Training   2

Mainframe-Based Training   3

Satellite-Based Live Video   5

The PC CD-ROM Era   6

Development of Learning Management Systems
and AICC   8

Enter Web-Based Training: The First Generation   10

Today: A Wide Range of Options   12

Lessons Learned in This Chapter   12

Chapter Two: The Business of Blended Learning   15

The Issue of Limited Resources   16

Portfolio Management: Identifying High-Impact
Investments   16

Program Portfolio Allocation   18

The Trap of "Cost Reduction" Programs   19

High-Impact Programs 21

Creating Measurable Goals 24

Certification Programs: A Special Case 26

Alignment with Business Objectives 27

Blended Learning Is a Powerful Business Tool 29

Lessons Learned in This Chapter 30

**Chapter Three: Blended Learning
Design Concepts** 31

How Do People Learn? 31

The Goal of Mastery 33

Six Modes of Learning 34

Research Supports the Value of Experiential Learning 39

Blending Works: Thompson Job Impact Study 40

Cultural Goals: Socialization and Gaining Attention 42

The Four Types of Corporate Training 45

Tracking and Reporting as a Program Characteristic 47

Lessons Learned in This Chapter 52

Chapter Four: Proven Blended Learning Models 55

The Two Approaches to Blended Learning 56

Five Specific Blended Learning Models 83

Lessons Learned in This Chapter 94

**Chapter Five: Eight Criteria for Selecting
the Blending Model** 97

Criterion 1: Program Type 98

Criterion 2: Cultural Goals 98

Criterion 3: Audience   101

Criterion 4: Budget   105

Criteriion 5: Resources   106

Criterion 6: Time   111

Criterion 7: Learning Content   113

Criterion 8: Technology   116

Lessons Learned in This Chapter   117

Chapter Six: Developing the Budget   **119**

Sizing the Budget: Define the Size of the Problem   120

Compute Cost Per Learner   122

Economics of Blended Learning   123

The Five Components of the Budget   124

Real Costs: The Blended Learning: What
    Works™ Study   129

Lessons Learned in This Chapter   142

**Chapter Seven: Media Selection:
The Right Blend**   **143**

Review of the Selection Criteria   144

The Sixteen Media Types   144

When to Use Instructor-Led Training   144

When to Use On-the-Job Exercises   146

When to Use Live vs. Self-Study   149

Program Type 1: Information Broadcast Programs   154

Program Type 2: Critical Knowledge Transfer Programs   155

Program Type 3: Skills and Competency Programs   156

Program Type 4: Certified Skills and Competencies   157

Media Selection   159

Lessons Learned in This Chapter   174

Chapter Eight: Content Development   177

The Instructional Design Team   178

Typical Content Development Challenges   179

Developing a Program Plan   180

The Instructional Plan   180

Developing Standards   181

Making Content Reusable   183

e-Learning Content Development Process   184

Working with SMEs   186

Developing Webinar or Live e-Learning Content   187

Development Tools   189

Simulations   193

Content Development Tips and Techniques   200

Outsourcing Content Development   202

Lessons Learned in This Chapter   204

**Chapter Nine: Learning Technology
and Infrastructure   207**

Review of Blended Learning Infrastructure   207

Using and Setting Standards   215

How Much Learning Infrastructure You Need   216

Do You Need an LMS at All?   217

Low-Cost LMS Approaches   218

LCMS and Development Tools   219

Lessons Learned in This Chapter   221

**Chapter Ten: Program Management:
Launch, Rollout, Support**   **223**

The Challenge of Utilizing e-Learning   224

Review the Program Schedule   225

Program Launch   226

Executive and Management Support   227

Specific Launch Events   229

Ongoing Marketing   230

Support and Operations   232

Learning Labs   233

Field Coordinators   234

Measuring and Reporting Progress   235

Communication with Upper Management   237

Communication with Line Management   238

Lessons Learned in This Chapter   242

Moving Forward   **245**

Why Blended Learning Is So Important   245

Where Blended Learning Is Going   246

Appendices   **249**

Appendix A: Case Studies and Solutions

Appendix B: Blended Learning Study: Financial Overview

Appendix: C: Case Study Business Strategies

Appendix D: Program Checklist

Appendix E: Eight Criteria for Media Selection

Appendix F: Sixteen Media Types and Descriptions

Appendix G: Glossary

Appendix H: Selected Samples of Courseware and Media

Appendix I: Sample Detailed Instructional Plan

About the Author   311

Index   313

Pfeiffer Publications Guide   321

Introduction

Internet-Based Learning: An Adventure

Corporate learning is a fascinating subject. Amazon.com alone has more than 117,000 titles that cover training, learning, corporate education, and knowledge management. According to a study done in 2002 by KPMG (now Bearingpoint), nearly 60 percent of corporate knowledge goes out-of-date within three years. Well-run companies know that a vigorous and ongoing investment in employee training is critical to staying competitive.

Ultimately corporate training can be viewed as a business investment. I tend to use the word "training" rather than "learning" because it reinforces the point that training should deliver just enough knowledge, skills, and competencies to drive a business outcome. Unlike other forms of learning, corporate training is very pragmatic. Every dollar invested in training must somehow increase revenue or reduce cost. Although sometimes difficult to measure, these business results do occur when companies focus on the design, development, deployment, and management of excellent programs. I find in my research that it is not unusual for training programs to drive returns-on-investment of ten to one-hundred times their original investment.

Since the advent of computers in the 1960s, organizations have been trying to apply technology to the learning and training process. Technology has the potential to add scale, speed, and efficiency to training. Today's application of technology to training is called "e-learning"—a term that implies the use of the Internet as the center of the process. Much has been written about the potential for e-learning, with one well-known executive, John Chambers of Cisco, claiming that "e-learning will make e-mail look like a rounding error."

This book is about the next step in this adventure: a concept called "blended learning." Blended learning, which we will define in this chapter, integrates the use of the Internet with a rich variety of other approaches and technologies to create an integrated learning experience. Excellent blended learning programs demand a clear understanding of business goals, technology, and the way people learn. Although the concepts of blended learning are not new, the applications in today's environment are.

What This Book Is About

This book is focused on the corporate training market. In my research into the training industry, I see companies rushing headlong into e-learning wherever possible. They are buying "learning management systems" and tools, hiring consultants, going to trade shows, and reading everything they can find. They want to understand which technologies to use when—and how and when to blend them together. My goal in writing this book is to simplify this process and give you a guidebook on the principles, best practices, and lessons learned in blended learning. Much of what you will read here are "guidelines for excellence" we have uncovered by working with many pioneers in the market.

If you are a training manager, program manager, executive, or new to e-learning, this book will give you:

- An understanding of what "blended learning" means;
- A variety of blended learning models (approaches) that have been proven successful;
- A set of tips and techniques for budgeting, selecting technology, developing content, and selecting media;
- A large library of case studies and examples that you can learn from; and

- A set of "lessons learned" in every chapter that you can apply directly to your job.

As an avid practitioner and researcher, I focus on practical examples of What Works™[1]. Although there are many books written about instructional design and theory, this book is focused more on real-world experience. It is filled with examples. I hope that this book gives you, the individual charged with putting training resources to work, the tips, insights, and models to make your programs more effective, efficient, and easy to manage.

Defining Blended Learning

The term "blended learning" has become such a buzzword—so that it has taken on many meanings. For the purposes of this book, we will use the following definition:

> Blended learning is the combination of different training "media" (technologies, activities, and types of events) to create an optimum training program for a specific audience. The term "blended" means that traditional instructor-led training is being supplemented with other electronic formats. In the context of this book, blended learning programs use many different forms of e-learning, perhaps complemented with instructor-led training and other live formats.

In the early days of Internet-based training (only a few years ago), people rushed to put as much content as possible onto the web. Reality has set in. Web-based training alone is not appropriate or sufficient for all problems. In some cases it is a breakthrough, extending the reach of training to people never before able to attend a class. In other cases it costs thousands of dollars and sits on the virtual "shelf." The goal of blended learning is to synthesize

---

[1]WhatWorks in e-learning is a trademark of Bersin & Associates.

training media into an integrated mix—one you can tailor to create a high impact, efficient, and exciting training program.

The e-Learning Evolution: From Novelty to Reality

e-Learning has become a very big business. According to the latest statistics from International Data Corporation, in 2003 the e-learning market reached more than $15 billion in products and services. Corporations report that more than 16 percent of all corporate training is now conducted through technology (*Training* Magazine Industry Survey, November, 2003). Hundreds of universities and for-profit educational institutions offer web-based offerings that supplement, complement, or replace traditional classroom offerings.

As this growth occurs, however, a realization is taking place. The big savings in travel and instructor costs are largely over. It is no longer enough to "put our content on the web" to save money and reach more people. Corporations are flooded with electronic content. Many workers complain that they do not have the time to take hours and hours of online training. In e-learning there is no coffee, no donuts, and no fellow student to chat with while you get away from work.

According to a recent study we completed with more than 1,200 training managers, the biggest challenge companies still face is "getting learners to take online courses" (Bersin & Associates study, Summer 2003).[2] Over and over again companies build or

---

[2]Study conducted through online survey to more than 8,000 corporate training professionals in June of 2003, 1,214 respondents. The two biggest challenges companies face are (1) "It takes too long to build courses" and (2) "Getting learners to take courses."

Does anyone remember Webvan? For a few brief years, many of us in Silicon Valley actually believed that all shopping was going to be done online. Just as we now know that not all shopping is done on the web, we also know that "not all learning will be done on the web."

Training organizations now have many different delivery options, each of which provides a different experience. Sometimes instructor-led training is the most effective approach. The art of e-learning is not the content itself, but building the best mix to optimize the problem at hand. The power is in the "blend."

buy e-learning courses expecting massive enrollments, only to find that the biggest trick is getting people to enroll, engage, and complete.

Why e-Learning Often Fails

Many e-learning programs do fail. In the early days of e-learning, programs suffered from dropout rates of 60 percent and higher. Any program that does not achieve its desired level of enrollment, completion, and business impact is a failure. I frequently talk with companies faced with this situation.

Why do failures occur? There are many reasons, and we walk through most of them in this book. One of the biggest problems is the paradigm itself. Workers today are busy doing their jobs, reading e-mail, and going to meetings. Unlike traditional training, e-learning is very easy to "opt out of." There is no "getting away from the office" to join an e-learning course. There is no "class" to chat with. It is very easy to disengage.

Even worse, Internet-based content is often boring, slow, and buggy. Many off-the-shelf courses are nothing more than pages of text with a few colorful graphics. We are asking people to squeeze this activity into an already overcrowded day of work, meetings, e-mail, family obligations, and commuting. The following quotes illustrate this point well.

> "The concept of 'build it and they will come' does not work. We have to continually market, evangelize, and promote our programs to remind people to complete the programs they have started." (Ceridian, 2003)

> "We tried e-learning alone . . . our e-learning programs simply did not take off. Learners repeatedly told us that they were too busy and could not take the time during the day to focus on our web-based courseware. We found that blending was the only way to move forward from 'awareness' to proficiency and mastery." (Large U.S. Insurance Company, 2003)

Blended learning solves these problems.

The Challenge: Defining the Blend

But how do you create the right blend? In corporate training every program has a slightly different strategy, goal, and audience. No single model or blend of media fits all. There are some basic guidelines (for example, sales training should include scenario-based exercises and practice sales calls), but the right blend depends on many criteria. These include business strategy, program type, audience, budget, resources, content stability, content duration, and technology infrastructure available. One of the goals of this book is to introduce you to these criteria so you can select the right blend more easily.

The other challenge in defining the blend is deciding what media types to use. We discuss sixteen different media types in the book, shown in Table I.1. Each of these media types has its own special strengths and weaknesses, and we will review these in detail in Chapter 7: Media Selection.

Focus on Practical Experience

After nearly five years of research into dozens of blended programs, I am still amazed at the innovations I see in real-world experience. Although instructional design and learning theory are important, best practices come from experience. In this book I take this experience and translate it into useful lessons to show you how to use blended learning for your particular situation. The book will introduce you to models, best practices, issues, technologies, and methodologies that have been proven effective. It will give you lots of examples. And best of all, it will give you the insights that others have learned by developing and launching programs of their own—learning along the way.

This Book: A Proven Approach

This book was written to give you an overall approach to blended learning as well as many detailed tips and techniques to make your programs effective.

Figure I.1. The Blended Learning Process

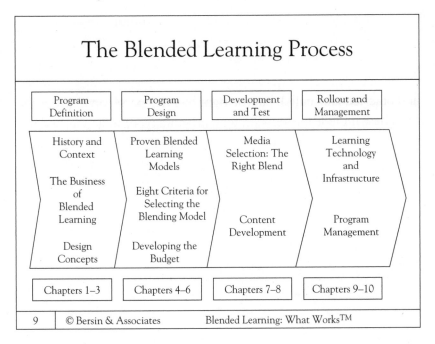

The Blended Learning Process

Program Definition	Program Design	Development and Test	Rollout and Management
History and Context The Business of Blended Learning Design Concepts	Proven Blended Learning Models Eight Criteria for Selecting the Blending Model Developing the Budget	Media Selection: The Right Blend Content Development	Learning Technology and Infrastructure Program Management
Chapters 1–3	Chapters 4–6	Chapters 7–8	Chapters 9–10

9	© Bersin & Associates	Blended Learning: What Works™

In Chapters 1 through 3 we will introduce you to the history, concepts, and business issues in blended learning. From there, in Chapters 4 through 6 we will show you specifically how to define a program and create a cost-justifiable budget. Once you have defined the budget, and program structure, in Chapters 7 and 8 we will walk you through the process of media selection and content development. Then in Chapters 9 and 10 we will describe the critical roles of technology and program management. These chapters give you what you need to know to launch, manage, track, and measure blended learning programs.

In each chapter we will give you detailed lessons learned, case studies, and tips you can use immediately. The Appendix includes a Glossary, details on some of our research, case studies, and job aids.

Lessons Learned in This Chapter

1. Blended learning is the combination of training media to optimize programs for a specific problem. It is not a new concept but today's options are very new.

2. e-Learning suffers the risk of low enrollments, low completion rates, and low impact if not applied correctly. People are busy, so blended programs must motivate, incentivize, and encourage people to engage.

3. There are sixteen basic media types available in blended learning. These fall into categories of synchronous (live) and asynchronous (self-study). Your challenge is deciding when to use which and how to blend them into an optimum program.

4. The approaches to Internet-based training and blended learning are changing and evolving every day, so you must look to best practices to keep current on what works in today's environment.

Chapter One

How Did We Get Here?

The History of Blended Learning

It is important to look at blended learning in perspective. This chapter looks at the history of technology-based training (see Figure 1.1). If you are itching to get into the business of blended learning, you could choose to skip this chapter, but remember to come back and read it later. We will refer to many of these principles throughout the book.

Figure 1.1.   Where We Are

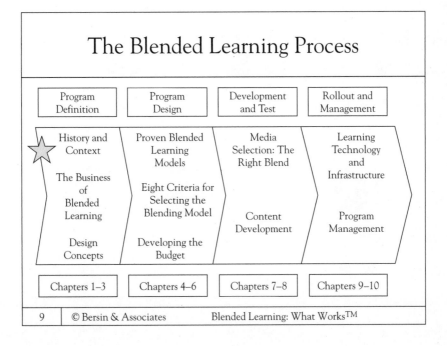

The Blended Learning Process			
Program Definition	Program Design	Development and Test	Rollout and Management
History and Context The Business of Blended Learning Design Concepts	Proven Blended Learning Models Eight Criteria for Selecting the Blending Model Developing the Budget	Media Selection: The Right Blend Content Development	Learning Technology and Infrastructure Program Management
Chapters 1–3	Chapters 4–6	Chapters 7–8	Chapters 9–10

9   © Bersin & Associates   Blended Learning: What Works™

The Evolution of Technology-Based Training

Blended learning is the latest step in a long history of technology-based training. What we describe in this book is the continuation of thirty years of experience using technology for training and education. Although this evolution is far from over, where we are today is an important place, built on several major steps and learnings in this exciting industry. This short chapter on history will prevent us from having to "relearn" what has been learned before.

In the evolutionary steps which led us to where we are today, we start with traditional instructor-led training. (See Figure 1.2.)

Instructor-Led Training

There will always be a role for the teacher, professor, or subject-matter expert to teach and entertain us in a classroom. Instructors convey enthusiasm, expert knowledge, experience, and context.

Figure 1.2.   Evolution of Technology-Based Training

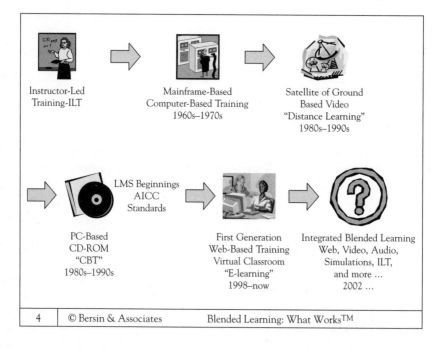

Instructor-Led
Training-ILT

Mainframe-Based
Computer-Based Training
1960s–1970s

Satellite of Ground
Based Video
"Distance Learning"
1980s–1990s

LMS Beginnings
AICC
Standards

PC-Based
CD-ROM
"CBT"
1980s–1990s

First Generation
Web-Based Training
Virtual Classroom
"E-learning"
1998–now

Integrated Blended Learning
Web, Video, Audio,
Simulations, ILT,
and more ...
2002 ...

4   © Bersin & Associates   Blended Learning: What Works™

They can answer questions and change the pace and direction of a class based on the audience. Even more importantly, as we have learned in e-learning, instructor-led training has a cultural effect: people interact and learn from one another.

The biggest challenge with instructor-led training is lack of scale. If you need to train thousands of students, there are only two options: large class sizes or lots of travel. Large class sizes greatly reduce effectiveness and travel is very expensive.

The second challenge with instructor-led training is long deployment times. Most business-critical training problems are time-driven. They must be accomplished within a tight deadline— and the number of hours available to learners is limited. We call these issues "deadline time" (time to complete the entire program) and "duration" (elapsed time for the program).

If a program relies on instructor-led training and has strict deadline times and limits on duration, you have a problem. You can schedule large classes (i.e., fly the entire organization to a convention center and sit them in a huge auditorium) or hire many instructors and send out to teach many classes at the same time. The large class approach (i.e., conference) has strong cultural benefits (it brings people together)—but makes one-on-one teaching and hands-on experience nearly impossible. Flying instructors all over the world is expensive and often impossible if you do not have a cadre of qualified instructors.

Technology is intended to solve these problems: extend the instructor model in space and time. Theoretically, if we use technology we can reach more learners in a shorter period of time—and as a bonus they can learn at their own pace and speed.

Mainframe-Based Training

The first technology-based training approach came with mainframe and mini-computers in the 1960s and 1970s. These systems had the limitation of character-based terminals but the benefit of reaching hundreds to thousands of people at their workplace. A pioneering example of such a system was Plato, a system developed in 1963 by Control Data and the University of Illinois. Plato pioneered the use of computers in traditional educational settings and still exists today.

As Figure 1.3 shows, mainframes were not graphical or visually interesting. Nevertheless, they provided the first platform to extend learning to large audiences through technology.

An Example of Blended Learning

My own experience in e-learning began in the mainframe era. In the 1980s I was first hired by IBM as an entry-level sales engineer. For my first fifteen months as a "trainee" I needed to learn how to sell, implement, and support many complex mainframe hardware and software systems. IBM had developed a well-structured blended curriculum for new hires made up of online product education at the local branch office and a series of classroom and simulation exercises in Dallas, Texas.

In the branch office we used a manual (job aid) and series of online courses (self-study) to learn about the basics of online systems, networking technologies, and business principles. Every exercise we completed at the branch was scored and graded and then sent to both our manager and the sales training organization in Dallas.

Figure 1.3.   Mainframe-Based Interface

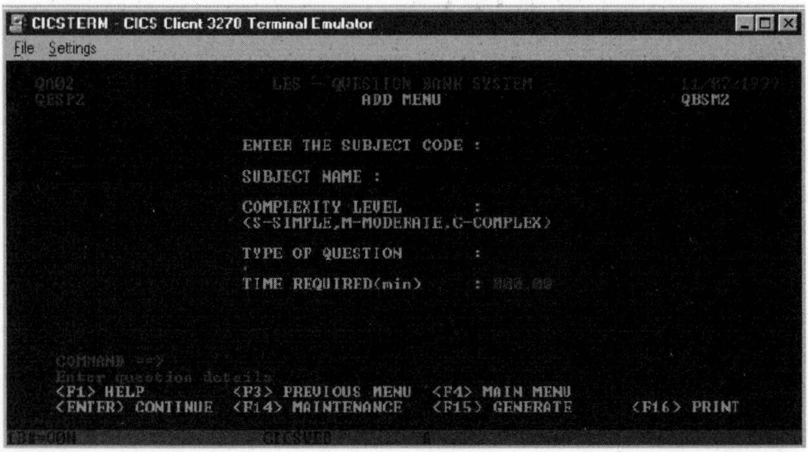

When we traveled to Dallas for our next set of real-world experiences the instructors already knew how well we had done on our branch exercises.

The entire fifteen-month program was a long, simulated sales call on a company called Armstrong Sporting Goods. During the program we learned how to make a sales call on the IT manager, the CFO, the CEO, and the VP of Sales. We learned how to deal with sales objections by performing real sales calls (which were graded). The instructors in Dallas simulated their job roles and treated us exactly as we would be treated when we went out in the real world.

This program had all the elements of a well-designed blended learning program. It was well-structured (all steps were well-defined and scheduled in advance); it took advantage of best-in-class media of the day (mainframe computers); it saved us time (we were working in the branch while taking courses); it created a social culture (learners spent a lot of time together); and it used demonstration and experiential learning (we actually had to "make the sale" in order to pass the course).

The lesson here is that creating a blended program is not dependent on technology. Rather it is a process of problem identification, defining the blending model, and carefully managing and measuring program execution. These are all topics we cover in detail throughout this book.

Bottom line on mainframe based training: it was the beginning of an evolution, and despite its clear limitations in user interfaces, formed the basis for our thinking about blending technology with instructor-led training.

Satellite-Based Live Video

As Figure 1.2 shows, the next step in the technology evolution came in the 1970s when companies started to use video networks to extend the live instructor. Take the problems with instructor-led training above and use TV-based technology to extend the live experience. Learners could sit in a classroom, watch the instructor on TV, chat and interact with other students, and even ask the instructor questions.

A well-run example of this approach is the Stanford University Interactive TV network, which is still used throughout Silicon Valley. Stanford invested in a community-based video network in the 1970s and 1980s that enables Stanford professors to teach courses all over the San Francisco Bay Area without leaving the campus. The students never have to leave their workplace to learn. They submit exercises and tests via courier.

I took live video courses at Stanford and also during my time at IBM. The experience is very close to a real classroom experience. The classrooms have TV cameras that enable the instructor to see the entire class. Students can push a button to ask questions. It truly extends the classroom model into a global delivery solution.

Live video continues to be an important training approach in many companies. General Motors, for example, relies heavily on video-based instruction to train dealers. If the audience is not particularly PC-literate or does not have access to computers, live video training is very appropriate. The challenge is expense: building and maintaining video networks is costly and this approach is rapidly being replaced by lower-cost digital IP-based systems like web-casting, web-based video, and conference calls. We learned from live video that the face, body language, and visual cues from the instructor are an important part of training programs.

The PC CD-ROM Era

To really understand the issues we face today with blended learning it is valuable to understand the CD-ROM era, which forms the basis for much of the web-based training we see today.

In the early 1980s when the first PCs arrived, trainers and educators rushed headlong into PC multimedia technologies. Training technologists love to work on the cutting edge. Computer companies saw this market and started to create special PC models and features designed for multimedia training. Microsoft even went so far as to create a Multimedia PC (MPC) specification.

I call this period the CD-ROM era. Vendors and training departments realized that computers could deliver graphics, sound, video, and rich interactivity. With the extensive storage media available in CD-ROM, these programs could be distributed with ease. The learning experience was rich and perhaps could completely replace the instructor-led model.

The leader in this market was a company called CBT Systems. This company is one of the only major players that successfully made the transition from CD to the web. CBT Systems was the largest provider of CD-ROM training for software and IT professionals. As the CD market started to wane, the company adopted a new web-based approach and relaunched itself as SmartForce around 1999 and then later merged with Skillsoft in 2002. They realized that the CD-ROM era was giving way to new approaches that leverage the web.

It's important to realize that, in the 1980s and 1990s, when companies developed content for CD-ROM they did not use the web-centric approach we have today. They typically relied on high-quality video, complex animations, and professionally developed sound. These titles, often authored in Authorware[1] from Macromedia or Toolbook[2] from Click2Learn, were designed to use high bandwidth media—video, audio, and interactions—elements that do not always translate well to the web. Developers learned that there is a fundamental difference between content authored to run in a CD-ROM (which can house large amounts of video and audio locally) and content authored for the web (where the bandwidth to the PC may be 56k or less in some cases).

---

[1]Authorware® from Macromedia is one of the widest used tools for development of CD-ROM courseware.

[2]Toolbook® from Click2Learn is one of the original and most widely used tools for CD-ROM and now web-based courseware. In 2004 Click2Learn merged with Docent and is now called Sum Total Systems.

Development of Learning Management Systems and AICC

The limitations of CD-ROM technology formed the basis for e-learning as we know it today. The first problem people faced with CD-ROMs was how to manage all the distributed copies of courseware. Who was using it? What were they doing? How could we tell if they were completing? This problem created the need for a "learning management system" (LMS)—a piece of software somewhere on the network that could track and manage all the CD-ROM courses people were taking.

One of the biggest users of CD-ROM technology was the airline industry. Boeing, for example, developed thousands of hours of content devoted to the support and maintenance of aircraft. If the content was distributed to hundreds of PCs, how could Boeing track who was taking these courses and what levels of completion and compliance they were achieving? The answer was the first network-based LMS.

The first LMS systems were developed primarily to manage the enrollment, tracking, and completion of CD-ROM-based content across a network. For this to work, however, the industry needed some standard way for courseware to communicate with the LMS about what the learner was doing. The LMS needs to know when you start a course, what scores you achieve in certain assessments, where you leave off when you are interrupted, and how much time you spend in the course.

To solve this problem, a group of airlines developed a new standard. The Aviation Industry CBT Committee (AICC) developed the most useful and widely implemented approach to enrollment, tracking, reporting, and book-marking electronic content. AICC standards are built into almost every course and every LMS available in the marketplace today.

Today, SCORM (Sharable Content Object Reference Model), a superset of AICC, is slowly becoming the new standard for content packaging and interoperability. SCORM builds on AICC and adds concepts such as reusability, sequencing, and searchable metadata.[3]

"More Experience" Is Not Necessarily an "Effective Experience"

One of the learning experiences from the CD-ROM era is that "more experience" does not necessarily result in an "effective experience." When developers realized that they could deliver audio, video, animation, and interactivity through the computer, they rushed into complex and expensive content production.

Learning requires a combination of **content** plus **context**. Content is meaningless unless it is fit into the context of the business challenge, the learner's abilities and background, the work environment, and the specific learning objectives. Today, this design "truth" continues to drive Internet-based media. We will discuss these issues in detail and give you guidelines to avoid building "the most wonderful course that no one takes" or "the most interesting course that teaches you nothing."

Cost of Maintenance and Deployment Emerge as Major Issues

One of the big issues we discovered in the CD-ROM era was the enormous problems of content deployment and content maintenance. It has been estimated that over the lifetime of a course (and lifetime is a measure of "content stability," which is discussed later), maintenance can become many times more expensive than the initial development. In the CD-ROM model, maintenance became a nightmare. With thousands of CD-ROMs distributed throughout

---

[3]Reusability refers to the ability to use a chapter or "sharable content object" (SCO) in multiple courses. Sequencing refers to making it easy for the learner to branch from chapter to chapter without coding this logic into every course. Searchable Metadata refers to "tagging" content so it can be searched easily with tools like Google.

an organization, it was nearly impossible to replace them with new versions.

Learnings from the CD-ROM Era

Table 1.1 summarizes the lessons learned from the CD-ROM era.

Although the CD-ROM industry grew, it never reached a size greater than $400M or so, largely due to technology limitations shown in the table. Many vendors found that high costs of developing and maintaining CD-ROMs would not sustain a profitable business. Many companies built CD-ROM programs that cost far more than their instructor-led equivalents. The trick was (and still is) to develop a highly interactive experience without going "overboard" on expensive video, authoring, and graphics that were not justified for a given application.

The industry learned extensively from this experience, and the ubiquity of the Internet—coupled with standardized PC software (Windows®)—has given us a whole new set of options. Already the web-based e-learning market is five times larger than the CD-ROM market ever was.

Enter Web-Based Training: The First Generation

In the last few years some important changes have taken place. Web browsers (Internet Explorer® primarily) are ubiquitous. Network access is now relatively common. Computers are fast enough to display sound, broad ranges of color, and video.

These new technologies create a platform that solves many of the problems that plagued the CD-ROM era. Now courseware can be published in one place and easily distributed to thousands of people. The pioneers of web-based training tried to take CD-ROM content and publish it to the web. This approach did not work. CD-ROM-developed content is designed with large video and audio files and "takes over the screen" with its own user interface. When published to the web, it generally results in a slow and sluggish

Table 1.1.   Learnings from the CD-ROM Era

Content can be very expensive to produce.	CD-ROMs were built on the concept of high interactivity, branching, and often video, and therefore took many months and often hundreds of thousands of dollars to build. *Often web-based courseware still suffers from this challenge.*
Content may be difficult to update.	Once cut, a CD-ROM becomes a published work, like a book. Updating it is a laborious process, so content rapidly became out-of-date. *Web-based courseware solves much of this problem, but still requires a maintenance strategy. Some courses are "disposable" and we call these "Rapid e-Learning."*
Technology was difficult to deploy.	CD-ROMs required a "player"—a piece of software that ran in your PC and displayed the content. If you did not have the player, it had to be included on the CD-ROM, which made running the content more prone to errors. Your PC had to have the right sound card, video card, and screen resolution. *Early Internet-based programs suffered from this problem as well, and many programs still do. PCs must have the right plug-ins, bandwidth, and hardware and software configuration.*
Multimedia was not standardized.	Because early PCs did not have standard graphics, sound, or video technology, many CD-ROMs did not run correctly. *In e-learning this problem has largely been resolved by Flash,* but continues to plague programs with video and some simulations.*
Tracking was difficult or impossible.	Some CD-ROMs had tracking, but many did not, so they were essentially books you perused at your own pace. Technology for tracking and reporting was not standardized until very recently (AICC**). *Today, thanks largely to this standard, it is fairly easy to track electronic content. However, we always recommend testing this interoperability, because the "standards" are simply reference guides and are often implemented differently among different vendors.*

*Flash, from Macromedia, is one of the widest used technologies for deployment of highly interactive content.

**AICC, the Aviation Industry CBT Committee, developed one of the most widely used standards for tracking and launching electronic courseware today. It is still the most used learning management system to launch and track learning courseware.

experience. The tools used for CD-ROM content (Authorware, as an example) were not designed to edit HTML and other technologies used on the web.

We now know that web-based training is new and different. It uses HTML and browser-based technologies like Flash®. It usually runs within a portal or an online learning environment. It leverages the power of search and linking, which is unique to the Internet.

Today: A Wide Range of Options

This brings us to where we are today. Today training organizations have a wide range of options for blended learning. Self-study (asynchronous) options include web-based courseware, simulations, EPSS systems, books, and job aids. Live (synchronous) options include webcasting, live video, conference calls, and instructor-led training. The key issues we discuss in this book are deciding which to use when and how to blend them together to solve a particular business problem.

Lessons Learned in This Chapter

1. Blended learning is not a new concept, but the tools available to us today are new.

2. The origins of blended learning are the simple but powerful desire to extend the classroom "people-centric" experience in space and time.

3. Blended learning can be accomplished through any variety of media, whether it is mainframe-based, video-based, or web-based. The key issue is not making the technology exciting but fitting technology seamlessly into a program appropriate for the problem at hand.

4. CD-ROM-developed media, while important in today's world, is authored differently from web-based media. It is

difficult if not impossible to use the same content for both delivery technologies. Web content can be distributed on a CD-ROM, but content authored for CD-ROM rarely works well in web delivery.

5. The web as a delivery and learning platform is new. It uses new tools and approaches which build from the CD-ROM world but are also dramatically different.

6. The history of technology-based training teaches us that problems such as appropriate content development, content maintenance, deployment, and distribution are critical in any program.

7. Standards like AICC provide excellent ways of tracking student progress. They were developed to track content usage and completion and are now embedded into most commercial LMS systems. SCORM, the latest specifications for tracking and content structure, builds on the principles of AICC.

8. Today's blended learning approaches build on years of experience but apply new technologies and delivery options that will continue to change.

Chapter Two

The Business of Blended Learning

In the corporate market, training is ultimately a business tool. All training programs are built with a business goal, which ultimately translates into increased revenue or reduced costs. Decisions about how to create the program and what media elements to use must be made in the context of this business goal. The larger the potential return, the more money you can justify spending.

Figure 2.1.   Where We Are

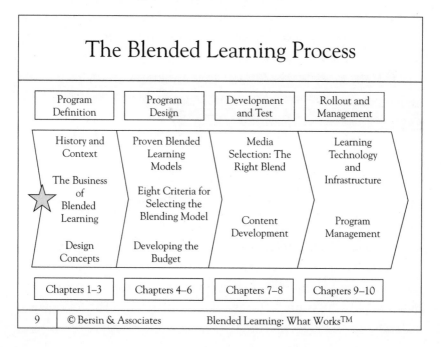

The Blended Learning Process			
Program Definition	Program Design	Development and Test	Rollout and Management
History and Context	Proven Blended Learning Models	Media Selection: The Right Blend	Learning Technology and Infrastructure
The Business of Blended Learning	Eight Criteria for Selecting the Blending Model		
		Content Development	Program Management
Design Concepts	Developing the Budget		
Chapters 1–3	Chapters 4–6	Chapters 7–8	Chapters 9–10

9   © Bersin & Associates   Blended Learning: What Works™

This chapter will give you the framework and tools to refine your business strategy so you understand how to make blended learning investments (see Figure 2.1).

The Issue of Limited Resources

My assumption is that your training organization has a limited budget. According to the American Society of Training and Development's 2003 survey (and this is consistent from year to year), companies spend between 1 and 3 percent of payroll on training. Although this budget translates into a large number of dollars, it is in direct competition with other corporate initiatives: hiring new sales representatives, increasing manufacturing capacity, or developing a new marketing budget. It is very easy to cut training budgets. Over and over again I hear training managers concerned that their CFO or VP of HR is going to cut the budget.

As a training manager, the issue you then face is how to best allocate this limited budget so that your executive team and line-of-business management remain convinced that your programs are driving business impact. The first challenge then, is to decide which programs to fund. From there you must then decide when and where to apply a blended approach.

It is important to realize that blended learning programs typically cost two to three times (and sometimes more) as much as instructor-led or e-learning programs do. With a limited budget, you have to make the first decision: where does blending make sense?

Portfolio Management: Identifying High-Impact Investments

Here is an excellent approach that we call the "Training Investment Model." I originally saw it at a major insurance company and later noticed it used in other companies. It is a powerful scoring methodology to help allocate training investments based on four quadrants. Every training program falls into one of the four quadrants shown in Figure 2.2.

Figure 2.2.   Training Investment Model

The Training Investment Model™

	Run the Business (Operational)	WIN in the Market (Strategic)
Custom to You	ERP Rollout Call Center Application Training Product Introduction	**Your Secret Sauce** Business critical skills, competencies, and processes for your company
Off the Shelf	IT Training Desktop Skills General Management Skills	Project Management Sales Techniques Customer Service Techniques

Highest ROI Apply Blended Learning Here

| 1 | © Bersin & Associates | Blended Learning: What Works™ |

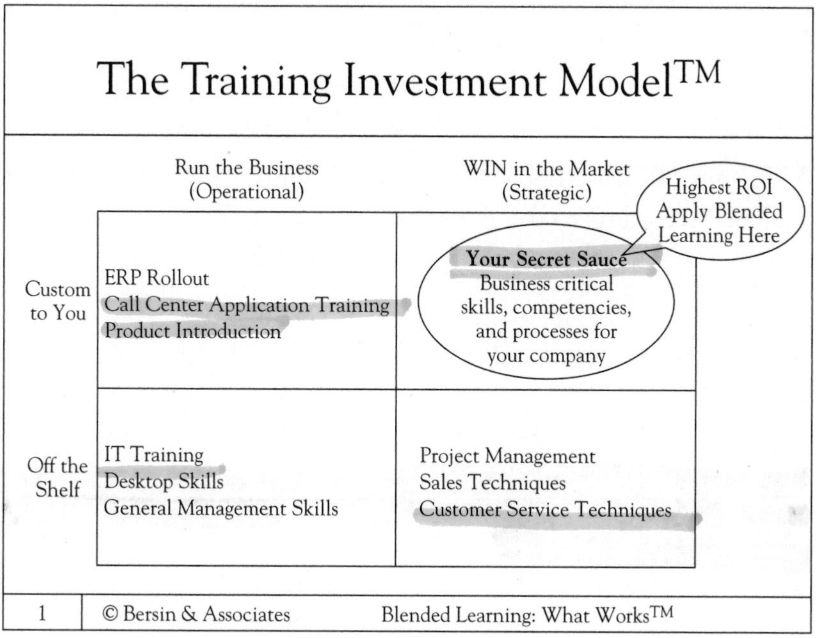

Each of your program's content falls into one of these four quadrants. On the vertical axis you see two categories: "off the shelf" and "custom to you." Off-the-shelf programs are those you can purchase from outside vendors. IT training, some sales training, some management training, desktop application training, and many other topics are available off the shelf. Custom programs are those you must develop internally. Examples of custom programs are training for your internal ERP systems, new hire training, first-time manager training, and most executive education.

Across the horizontal axis are two other categories: programs required to run the business and programs that drive strategic competitive advantage. Run-the-business programs are those that reduce costs, increase efficiency, or maintain sales growth or revenue. We often call them operational programs. "Competitive advantage" programs are those that increase market share, drive strategic corporate transformations, align organizations, or otherwise make your company "win" over the competition.

Every company will have different programs that fall into the left column versus the right column. In a typical insurance company, for example, IT training is a run-the-business program, because IT skills are critically important but will not create competitive advantage. In a consulting and services firm like EDS, however, IT skills will fall into the right column because these skills will make the company win in the market.

As you try to map your programs into these four quadrants you will find that a large number of your programs (and much of your time) are spent in the left side of the quadrant. You will realize that only a small number of strategic programs go into the upper right. Programs in the upper right are those that will typically generate very high returns on investment and *these are the ones you should target for blended learning.*

Program Portfolio Allocation

One of the big benefits of this mapping approach is that it helps you create a budget allocation model. The insurance company mentioned above, for example, decided that they will allocate their program dollars as follows: 40 percent to the upper right quadrant, 30 percent to the lower right quadrant, 20 percent to the upper left quadrant, and 10 percent to the lower left quadrant. In essence then, 70 percent of their discretionary training dollars are going into strategic programs. Although this may seem like a ruthless approach, it forces them to be strategic with their time and investments. I have recommended this to many companies, and the methodology is powerful.

For our insurance company client, their allocation resulted in the model illustrated in Figure 2.3. The most strategic programs in their company are policy pricing, claims investigation, claims reserving, and performance management. Later we will show you how they apply blended learning to the challenge of performance management.

**Figure 2.3.   How an Insurance Company Allocates
Its Training Budget**

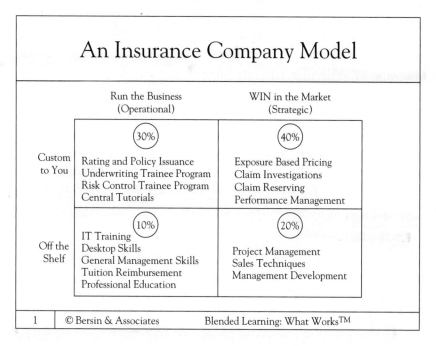

One interesting thing this chart shows is that IT skills, professional education, and much off-the-shelf content often fall into the
lower left quadrant.

Lesson

Use the four-quadrant "Training Investment Model" to prioritize your program investments based on strategic value and apply
blended learning to those with the highest overall impact on
your organization's strategic objectives.

The Trap of "Cost Reduction" Programs

At the time of the writing of this book, the U.S. economy is coming out of one of the deepest recessions in fifteen years. Much of the
growth of e-learning and blended learning has been a drive to
reduce the cost of training.

As we described in the history of technology-based training, e-learning technologies have always been used to extend the classroom experience to more learners and at a lower cost.

In considering blended strategies, you should try to categorize your training programs into two broad categories: *cost reduction programs* and *high-impact programs.*

"Cost Reduction Programs"

If you are embarking on blended learning and e-learning to reduce costs, let me warn you about a few traps. First, *e-learning may not reduce costs.* It will shift costs from variable (instructor salaries and travel) to fixed (LMS infrastructure, content development, and technology upgrades). In this shift, you will have to incur significant new investments, hire new people, develop new skills, and generally spend time and money on infrastructure which, by itself, trains no one. Only by carefully managing this capital investment will e-learning truly save money.

Second, most cost reduction programs only save costs one time. Once you have shifted a program from instructor-led-training to web-based or blended, those cost savings have been captured. You cannot go back year after year and continue to save more.

Third, and most importantly, by focusing on cost reduction you have suddenly changed your training organization from a strategic resource into a cost center. *The business impact of reducing the cost of training is virtually zero.* If, as the ASTD data tells us, training is an investment of 1 to 3 percent of payroll and you cut the training budget by 30 percent (a very large number), you may be reducing overall company costs by .33 to 1 percent of payroll. These savings will typically have little or no effect on the bottom line. There is just not that much money to be saved.

This is not to say that you should not be focused on training efficiency. Indeed, your ability to reach more people at a low cost is one of your most important goals. *But do not try to measure the ROI of a training program based on how much money you saved.*

These are one-time savings, and my argument would be to think about how high the ROI would be if you eliminated that program altogether!

High-Impact Programs

On the other hand, examine the metrics of focusing training on high-impact problems. If every dollar you spend on training increases worker productivity by a few percent, your training programs will generate enormous returns on investment.

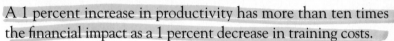

> A 1 percent increase in productivity has more than ten times the financial impact as a 1 percent decrease in training costs.

One of our research clients, a large Canadian telecommunications company, spent two years developing an enterprise-wide catalog of e-learning programs solely to reduce training costs. They centralized LMS systems, signed a large agreement with a catalog content provider, and shut down many of their instructor-led programs. The program manager developed slide after slide showing top management how much money they had saved. Two years later when I talked with them, they were rebuilding many of their initiatives in field service training, call center training, and project management training because they had lost focus on the high-impact (or upper-right quadrant) programs.

What are some examples of "high-impact" programs? Let's look at programs from three companies: the global manufacturer Siemens, a large manufacturer, and a major U.S. retail electronics chain.

In 2000 and 2001 Siemens decided that in order to drive a higher market capitalization it needed to be listed on the New York Stock Exchange. To accomplish this the company was required to make a complete switch from German accounting rules to U.S. Generally Accepted Accounting Practices (GAAP). (There are many differences in depreciation rules, accounting for inventory, and other important items.) This change affected every one of

Siemens' 1,000+ business units and required re-training of the accounting and financial professionals in each of these units. Clearly this was a time-driven mission-critical problem.

Siemens, with help from Accenture, developed a powerful blended program built around a series of business simulations. Every financial professional in Siemens was required to become "certified" by successfully completing these simulations. The Office of the CFO created a list of all employees who must be certified, created an extensive website, assigned local coordinators, and created a strict program timeline for completion. Learners were required to successfully complete each individual simulation before they even received the next one. The program was very carefully developed, rolled out, and managed.

The result: one of the fastest accounting transformations possible. Siemens switched accounting practices in less than two years and is now listed on the NYSE. As you can imagine, the benefits of this program run into the billions of dollars. Blending was easily cost-justified.

The second example of a high-impact blended program is one that most companies face: a major ERP software upgrade. This company, a major distributor of industrial products (we call them Company W), was rolling out a new version of SAP. This particular company is one of SAP's largest customers and processes tens of thousands of transactions per day. Any glitch in the changeover could potentially cost millions of dollars in lost sales. The CEO mandated a strict and well-managed blended learning program to make sure that all order entry and sales personnel were well trained before the switchover took place.

The company built a blended program that included a series of field kickoff meetings, online simulation exercises, conference calls, and job aids. The program was built and rolled out under close management with several dedicated project coordinators in the training organization. In order to give sales teams high levels of support and motivation, the training organization recruited the help of local field coordinators in each sales location. This extensive change management process dramatically increased the expense of the program but was easily justified by the size of the change taking place.

Needless to say, the program was a success. In the process this company found that the biggest challenge they faced was a skills gap in understanding the business processes of order entry, discounting, returns, and customer service. These basic processing skills were fundamental to understanding the SAP system. As a result, new modules and exercises were added to develop and reinforce these strategic business skills.

"We could not afford this program to fail," said the CEO of this particular company. "This order system processes, many millions of dollars per day and controls our interface to the customer. Training was critical to our successful cutover."

Our final high-impact example is the development of a blended sales curriculum for a large consumer electronics retailer (Company C). They faced a daunting challenge: rapidly changing products that use complex technology and a labor force of young, high-turnover sales and service personnel. Their traditional "back of the store" sales training was not keeping up.

This company's first effort at online training was a large curriculum of e-learning courses delivered through PCs in the back of the store. Although this resulted in a lot of training, it was not clear that it resulted in improved sales and customer satisfaction. Over time they realized that each sales representative needed a specific curriculum that certified his or her skills in "Audio," "HDTV," "PCs," or "Phone and Wireless." In addition to product skills, employees needed certification and training in customer service, objection handling, and negotiation.

The result was a series of manager-facilitated learning tracks that require line managers to work directly with employees during these online certifications. As we describe later in the book, by blending e-learning with manager interventions, this company dramatically increased effectiveness and employee satisfaction.

"We have more than six hundred stores nationwide that distribute retail electronics to a variety of customer types. Some of our customers are very sophisticated and challenge our salespeople. Our salespeople are often young and unfamiliar with the selling process, and one of our biggest challenges is turnover. The original goal of our blended learning program was to increase sales but we found that the biggest impact of the program was an increase in employee confidence and a resulting reduction in turnover. We now see this blended learning program as a required infrastructure to staying competitive in retail electronics." (Senior VP of HR)

Typical high-impact programs focus on business initiatives such as:

- Increase sales per employee;
- Improve sales productivity;
- Enable the rollout a new product or IT system quickly;
- Reduce errors in manufacturing;
- Develop new management skills, which results in improved morale or reduced turnover;
- Improve employee job satisfaction and productivity;
- Roll out and implement a change in company structure or processes;
- Implement a new IT technology quickly and seamlessly; and/or
- Reduce the time to productivity of new employees.

These programs warrant blended approaches.

Creating Measurable Goals

One issue that comes up continually in corporate training is the problem of measuring impact. We completed a large survey of training measurement practices in the Fall of 2003 and found that, among more than 8,000 training professionals, only 11 percent even attempt to measure the business impact of their programs (Bersin & Associates, 2003 study).

Why is this? The tools and processes of measuring the business impact of training are not easy to use or well-defined. Rather than focus on measurement techniques in this book, I would like to highlight one important business strategy in blended learning: *create a measurable goal.* If you have a measurable business goal, you will be able to cost-justify your budget (see Chapter 10).

Some examples of measurable business goals include:

- "This blended program to roll out our new mobile commerce solution will drive sales increase of $3M in the first year, and we will do this by making sure that 80 percent of our sales representatives pass a simple qualification assessment." (Focus on sales output/*British Telecom*)

- "This blended program for field service training will eliminate the backlog for training from six weeks to 'just in time' and maintain the learning results we achieved with our instructor-led model." (Focus on training throughput and cost savings/*Verizon*)

- "This blended program for manufacturing certification will enable us to triple the number of engineers who are certified and improve manufacturing quality by making all plants 90 percent compliant." (Focus on manufacturing quality/*Large Semiconductor Manufacturer*)

As a program manager you have many decisions to make. Your overriding business goal should be your guiding light. If your goals are vague, such as to "increase awareness" or "educate about a new regulation," you will find it difficult to decide how much money, time, and effort to spend on various media in your blended learning. Specific business goals help you decide how much money to spend and what kind of blended program to build. Typical business measures that can be correlated to training include:

- Sales: time to quota (new hire training);
- Sales: product revenue increase (new product launch);
- Sales: sales volume per customer (solution selling);
- Sales: sales per hour or per customer (call center sales);
- Service: time to resolution (call center);
- Service: number of "second calls" (call center, field service);
- Service: customer satisfaction ratings (call center, field service);
- Service: number of service calls (customer training);
- Employees: retention rate (any type of job training influences this);
- Employees: productivity (manufacturing, IT, many areas);
- Employees: job satisfaction (corporate university training);
- Employees: satisfaction with company or manager (corporate university training);
- Manufacturing: rework rate or scrap rate (quality or process training);
- Manufacturing: error rate (quality or process training);
- Manufacturing: productivity (quality or process training); and
- Many, many more.

Your goal should be to decide which of these metrics you are trying to affect, and then to set in place a plan to measure this metric before, after, and long after training. We plan to dive into this process in much more detail in a book on training analytics.

Certification Programs: A Special Case

In many industry, government, and military programs the business goal is simple: we must be certified. Period. The term "certification" means that people must achieve a certain standardized level of learning (typically measured by an assessment or completion status) and maintain that level over a period of time.

Many industries (healthcare and financial services, for example) have strict certification rules. In the healthcare industry all employees must be certified that they understand the U.S. Government HIPAA rules for patient privacy and protection of confidential information. In financial services and accounting, many professionals must be certified that they understand the compliance rules of the Sarbanes-Oxley regulations.

In the next chapter we will introduce the concept of "mastery" and the four types of training programs. Certification programs are one of these four types. They set very specific learning and completion objectives. In particular, blended learning programs for certification require much more measurement. Typically, these programs require a more advanced learning management system with tracking of assessment results—and they often have expiration rules. These additional features result in additional cost and complexity. From a business standpoint, then, you must make sure that if you are creating a certification program it is well worth the extra time and expense.

Alignment with Business Objectives

The term "alignment" is often used in training. Training investments must be "aligned" with strategic corporate objectives. We have done much research on this topic and typically find that highly effective training organizations have steering committees and quarterly or semiannual meetings between training management and line-of-business management. This process ensures that programs are aligned with the most current and urgent business objectives.

Your challenge in blended learning is not only alignment but time. The development of a blended program typically takes months, and rollout may take many more months. You must have advanced knowledge about a strategic new product initiative, a merger, reorganization, or other business change that requires a blended learning program.

In some cases you will find that in order to solve a particular pressing business problem there are long-term skills gaps that must be closed.

In the case of a the distributor of industrial products mentioned above (Company W), the training organization found that the biggest challenge they faced was a skills gap in understanding the business processes of order entry, discounting, return, and customer service. Understanding these basic business processes was fundamental to understanding the SAP system. As a result, the SAP upgrade training program needed modules on the fundamentals of these business processes.

As you go through the alignment process, make sure that you seek out skills gaps—not just company initiatives. The type of blend and media you select can be used to close these gaps, but only if you identify them in the business alignment process. As we will describe in the next chapter, blended programs are best used when the business problem requires that you develop "mastery."

Figure 2.4, compliments of Accenture, shows a proven approach to integrate learning with business objectives.

Figure 2.4.   Aligning Training with Business Needs

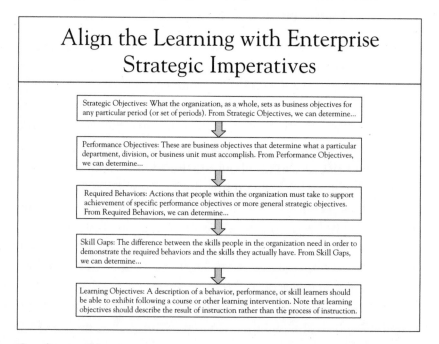

Align the Learning with Enterprise Strategic Imperatives

Strategic Objectives: What the organization, as a whole, sets as business objectives for any particular period (or set of periods). From Strategic Objectives, we can determine...

Performance Objectives: These are business objectives that determine what a particular department, division, or business unit must accomplish. From Performance Objectives, we can determine...

Required Behaviors: Actions that people within the organization must take to support achievement of specific performance objectives or more general strategic objectives. From Required Behaviors, we can determine...

Skill Gaps: The difference between the skills people in the organization need in order to demonstrate the required behaviors and the skills they actually have. From Skill Gaps, we can determine...

Learning Objectives: A description of a behavior, performance, or skill learners should be able to exhibit following a course or other learning intervention. Note that learning objectives should describe the result of instruction rather than the process of instruction.

Compliments of Accenture.

If you use a methodology such as this, you will make sure that you stay aligned and also keep a clear eye on the business objectives, performance objectives, and learning objectives for your program.

Blended Learning Is a Powerful Business Tool

Let me add one more thought here. Blended learning programs that drive major business impact are not easy. They have many moving parts. There are myriad options for technology, processes, and architectures that may meet a particular need. You have to think about media, content development, technology, business processes, budgets, and program management. You must consider business issues, people issues, cultural issues, and technology issues. In deployment you must manage all these parts into a cohesive and trackable program.

On the other hand, the tool of blended learning has tremendous impact. If you succeed, the programs you develop by using this approach will generate millions of dollars of business benefit for your company. As a training professional, one of your jobs is to show your organization how this powerful tool can be used to drive impact today.

My goal here is to give you a toolkit. You will not apply the same approach to every problem. This book will show you how to use all the resources at your disposal to apply just enough e-learning (and the right types) for the problem at hand. The Internet is a rich and complex set of technologies and media. If you spend some time learning about all the tools at your fingertips, you will end up with a better result.

One final preamble thought. *Training and education are all about people.* Our goal is to inform, educate, and change the behavior of people. Blended learning forces you to think about your audience in detail. It forces you to think about the exercises, collaboration, and activities that will drive your program home. As you explore the blended learning process, you will find that you are forced to think hard about the people you are reaching—their motivation, skills, background, jobs, technology savvy, and even lifestyles. Such a process always leads to a more interesting, effective program. Let's dive in.

———

Lessons Learned in This Chapter

1. Training organizations live in a world of limited resources, so you must focus on the most cost-effective use of program dollars to drive high impact.

2. Training programs must be prioritized (using the four-quadrant "Training Investment Model") to understand where to apply blended learning to obtain the highest return. Select your own allocation model so you can make sure you are not over-investing in low-return programs.

3. Cost-reduction programs are not a strategic way to invest in blended learning. Consider cost-reduction a trap.

4. Create measurable goals at the outset to serve as your guiding light for budgeting and program design.

5. If you define a need for certification programs, make sure the business goal is warranted because costs and complexity will be much higher.

6. Business alignment is strategic and important. Align regularly to make sure that you can stay "ahead of the business" with blended learning programs. Look for skills gaps and "mastery" problems.

7. Blended learning is a powerful tool that requires you to stay vigilant, open-minded, and creative. Think about it as a tool that improves performance, not a tool that reduces cost.

Chapter Three

Blended Learning Design Concepts

In this chapter we dive right into blended learning in practice. The key to making blended learning work is understanding some of the theories and concepts that have been proven in practice. We will introduce a very important concept: the *four types of corporate training*. These four types give you the framework for building the right blended model. Then we will discuss two approaches and five models in detail, so that you can select the right one for your needs.

The term "model" refers to a proven approach I have seen used in multiple successful implementations. You can build any blended learning model you wish—and we expect that as technology changes new models will appear. For the purpose of this book you should consider a *model* as an instructional template that helps you decide how to select and blend media for best results.

As you can see from Figure 3.1, we are entering the meat of the first phase of blended learning: program definition.

How Do People Learn?

No discussion of blended learning should leave out some principles of instructional design. Much research has been applied to learning styles, and we can apply this research to blended learning design.

Years of research into primary and secondary education has proven that people learn in different ways. There appear to be

Figure 3.1.   Where We Are

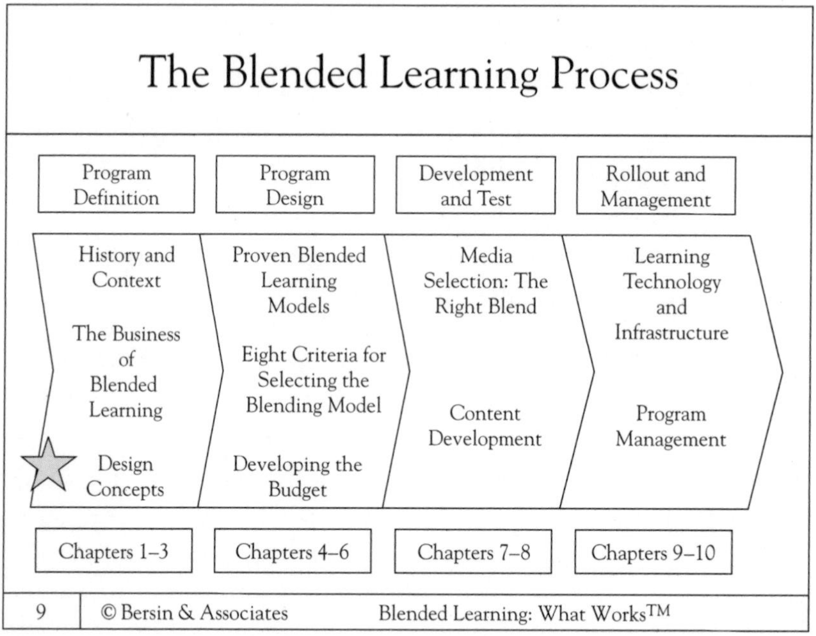

Program Definition	Program Design	Development and Test	Rollout and Management
History and Context	Proven Blended Learning Models	Media Selection: The Right Blend	Learning Technology and Infrastructure
The Business of Blended Learning	Eight Criteria for Selecting the Blending Model	Content Development	Program Management
Design Concepts	Developing the Budget		
Chapters 1–3	Chapters 4–6	Chapters 7–8	Chapters 9–10

9   © Bersin & Associates   Blended Learning: What Works™

three primary ways an individual learns—and each individual favors one or two as their primary approaches:

- *Visual Learners:* Approximately 50 to 70 percent of the population are characterized as "visual learners," meaning that they relate most effectively to written information, diagrams, images, and pictures. Visual learners like to take notes, write on the whiteboard, and create and view PowerPoint® slides with graphics. Most Internet-based courseware is targeted toward visual learning. (I know that I am a visual learner, because my best ideas and concepts come from diagrams and pictures.)

- *Auditory Learners:* Approximately 20 to 40 percent of the population are characterized as "auditory learners," people who learn best by hearing. These are people who like to listen to lectures and take notes later, and who often excel at public speaking and direct interaction. (My son is an auditory learner; he seems to remember every conversation we have ever had.)

- *Kinesthetic Learners:* A smaller percentage of the population (5 to 20 percent) learn best through touching and doing things. These are people who learn by imitating, trying, holding, and feeling things.

We also know from experience that the deepest learning takes place by doing, often called "experiential learning." In corporate training we usually focus on developing and refining specific skills: "how to handle a sales objection" or "how to enter an order into SAP." No amount of lecture or images truly develops these skills until the learner actually attempts to perform the work—and then learns from his or her mistakes.

The Goal of Mastery

In corporate training, I use the word "mastery" to describe the depth of learning for a given subject or process. To develop *mastery* of a subject or a process, you must be highly *proficient* (you can perform the task correctly) and *experienced* (you can undertake the task under a wide range of conditions). Experience is key: it creates retention—the ability to remember and apply these skills rapidly when needed. (Consider the example of driving a car. You can learn to drive in driver's education . . . but you do not truly become a safe driver until you have driven at night, in the rain, on mountain roads, and in many other conditions.) Here is my definition of mastery:

$$\text{Mastery} = \text{Proficiency} + \text{Retention}$$

For any given business problem, you as a training manager must decide *how much mastery you want to achieve.* (Or, more importantly, how much mastery the business problem justifies.) Programs that drive higher levels of mastery are more expensive and complex to build and deploy. However, as learners reach higher levels of mastery, their productivity, effectiveness, and motivation go up. In every learning situation mastery is valuable, but from a business standpoint it may not be cost-justified. A few examples will help explain this tradeoff.

> High Degree of Mastery–Intel: In Intel's manufacturing excellence program the goal was to develop a high level of mastery of semi-conductor manufacturing processes. Mastery was cost-justified by the impact on yields and manufacturing costs. Expert manufacturing drives higher yields, which in turn can result in hundreds of millions of dollars of profit. The result: a mastery-driven certification program (in blended form) that cost millions to develop and takes months to complete.

> Lesser Degree of Mastery–Novell: Novell launches twenty to thirty new products and services to their channel partners every year (several per month). The goal of Novell's product introduction training is not mastery but awareness—enough awareness to enable channel partners to position, introduce, and sell these new products. Novell's channel training programs seek to introduce new material and show resellers how to fit these new products into their existing skills in selling and servicing Novell products and services. Mastery goals were low, and the blended program was much simpler.

Is mastery your goal? Not always. As we will discuss later under the heading "Four Types of Corporate Training," some business-critical programs should not necessarily try to drive high levels of mastery.

Six Modes of Learning

If you decide that your goal is to obtain a high level of mastery (and we will discuss how you make that decision in this chapter), what instructional principles and techniques should you rely on? Here is an easy way to understand this problem.

Consider the following hierarchy of six modes of learning shown in Figure 3.2.

Figure 3.2.   Six Modes of Learning

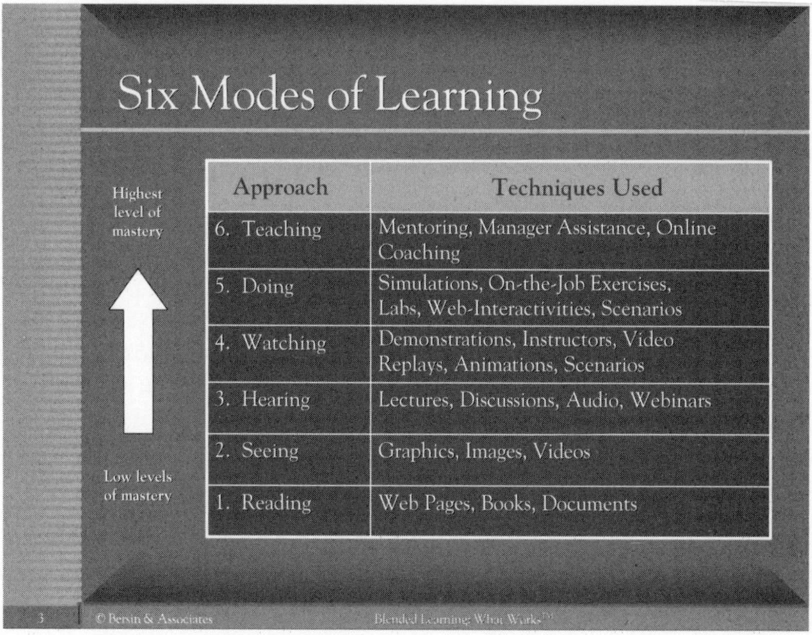

Six Modes of Learning

	Approach	Techniques Used
Highest level of mastery	6. Teaching	Mentoring, Manager Assistance, Online Coaching
↑	5. Doing	Simulations, On-the-Job Exercises, Labs, Web-Interactivities, Scenarios
	4. Watching	Demonstrations, Instructors, Video Replays, Animations, Scenarios
	3. Hearing	Lectures, Discussions, Audio, Webinars
Low levels of mastery	2. Seeing	Graphics, Images, Videos
	1. Reading	Web Pages, Books, Documents

3   © Bersin & Associates   Blended Learning: What Works?

1. Reading

The easiest way to "teach," of course, is to give people things to read. When material is in a well-designed book form, reading is very effective for visual learners. In web form, reading is less valuable because people will not and cannot read long manuscripts on the web. For people who are not visual learners (this is the vast majority of workers in corporate positions), reading is a source of reference material, not learning.

2. Seeing

The next technique up the hierarchy is "seeing." Here we take text and add diagrams, photographs, and images. As we all know, visual images add tremendous new conceptual understanding. In a web form, visual images can be animated to show moving processes and can even include interactivities (slider bars, push buttons, knobs)

Figure 3.3.   Example of Typical Page-Turning
Web-Based Courseware

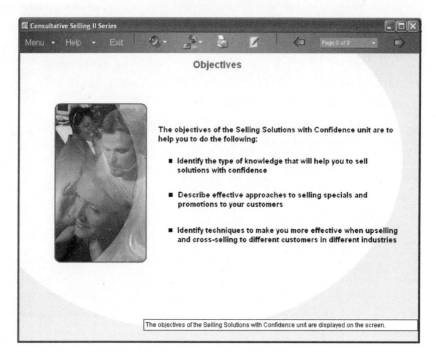

to turn them into mini-animations. In many cases, the diagrams and images are static, and we end up with a web-based book.

Most traditional early web-based courseware used this technique. It is sometimes called "page turning" because it is very much like a book. An example from the Thomson NETg library is shown in Figure 3.3.

3. Hearing and 4. Watching

The next set of techniques add sound, motion, and demonstrations. These techniques include instructor lectures, demonstrations, videos of real-world examples, and scenarios. We have taken the learners one step up the learning ladder because now they can see and hear people actually explain and demonstrate concepts.

In the example above, the learner can choose to listen to a narrator read the text. This adds auditory learning to the mix, improving interest and retention. Here's another example.

> Ninth House, Inc., a leading e-learning provider of management and executive education, has invested in millions of dollars of TV-quality videos to help teach leaders how to handle various leadership and motivational situations. These high-quality programs, while expensive to produce, drive understanding and mastery at a much higher level than do traditional books or web-based courseware. Examples of Ninth House, Inc. content are shown in Chapter 8.

5. Doing (Experiential Learning)

The highest level of mastery comes from experiential learning: learning by doing. Ask a call center agent to take a live call. Give a telephone repairman a phone to fix. See if the order entry clerk can enter a product return. These are the learning activities that create high levels of understanding, context, and retention. Most instructional designers and teachers will tell you that no one ever truly masters any subject until he or she has actually done the job for an extended period of time. Blended learning should strive to create experiential activities.

The biggest trend in experiential learning in web-based instruction is simulation. Simulations are a special form of web-based training that immerse the learner in a real-world situation. There are several forms of simulation, which we will cover in Chapter 8, Content Development. An example of an online simulation is shown in Figure 3.4, from the NETg Call Center course. The characters shown here behave differently depending on how the learner answers a given question.

Of course learning by doing is also possible through on-the-job exercises and other real-world activities.

Figure 3.4.   Simulation—Learning by Doing

Compliments of Thomson NETg.

6. Learning by Teaching

By far the most valuable way to master a subject is to teach it. This approach is often applied in corporate training. Let me give you a personal example.

> When I was at IBM fifteen years ago, one of the most valuable developmental programs for sales management was to teach new hire sales training. Bright, high-potential managers were given a two-year rotational position at the Entry Marketing Education center in Dallas. This position took people out of the field and into a full-time job as a training manager and teacher.
>
> There were many benefits to this approach. First, sales managers who spent two years in this program became some of the most effective sales executives in the company. Through the process of training new hires, they came to understand all the intimate and subtle issues in sales management, sales techniques, and the training of new employees. Second, this process

gave the program a huge degree of legitimacy and "buy-in" from the IBM sales organization. Everyone knew that sales training was important and understood that the instructors were competent leaders who would one day be running major organizations in the company.

We will introduce many other approaches to "learning by doing" in the media selection and content development sections of this book.

Research Supports the Value of Experiential Learning

To help you understand the power of experiential learning, let me share two research studies in this area. The first, conducted by the National Training Laboratory in 2001, exposed people to a wide variety of learning approaches to teach basic IT desktop skills. After participating in different events, individuals were assessed three months later to measure retention. Results clearly showed that experiential learning drove much higher retention rates, as seen in Figure 3.5.

Is it possible to create experience through web-based training? Yes. In e-learning, experiential learning is accomplished with simulations, scenarios, and interactivities. We will discuss these in detail throughout the book. *Simulations* attempt to give learners a real-world situation online—whether it is a software application, a business to run, or a person-to-person interaction. *Scenarios* are a form of simulations used for soft-skills and sales training where learners are given real-world situations and they must make decisions about what to do next. *Interactivities* refer to small web-based objects that require the learner to slide a bar, select from a list, take a small test, or match boxes to test their learning and "see what happens."

The goal of a blended program is to try to intersperse these learn-by-doing events within an overall program.

Figure 3.5. Experiential Learning Increases Retention

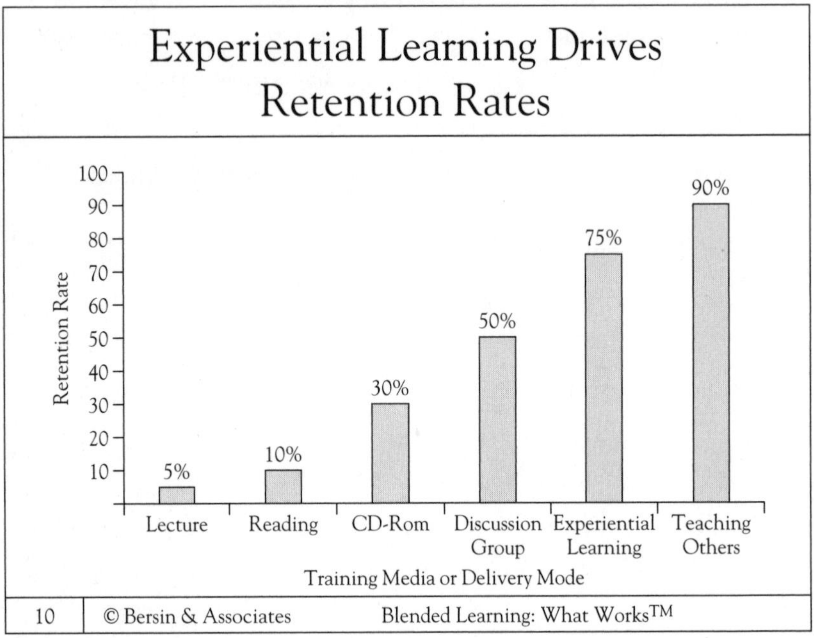

Experiential Learning Drives Retention Rates

Lecture 5%, Reading 10%, CD-Rom 30%, Discussion Group 50%, Experiential Learning 75%, Teaching Others 90%

Training Media or Delivery Mode

10 © Bersin & Associates   Blended Learning: What Works™

Blending Works: Thompson Job Impact Study

In blended learning the challenge is deciding how to blend these different approaches. An interesting study that measured the impact of blended learning was the Thompson NETg Job Impact Study.[1] This study looked at five different training techniques and tried to understand the impact of blending, that is, giving a learner two or more techniques for a single learning problem.

The study uses Microsoft Excel® skills as the learning problem. They trained a small group of learners on Excel topics using five different methods:

- Blended instructor-led training—the learner had a classroom experience coupled with a textbook, reference card, scenario-based exercises, and web-based instruction;

[1]The Thomson NETg Job Impact Study is available for download at www.netg.com.

- Blended text-based training—the learner had all the supporting materials in text form, but no instructor;
- Blended scenario-based training—the learner was given the scenario-based exercises and supporting material, but no instructor or text background;
- e-Learning without scenarios—the learner had a traditional web-based course without instructor or scenario-based exercises. This represents the "unblended" e-learning model; and
- Control group—no training at all.

After the training each group was given a series of Excel tasks to perform. They were assessed on two criteria: accuracy (proficiency) and speed (retention). Speed is a measurement of retention because it shows how well the learners remember the detailed processes they learned during the training. There were two interesting findings:

First, the students who were trained with more than one media type (the blended groups) *performed 30 percent more accurately than the group that had e-learning alone*.

Second, the blending groups *finished problems more than 40 percent faster than the group that used e-learning alone*.

This indicates that blended learning results in better retention (the learners could recall the steps to complete much more quickly).

This demonstrates that the blending process itself, which gives people more than one way to master the subject, has significant impact on mastery. These individuals had higher learning outcomes, and therefore higher productivity (presumably they would make fewer mistakes). The researchers reported:

"Regardless of the specific instructional components used, a well-defined blended learning solution designed around scenario-based exercises heightens overall on-the-job performance (speed and accuracy) over non-blended learning." (Thompson Job Impact Study, 2003)

Although this study applied only to a limited set of training problems (software application training), it reinforces what we intuitively believe: *people learn better when they have more than one media to use*. The simple fact that there are two or three different types of training (reading a book, trying out a skill on an exercise, listening to a lecture, and interacting with a web-based course) has a significant impact on mastery and retention.

Classroom instructors have known this for years—hence the reason for homework, exercises, and group discussion. In technology-based training, the questions are how to accomplish this blend in a cost-effective way and when to select which media elements for a given problem.

Lesson

Blending of any type increases mastery. If you can add only a single new learning media it will have a significant impact on learning results.

Cultural Goals: Socialization and Gaining Attention

An important issue to consider in blended learning is what I call the "cultural factor" of the program. In a traditional instructor-led program, there are two outcomes that typically do not exist in technology-based training:

- First, there is a *socialization process*, in which students talk to each other, get to know each other, ask questions, and "enter" the learning environment. This socialization itself is the goal of many programs such as new hire training, sales training, and management training.

- Second, there is an "*attention getting*" process where the students leave their work or home life, enter a classroom or laboratory, and are motivated and excited by an instructor. Gaining attention is critically important in corporate training because people are busy and take training by choice.

These two factors (socialization and gaining attention) are critically important to consider in any program. *Most early failures in e-learning were caused by overlooking these factors.* Technology-based training can be a lonely experience—the learner sits at his or her desk, reads and interacts with the computer, and must complete the material on his or her own. If the learner has a question, there is no one there to talk to. There are no classmates or peers to interact with. The process and environment are very different from a classroom. Traditional e-learning ignores the social and attention-getting factors.

You as a program manager must decide what the cultural goals are for your program. You should ask yourself the following question: how important is it to develop a sense of culture and social experience in this program? In some cases such as new hire training, sales training, and management training, the cultural and social objectives are as important as the learning objectives. New hire training in particular strives to introduce people to a company's culture and to their peers and co-workers.

Example: New-Hire Training

When a large global oil company (Company S) decided to redesign their entry-level engineering training on petroleum practices, they realized that socialization was critical to the success of the program. They wanted new hires to meet other new hires and go through the program together, developing a sense of community and teamwork in the process. Their blended program, which is months in duration, uses online and face-to-face activities in a structured mix. The program includes self-study web-based modules, classroom instruction, synchronous online chat, and online assessments. From course to course the arrangement of these media varies. In the "Introduction to Petroleum Processes" course, for example, employees have to go out into their local refinery and identify specific pieces of equipment and then answer questions about this equipment online.

Online learners are put into small groups, a powerful technique that makes online learning more personal. These small groups enter chat rooms together at scheduled times and grade each other's exercises (once per week). Since these people are located all over the world, they gain cultural connections and a feeling of belonging to a global community within Company S.

Near the end of the program people fly to a training facility and meet each other. This classroom experience is exciting and fun for the learners because it reinforces the cultural community they have created online.

A second example uses socialization in a more focused and tactical training program: training employees on a new ERP system rollout.

Example: ERP Software Rollout

We described Company W in the prior chapter. They are one of the world's largest distributors of industrial products. Their sales agents enter thousands of transactions into a SAP system every day. When Company W rolled out a new version of SAP, their goal was to assure that sales agents would be completely proficient before the new system went live. Yet there was no time during the software rollout to let people practice.

In an earlier attempt at a SAP upgrade Company W found that its biggest challenge was gaining the attention of busy telephone sales representatives to take online courses. People were just too busy to take the training. As a result, the first upgrade of SAP was a disaster.

In this subsequent SAP upgrade, the company solved this problem by focusing on cultural factors. They created a blended program, starting with a series of conference calls and local meetings held by regional coordinators. The coordinators brought people together and created a local "social context" for the training. They worked with local managers, explained the motivation for the course, and helped people complete. By adding this socialization and local presence, learning results were three to four times higher than the previous e-learning program, resulting in a flawless SAP upgrade.

Lesson

Think about your cultural and motivational goals in the program. These goals often overweigh the learning goals and will affect your media mix.

The Four Types of Corporate Training

Let us now examine one of the most important principles in this book: categorizing your program into one of four types.

It is important to realize that not every problem demands deep levels of learning and mastery. Some problems are far simpler. We address this issue by categorizing all training problems into different types. *These types define training not by content, but rather by the business problem you are trying to solve.*

I developed these four types after looking at dozens and dozens of programs. They will greatly simplify your challenge in building a blended program, and we refer to them throughout this book.

Let's examine the four types under the following conditions. You are the training manager at the Cadillac division of GM and the company is making a change to the product pricing model. Your problem is to develop a series of training programs to make sure the dealer and field organization understand the new price structure. Table 3.1 shows the four different ways we can approach this problem.

The first step in blended learning (or any content development) is to identify which of the four types meets your particular

Table 3.1. The Four Types of Corporate Training

Program Type	Problem Definition	Example for Cadillac Price Change
Type 1: Information Broadcast	Distribute information to a large audience quickly.	"We just raised prices on the Cadillac Escalade by 10 percent, and everyone needs to be aware of this."
Type 2: Critical Knowledge Transfer	Rapidly transfer critical knowledge (information, context, and ability to use it) to a large audience and verify that they received it.	"Here is the price sheet for the new Escalade and an explanation why the prices have been increased, so you can explain to customers."
Type 3: Skills and Competency Development	Develop new skills and competencies in an audience that needs them in their work.	"You need to learn the entire Cadillac pricing model so you can be qualified for discounting."
Type 4: Certification Programs	Certify and assess the skills and competencies developed in type 3. To certify means to "meet a standard," meaning the learner meets a standard established by the company, government, or educational institution.	"If you take this course and pass, you become a certified pricing manager for your office and you can discount up to 15 percent."

business needs. The program type is driven by the *business need,* not the content or learning issues themselves. For any given learning problem, you can build a type 1, 2, 3, or 4 program. It is up to you to decide which is appropriate based on business needs.

When introducing a new product, for example, is your strategy to update salespeople with information that fits into their existing skillset (type 1 or 2)? Or is it to train them in a whole new way of selling (type 3 or 4)? It may depend on the audience, product, and a variety of management factors. We discuss these later.

The Program Type Drives Program Design and Content Mix

One of the reasons that the four types are so important is that they drive the program characteristics, schedule, investment, and blend. They also drive the time to develop, tracking needed, assessment process, and total investment justified. Table 3.2 shows the design characteristics that define the program design for these different types.

As you can see, in type 3 and 4 programs you must be concerned about assessment, scoring, and tracking. This greatly affects your media and program mix. In types 1 and 2, you can rely more on "broadcast" media, with some or no tracking and assessment.

Applying the Four Types to Media Selection

These program types are very helpful. When people ask me, "How should I implement the following program?" my first question is, "What is our business objective?" If you do not understand which type your problem falls into, you will have a very hard time deciding what type of blended learning model to adopt. *Remember, the blend is not dependent on content per se, but on business need.*

Table 3.3 lists some examples of each type and the typical blends that make sense.

Tracking and Reporting as a Program Characteristic

One of the critical issues we will raise throughout the book is the issue of tracking and reporting of progress and results. A critical question you must ask early in the process of developing any learning program is *how much tracking do you need?* Tracking refers to the technology and processes to measure the enrollments, activity,

Table 3.2. Program Design Characteristics for the Four Types of Corporate Thinking

Program Type	Typical Time to Develop	Typical Shelf Life of Content	Time Learner Can Dedicate to the Content	How Many Programs You Develop Per Year in a Major Corporation	Tracking Required	Typical Budget Per Program
Type 1: Information Broadcast	Hours to days	Days to weeks	An hour or less	Hundreds to thousands	Little or none. Enrollment optional.	A few hundred to a few thousand
Type 2: Critical Knowledge Transfer	Days to weeks	Weeks to months	1 to 2 hours	Hundreds	Enrollment and completion	$10k to $30k
Type 3: Skills and Competency Development	Weeks to months	Months to years	Days to weeks	Tens	Enrollment, completion, score	$10,000 to $100,000+
Type 4: Certification Programs	Weeks to months	Months to years	Days to weeks	Tens	Enrollment, completion, score, and pass/fail	$10,000 to $100,000+ and more

Table 3.3. Examples of the Four Types of Corporate Training

Example	Typical e-Learning or Training Interactivities	Typical Blended Media
Type 1: Information Broadcast. Example: Kinko's has a new pricing announcement that dramatically reduces the price for color copying.	Read, listen, watch	Conference call, webinar, e-mail, or newsletter
Type 2: Critical Skills Transfer. Example: Novell introduces a new product to their 6,000 channel partners and needs to drive awareness and sales volume quickly. Sales reps must position correctly and compete to drive sales.	Read, listen, watch, and ask and answer questions	PowerPoint-based courseware, live e-learning webinar, track completion but not scores
Type 3: Skills and Competencies. Example: Intel rolls out a new manufacturing process and all worldwide plant engineers must understand how to use it effectively by 12/31 when the new equipment is enabled. If they are not trained, yields fall and huge losses could occur.	Read, listen, interact, practice, ask questions, answer questions, interact with others, take an exam, get feedback	Web-based courseware, instructor-led class, conference call, onsite labs, simulations
Type 4: Certification: Example: Royal & Sun Insurance must submit certification records for all insurance brokers that they are certified insurance and financial planners by a fixed date. These individuals will be audited and must train others.	Read, listen, interact, practice, answer questions, take an exam, get feedback, pass or fail	Type 3, plus external or internal testing, tracking by LMS for completion and expiration date. Certification means: "to attest as being true or as represented or as meeting a standard," implying that there is some standard that must be met.

Note: Interactivity is a term used in e-learning for some kind of technology or activity that requires the learner to practice or directly interact with the content. As we all know, people learn by doing. There are many types of interactivities (fill in the blanks, match boxes, slide a slider bar, and so on) used to illustrate a concept, and they also are used to practice an application rollout.

completion, and scores of the program. The five levels of tracking are

1. Enrollments	Has the student enrolled? How many enrollments so far? When did he or she enroll?
	In most blended learning media, tracking enrollments is easy. If you have an LMS, it will be handled there. For example, in retail sales training, the primary measure of usage is whether or not learners are enrolling in courses. Completion is not critical.
2. Activity	Is the student actually using the content? When was the last time the learner logged in? How many total hours has the student logged? What percentage of the work has been completed?
	This information is problematic and very dependent on the technology you use. We will cover this in the next chapter. For example, in a bank's call center training, each step is dependent on the last step, so percentage complete is a critical measure of the overall progress of a group of learners.
3. Completion	Has the student completed? Completed is hard to define. Does it mean reaching the end? Does it mean that the learner interacted with every chapter? Does it mean passing a final assessment?
	Completion information is usually stored in the LMS, but often is not. You, as a program manager, must decide what defines "completion," and from there you can select media that will give you this level of information. For example, in British Telcom's Mobile-Commerce sales training the company decided that learning required total completion of all

materials, so the company does not mark a student complete until he or she has completed every step in the blended program.

4. Score

Is there a single score for the entire course or one per module? How do you compute the overall score for the course? Is this an absolute score or a percentage of total possible? (See Appendix for AICC "mastery score" concept.[2])

You can usually decide whether or not you want scores and decide whether they are absolute or percentage of grade. For example, in Cisco's sales curriculum it is critical to have a passing grade to be marked complete. This passing grade varies from course to course and is set by the instructor.

5. Certification

Is the learner certified?

Certification does not mean just passing a test. Certification means "to attest as being true or as represented or as meeting a standard." A certification program (type 4) sets out some kind of standard that must be met in order for a learner to pass.

Typically certification programs require (A) completion, (B) a certain score to become certified, and often (C) manager validation and approval. Certification programs typically also have expiration dates: an individual's certification will expire after a certain period of time. They also have "certification windows," which require that an individual become

---

[2]Mastery score is defined in the AICC specification as the score (percent correct) that denotes a passing grade or mastery completion of the course or learning object.

certified within a certain time window after beginning a course. (This prevents someone from starting a course in 2001 and completing in 2003, by which time they have forgotten all the original material.) If you want to certify people, you must define all these criteria and must find media and/or LMS that give you this information.

One more: Satisfaction

How satisfied are learners? Do you want an end-of-course or end-of-event survey?

We always recommend a survey (or Kirkpatrick Level 1 assessment). For example, retailers like Kinko's, Pep Boys, and Circuit City regularly survey their retail users on each program to make sure they are developing programs that satisfy regional sales manager needs. The challenge for you is to understand how you will implement this survey in the context of the blended program you create.

In the next chapter we will start discussing the issue of selecting media. You will see that tracking and reporting characteristics are critical factors in this process.

Lessons Learned in This Chapter

1. People have three basic styles of learning: visual, auditory, and kinesthetic. Although people tend to prefer one style, research shows that use of all three drives higher mastery. Use all three approaches to blend programs.

2. "Mastery" is a combination of proficiency and retention. *Proficiency* measures the ability for the learner to perform the task accurately. *Retention* measures the ability for the learner

to remember and apply the task to many different situations. The level of mastery you desire varies from program to program.

3. There are six main modes of learning. Research proves that retention is much higher for experiential learning than for more passive methods of learning.

4. Research shows that blending more than one approach improves retention and proficiency by 30 to 40 percent and higher. Regardless of the blending model you select, blending multiple media types has a very positive impact on learning.

5. e-Learning lacks many socialization and attention-getting benefits of traditional training. You should decide cultural and socialization goals because they are as important as learning goals in the development of a program design.

6. There are four types of corporate training programs that can be applied to any learning problem. The type you select depends on the business requirements, not on the content itself.

7. The four types drive program design, media selection, and many infrastructure and assessment decisions.

8. Tracking and reporting are important factors in blended learning program design. There are five types of reporting, and business requirements drive which levels of tracking and reporting you need.

Chapter Four

Proven Blended Learning Models

In this chapter we take the design concepts from Chapter 3 and illustrate some proven models you can use (see Figure 4.1). The models we discuss are examples. No two training programs are identical, so it is unlikely that you will copy one of these models precisely. However, the approaches, benefits, and lessons

Figure 4.1.   Where We Are

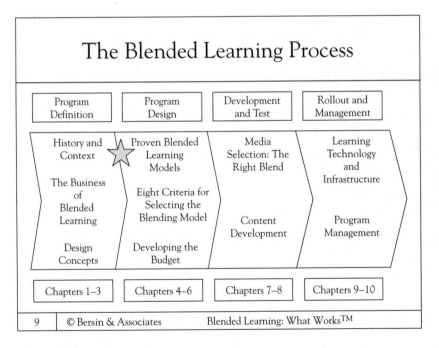

learned in these models will make your program design much easier.

The Two Approaches to Blended Learning

To begin, it is important to understand the two general approaches to blended learning. Remember from the Introduction that we define blended learning as "the combination of different training 'media' (technologies, activities, and types of events) to create an optimum training program for a specific audience."

The term "blended" comes from the concept that traditional instructor-led training is being supplemented with other electronic formats. In the context of this book, "blended learning" programs use many different forms of e-learning, perhaps complemented with instructor-led training and other live formats.

The first approach we call the *"program flow model."* In this model one creates a step-by-step curriculum that integrates several media into a chronological program or syllabus. It is analogous to the process of taking a college or high-school course. Each chapter or step is orchestrated to build on the one before. The program has a strict outline and requires that learners step through material in a linear fashion. At the end, a final step typically includes an exercise or assessment to measure total learning.

The second approach is what we call the *"core-and-spoke"* model. In this model the designer creates one fundamental training approach (typically onsite classroom training or web-based courseware) and then delivers other materials, interactivities, resources, and assessments as "supporting materials," optional or mandatory materials that surround and complement the primary approach. In this model, there may be exercises or references to multiple media, but they are not arranged in a step-by-step manner.

Every blended learning program is really a combination of both, but for simplicity it is easy to consider the two as a way to get started.

> ### The Spray and Pray Approach: Throwing Things Against the Wall to See What Sticks
>
> Let me digress slightly here with a lesson learned. Throwing lots of "stuff" at learners does not work. If you believe that learners need access to books, diagrams, simulations, and other media, *integrate them into the program itself.* In the program flow model, they should be explicitly *assigned* at a point in time. In the core-and-spoke model they should specifically be *referenced* in an exercise. Materials that are built as "supporting" but not integrated into the curriculum are rarely used and usually waste resources, time, and money.

Approach 1: Program Flow Model

The easiest way to understand this approach is to consider a typical thirty-hour instructor-led training program like that in Figure 4.2. You usually have each hour blocked out into a lecture, quiz, group exercise, discussion, or test. In a thirty-hour program (probably a week-long program) you will probably have fifteen to twenty of these individual learning activities. In most corporate training organizations, many of these programs already exist and have been developed over a period of years.

To apply blending concepts to the program flow model you replace some of the physical events with self-study or e-learning activities. For example, suppose you have a well-developed week-long class for new hire training. Instead of the introductory lecture, for example, you create a mandatory pre-class assignment on the web, which may consist of an audio-based PowerPoint presentation (which we call "Rapid e-Learning") with a short assessment at the end. The instructor knows from experience that students arrive at the class with different levels of proficiency. This introductory learning activity is like a prerequisite book: it brings everyone to the same level before class begins. If you are using an LMS, the

Figure 4.2.   Program Flow Model

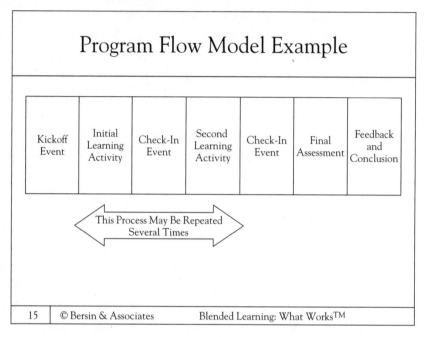

Program Flow Model Example

Kickoff Event	Initial Learning Activity	Check-In Event	Second Learning Activity	Check-In Event	Final Assessment	Feedback and Conclusion

This Process May Be Repeated Several Times

15	© Bersin & Associates	Blended Learning: What Works™

instructor can even review the scores of each student before class begins to see where to focus attention.

This simple blend solves many problems: first, you have forced people to come prepared, making the classroom experience far more efficient. Second, you have made the classroom experience more relevant because the instructor knows the level of competency of the students before they arrive. Third, you have saved money (if the audience is large enough to offset the cost of the web-based module) because the total time in classroom is reduced. Finally, in most examples, you have improved the learning results because the program is now more aligned to the specific needs of the learners.

In most content flow programs, the *kickoff event* is a conference call, set of e-mails, or meeting with a manager to explain the program goals and motivation. It sets out the agenda and communicates the consequences of *not completing*. In the corporate world, the kickoff is a critical event because it gives the learners the information they need to budget their time and decide how seriously to take this particular program. In the case of Company W's SAP rollout program, for example, this kickoff event consisted of a conference call with local representation by field coordinators. In terms of the prior chapter, this is the "attention-getting" event.

The *Initial Learning Activity* is the first experience the learner has with the content or instructor. This is when the learner immediately decides how "good" this program will be. If the initial activity is weak, you will suffer from low completion. You only have a few minutes to win them over, and this is the critical place to do it. Make sure that this particular module is carefully designed and tested.

The initial materials also tell the learner what will be expected of them, how the technology works, and how difficult the material will be. (Remember this simple strategy: tell them what you're going to tell them, tell them, and then tell them that you told them.)

The initial learning activity may be an e-learning course, a conference call, a webinar, or a physical meeting. In the case of Verizon's field service training, for example, the initial learning activity was actually a whole series of e-learning modules that introduced the learners to safety procedures, time-card processing, and other administrative aspects of their jobs. The first physical class takes place after many hours of online training.

The following series of events is usually delivered in a cycle, combining self-study with a live check-in process of some kind. In a long self-study e-learning program, these may be individual chapters or modules of the class. In a live e-learning program, these may be a series of live events interspersed with a reading assignment or check-in with an instructor.

Lesson

Try not to give learners more than one or two hours of self-study modules to complete between some live check-in process. In most corporate audiences, people will not complete more than one or two hours of self-study per week unless you explicitly allocate time from their work schedule.

Example

In Company F's (a major U.S. bank) new-hire call center training program, for example, the core of the program is a series of simulations of the bank's call center software interspersed with brief facilitated meetings. In the meetings learners demonstrate their proficiency and receive feedback from instructors. The meetings are important because they reinforce the online material and give the students the confidence to go out and work on the real system. Table 4.1 describes the curriculum plan for this program.

In this program, the blend includes instructor-led training, web-based training, collaboration, and on-the-job training. Because the material is very technical (learning to use the bank's online applications), the web-based self-study section is designed to let each learner proceed at his or her own pace. This empowers the learners to move at whatever pace they wish during this period, and then they all catch up at the break.

In most program flow programs, the *final assessment* is an event or module that wraps up the program and assesses the learner. In some e-learning programs, assessments are interspersed throughout

Table 4.1.   Sample Blended Curricula for Bank's New Hire Call-Center Training

Time	Activity	Type
15 minutes	Daily Introduction	Facilitated Full Group
60 minutes	Web-Based Training	Self-Study
30 minutes	Web-Based Training	Self-Study
	Break	
30 minutes	Sales Referral Process	Facilitated Full Group
75 minutes	Role Plays	Collaborative
	Break	
90 minutes	Structured On-the-Job Training	OTJ
15 minutes	Daily Wrap-Up	Facilitated Full Group

Proven Blended Learning Models   61

the program. In some type 1 and type 2 programs, assessments are often eliminated. In programs that are manager-centric, the assessment consists of a meeting with the manager. IBM's GenX diversity training, for example, uses a meeting with the employee's manager as the final assessment. In this meeting the manager discusses the material with a group of employees to make sure all questions and concerns have been *answered*.

The *feedback and conclusion* event is usually a survey or a meeting that enables learners to give direct feedback to instructors and content developers. In type 1 and type 2 programs, this conclusion is often omitted. However, I strongly recommend that you develop a short survey for feedback in every single program. As a training and educational professional, feedback is your lifeblood. It gives you the information that enables you to iterate and improve your training programs over time. Feedback also gives learners the feeling that you care about the program and its effectiveness.

Benefits of the Program Flow Model

1. It creates a deep level of commitment and a high completion rate. Learners feel engaged and can plan their training over time. It gives learners the time to fit training into their existing schedules, but forces them to continue until the conclusion.

2. It enables you to formally track progress. Each step in the program can be carefully monitored and tracked. If people are dropping out or missing steps, you know precisely where you have a problem.

3. It fits into the normal flow of classroom training that most people expect. Learners are conditioned to learn this way through their academic careers, which flow in quarters, semesters, and years. This is also the model most existing content uses, and it fits into most instructional-design paradigms (learn/try/assess).

4. It serves well for a certification program, in which you must assure that learners complete each step. If you need to make sure that learners complete every module, this approach is needed.

5. It is easy to modify and maintain. If you find that one of the elements in your program is unsuccessful, you can eliminate it or replace it easily without impacting the overall program. Over time you will modify elements to meet changing business needs—and such changes are easy to accommodate in the context flow model.

Figure 4.3 shows a blended learning program used by two companies (Roche Pharmaceuticals[1] and Company W) to roll out a major upgrade to their SAP order processing system.

Figure 4.3. Program Flow Example: SAP Rollout

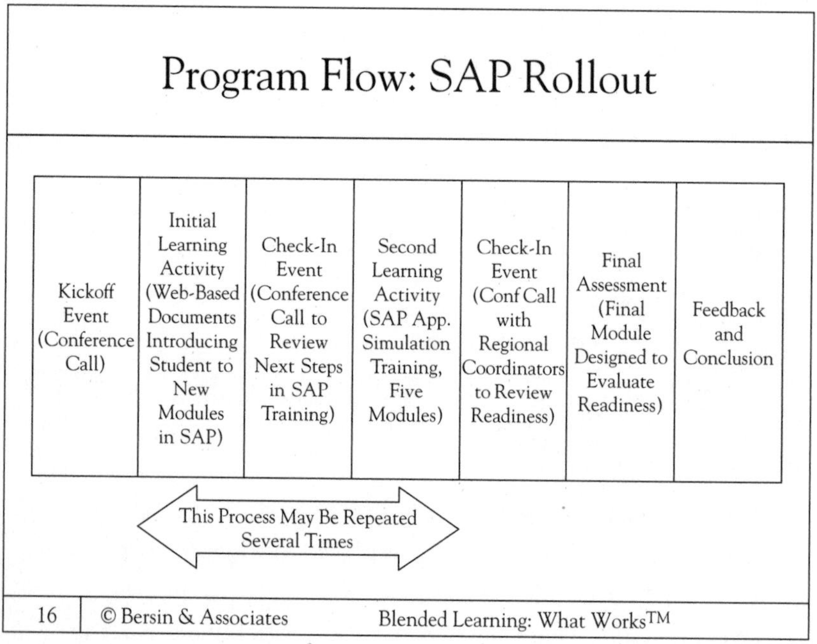

Program Flow: SAP Rollout

| Kickoff Event (Conference Call) | Initial Learning Activity (Web-Based Documents Introducing Student to New Modules in SAP) | Check-In Event (Conference Call to Review Next Steps in SAP Training) | Second Learning Activity (SAP App. Simulation Training, Five Modules) | Check-In Event (Conf Call with Regional Coordinators to Review Readiness) | Final Assessment (Final Module Designed to Evaluate Readiness) | Feedback and Conclusion |

This Process May Be Repeated Several Times

| 16 | © Bersin & Associates | Blended Learning: What Works™ |

---

[1]Roche Pharmaceuticals SAP Training.

In both of these programs, the main education consisted of an application simulation (multiple modules) built using a tool called InfoPack from RWD Technologies. This particular tool simulates the actual SAP application and helps learners walk through the application workflows in detail. It uses application simulations as the primary learning activity and surrounds this program with a conference call, web-based support materials, and a final assessment done online.

About Software Application Training

One of the lessons learned from these programs and similar application rollouts is that process training is just as important as application training. When first exposed to the application simulation, these users could not understand the new SAP application process. The company had to go back and develop a face-to-face module, which included whiteboard pictures and diagrams, to explain the business processes from a functional perspective. It was after this took place that the blended learning model started to work.

Example: Ninth House, Inc. Leadership Training

Ninth House, Inc., a leading provider of executive and leadership training, uses web-based video and simulations to deliver a step-by-step blended program focused on management and leadership training. This blended program has been developed and used by hundreds of companies and is customized from company to company with case studies, discussion groups, and assessments interspersed depending on a company's interest. It is shown in Figure 4.4.

The High-Impact Hiring program has four major modules and includes a series of scenarios, quizzes, and workbooks to help learners master the material.

Ninth House, Inc. has found that each company takes the library of content and combines it slightly differently. Depending on their culture and the amount of time learners can commit,

Figure 4.4.   Ninth House, Inc. Program Flow:
High-Impact Hiring

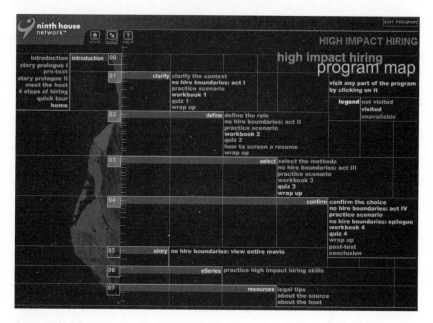

Reprinted with permission from Ninth House, Inc.

sometimes companies insert discussion sections; sometimes learners must write essays; and sometimes companies have instructor-led programs interspersed into the program. The lesson here is that you can easily use off-the-shelf content and turn it into a blended program.

Lesson

Use a blended model to add process understanding and context setting to the program. Although you may believe that you are teaching skills and techniques, the business process and motivation behind these skills may be even more important in driving understanding. These topics can be conveyed through a conference call, webinar, or other form of synchronous or onsite briefing that adds value to your program.

Example: BT Sales Training

BT had a major new product set to launch called M-Commerce. They believed that the entire training program to cover all topics would take nearly five work days to complete. Since BT sales agents can handle a maximum of three weeks of training per year, this was considered too long to handle. The company developed an innovative blended learning program that solved this problem, shown in Figure 4.5.

Prior to beginning the curriculum, the students (total of 260) were placed in groups of twelve to sixteen learners. Each group had a mentor who acted as the instructor, introduced the students to the curriculum, set the deadlines, and provided subject-matter expertise.

Figure 4.5. BT M-Commerce Sales Program

Program Flow: British Telecom M-Commerce Sales Training

Kickoff Event (Conference Call Introducing Program)	Two-hour e-Learning Program Students Have Three Weeks to Complete	Check-In Conference Call to Answer Questions and Kick Off Second Module	Second 1-2 Hour e-Learning Program Students Again Have Three Weeks to Complete	Instructor-Led Event (1 day) Where Students Must Practice Real-World Selling Techniques and Demonstrate Proficiency to Peers and Instructor

17 © Bersin & Associates Blended Learning: What Works™

This blended program was broken down into five carefully scheduled components:

- The program begins with a conference call hosted by the instructor. The purpose of the initial call is to introduce the program, including the objectives and schedule, then to answer questions. The instructors were members of the training staff who had been account directors.

- Next the formal instruction begins with an e-learning model of one to two hours' duration (see Figure 4.6). The students are given three weeks to complete this module, which includes collaboration features that allow students to send questions to the instructor via e-mail and also collaborate with one another.

- Three weeks later, students are brought back to another conference call hosted by the instructor. The instructor briefly reviews the content covered in the first e-learning module and then discusses questions that have been submitted by the learners.

Figure 4.6.   BT Content Sample

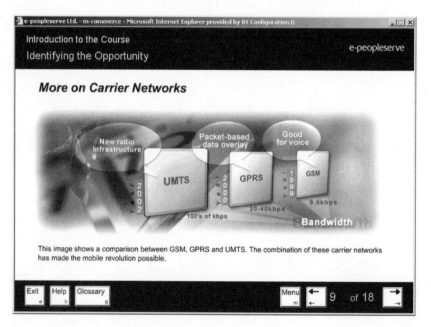

Students are also given the opportunity to ask questions and discuss the material. The next e-learning module is also introduced.

- Now formal instruction continues with another e-learning module of one to two hours' duration. The students are given another three weeks to complete this section.

- Finally, the program concludes with a single instructor-led event that allows students to practice what they have learned. Role-playing sessions give the learners a chance to rehearse their sales pitch to a prospective customer.

Example: Call Center Training at Company F, a Major U.S. Bank

A major bank (Company F) has more than 3,000 phone bankers in twelve call centers throughout the country. Each year, due to turnover and job changes, there are 2,400 new employees to train. Before blended learning, the new hire curriculum took six weeks to complete. The goal of the blended learning program was to reduce this to four weeks while improving the proficiency and self-confidence of the phone bankers.

After evaluating the job requirements of these individuals, the team found that there were two blended curricula needed: one for sales and a second for service. Both programs needed a core component of software application training to show employees how to use the highly complex online systems for bank transactions. This "thread" or learning goal demanded a set of application simulations and small exercises that taught phone bankers how to handle a wide range of inquiries and process them online.

The goal of this component of the training was true mastery. These individuals open new accounts, enter transactions, cancel credit cards, and perform many other business-critical functions. They must be fully competent on each step.

To drive mastery, the design team developed a blended program that includes a series of web-based training courses, simulations, role plays, and briefing sessions with the manager. The training program follows a series of scenarios (for example, a new customer opens an account, an irate customer calls for service, a customer calls to cancel a credit card). For each scenario, the learner has to take the web-based course, enter the right transactions into the application simulation, and then discuss in a group session why they did what they did.

An important aspect of this blended program is how the blend shifted over time. During the four-week period the blend shifted from web-based self-study and instructor-led training toward on-the-job exercises (see Figure 4.7). The first week focused on socialization and developing basic skills, so it had a high percentage of instructor-led training and web-based self-study courseware. Over time, the web-based component was reduced and the on-the-job training increased. On-the-job exercises serve to drive retention and increase confidence. By the end of the four-week period, these learners had to get on the phones and take calls.

Figure 4.7.   Call Center Program at Bank F

Call Center Training at Bank F

Week 1	Week 2	Week 3	Week 4
Collaboration 15%	On-the-Job 15%	On-the-Job 30%	On-the-Job 45%
Instructor-Led 50%	Collaboration 30%	Instructor-Led 40%	Collaboration 10%
	Instructor-Led 15%		Instructor-Led 30%
Web-Based Courseware 35%	Web-Based Courseware 40%	Web-Based Courseware 30%	Web-Based Courseware 15%

This program took nearly twelve months to build and roll out. It is very strategic to the bank and touches one of the bank's most profitable and strategic operational units. This program is clearly an upper right quadrant problem in the learning investment model.

The program had excellent results. Facilitators report that learners feel ready to take customer calls within the first eight days, a much faster time-to-competence than in the prior instructor-led program. Here are some of their comments:

- Instructor: "Today is the eighth day of training, and some of my star students are ready to start taking calls. In the old instructor-led curriculum, this would not have happened until week 5."

- Student: "The confidence I feel through this course gives me the desire to move to the phones as quickly as I can."

Lesson
Self-study training is an excellent way to build skills that can be transferred to on-the-job exercises over time, resulting in mastery and confidence. Traditional single media programs cannot make this transition.

Example: CNA Insurance: Leadership and Executive Training Worldwide

CNA Insurance is a pioneer in blended learning. In 2001 the company had a huge challenge: they needed to roll out an entirely new performance planning process to more than 2,000 managers before the end of the year. e-Learning efforts in the past were disappointing due to low enrollment and lack of interest. The CEO was driving this initiative. How could the chief learning officer and training organization solve this challenge?

The answer was blended learning. The company implemented an innovative web-based platform that enables learners to enter the blended environment online. This platform and solution were

Figure 4.8.   CNA Blended Learning Example

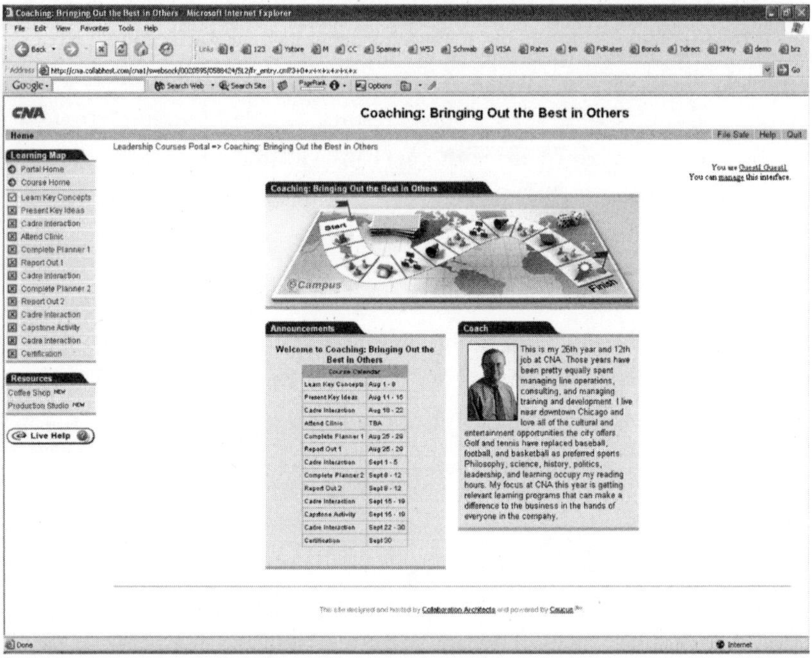

excellent examples of the components you should consider for largely web-based leadership programs.

Figure 4.8 shows the interface. Each step in the program is shown graphically and, as the student steps through the program, a variety of tools and collaborative techniques are used.

Online Collaboration and Interactivity

In a traditional program, each learner is a member of a class. At CNA, each student is a member of a similar group called a "cadre." A "cadre" is the equivalent to a class in traditional training, although people are not physically located together (see Figure 4.9). The cadres are teams of fifteen to thirty people who work through the program on the same schedule, score each other's exercises, and

Figure 4.9.   CNA Cadres Form Virtual Classmates

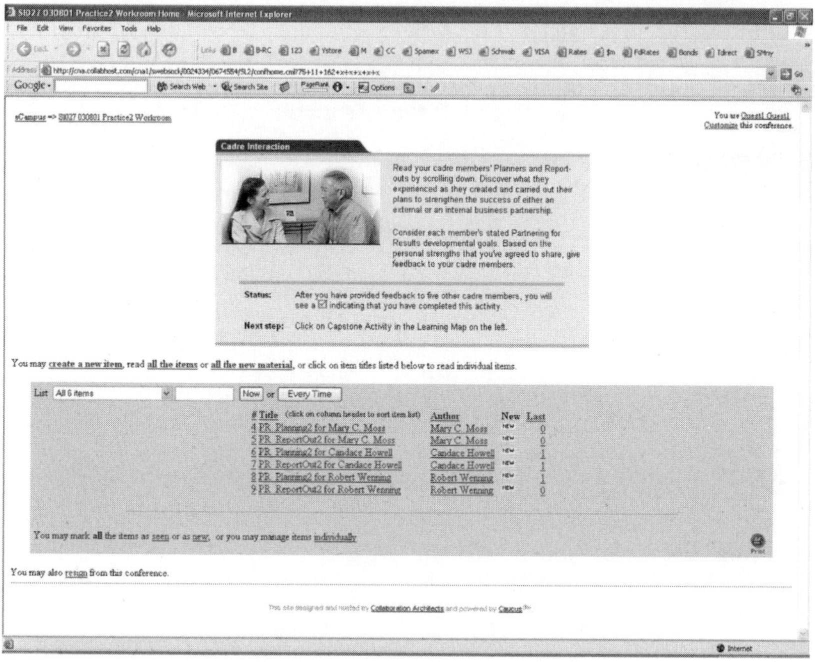

continuously interact throughout the program. How they interact varies from program to program.

In the program on "how to develop performance plans," for example, each member of the cadre is required to write a "smart" performance plan and post it to the website so that other members of the cadre can see it. Each learner is then required to read and critique at least three other plans.

Because the cadres are selected randomly, in most groups there are executives, supervisors, and line managers all mixed together. This means that learners may have the chance to critique an executive's performance plan, or vice versa. This level of interaction makes learners feel engaged and committed to the program.

The second key role CNA created is that of an online coach. The coach is a specially assigned instructor who serves as a tutor, advisor, and teaching assistant. When a student submits an exercise, the coach reads it and sends feedback to the learner. Coaches are instructors or subject-matter experts who agree to collaborate with learners. Because of the efficiency in the platform, coaches can handle multiple cadres. The platform has many tools that make the coach's work easy and efficient.

The "coffee shop" (shown in Figure 4.10) is an example of how the cadres and coaches are used. In the coffee shop learners can chat with each other and interact with the coach or submit exercises to be graded.

The lessons in the CNA experience are many: interaction, coaching, mandatory exercises which are graded, and organizing people into small groups. Although in their programs there is no instructor-led training per-se, they create a high-impact blended learning through their platform.

Figure 4.10.   CNA "Coffee Shop"

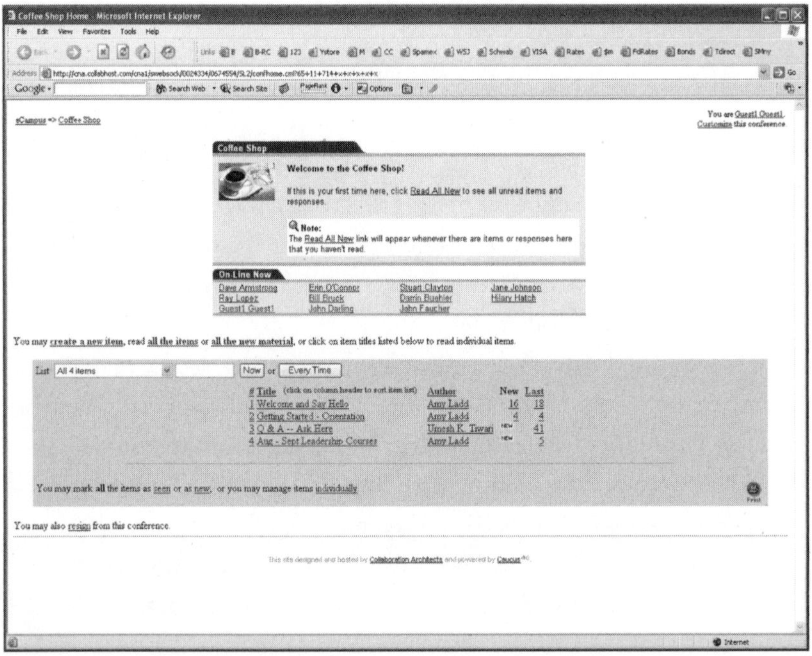

> **Lessons**
>
> The program flow model is the easiest to understand and efficiently mixes different media in a flow just like a traditional university curriculum. You can develop such a model with only a few different media and learner satisfaction and business impact will go up dramatically.

Approach 2: Core-and-Spoke Model

Many programs are not complex enough to justify the investment in a program flow model. In these programs (and for many off-the-shelf e-learning programs) you should consider the core-and-spoke approach, as shown in Figure 4.14 on page 77.

In this approach the program is designed with a single course using a single media (electronic or live) and uses other media or learning activities as optional or supplemental materials. The main difference between the core-and-spoke approach and the program flow model are as follows:

- In core-and-spoke
  - The supplemental materials are optional and not explicitly scheduled;
  - Students decide which supplemental materials to use; and
  - All students do not necessarily complete the course at the same time.

This is called the core-and-spoke model because the additional exercises, materials, events, and references are supplemental to the core and are used to reinforce, supplement, and complement the main course. You track and certify people based on the main course, not necessarily on the spoke materials.

This model is widely used in IT training, where there is a linear series of modules but one or more reference books available to assist with exercises. Many of the companies that implement this model are catalog content providers. NETg, ElementK, and Skillsoft, for example, provide a wide range of resources and tools that add to their IT training. These resources are provided as backup and supplementary materials, not necessarily weaved throughout the course. Both Skillsoft and NETg provide "online mentors" or tutors who can grade exercises and answer questions. Skillsoft's Books 24×7 division and NETg's partner, Safari Online, provide online books that enable learners to look up topics while they are in the courseware.

The biggest benefit to this model is deployment simplicity. When the blended learning elements are optional and involve self-study, you can have hundreds or thousands of people in the program moving at their own pace. You have the benefits of blended learning available to learners, but you do not have to schedule, manage, and track learners through a series of linear steps.

Online References Example: Thomson NETg—Safari Books Online

Thomson NETg partners with a company called Safari Books Online to provide online access to books in business and IT topics. NETg integrates these books into their online courses. Typically, the most popular use of online reference materials is for IT training, where programmers want to look up code samples and specific references and definitions (see Figures 4.11 and 4.12). The following shows an example of a resource provided for technical training.

Online References Example: Books 2437 by Skillsoft

Skillsoft, another large provider of online courseware, has a similar offering from a division called Books 24×7. Their offerings are integrated into Skillsoft's courseware and platform, making it easy for learners to look up reference materials from within a course (Figure 4.13).

As you can see from these two examples, reference materials are one easy way to build a core-and-spoke model. One thing to

Figure 4.11.   Safari Technical Books Online
The following shows an example of a resource provided for business-oriented training.

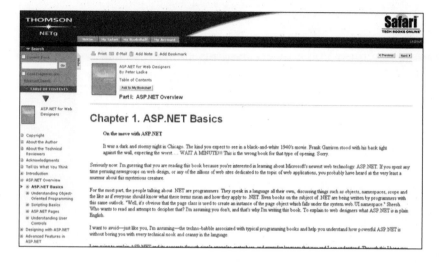

Figure 4.12.   Safari Business Books Online

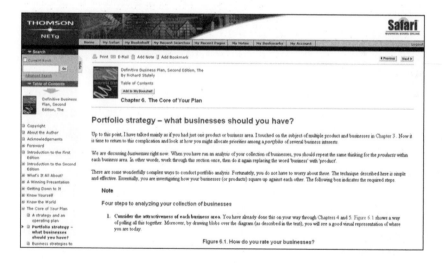

beware of, however, is that books are not typically licensed for online use. If you want to offer books as part of your program, you must purchase them through one of these suppliers or license the book for broad distribution from a publisher.

Figure 4.13. Books 24×7 Online Reference Materials

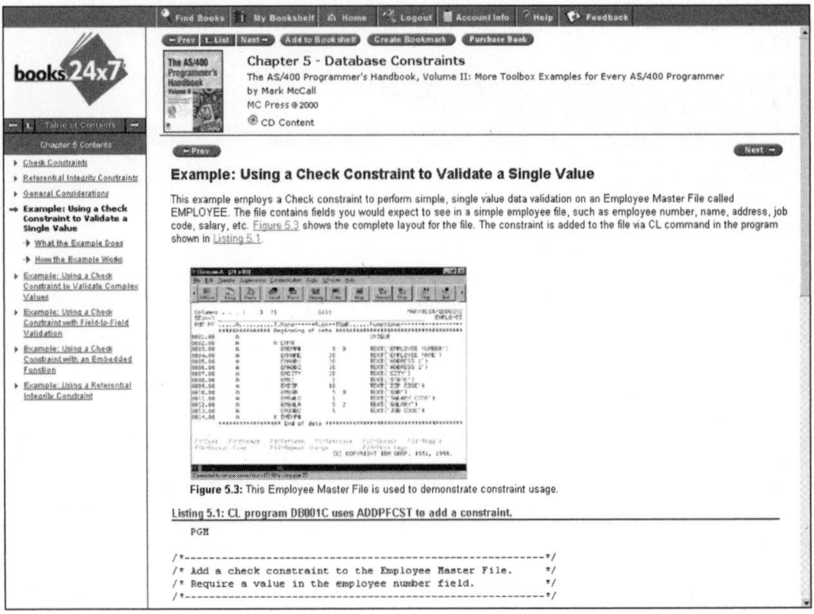

There are many examples of this model throughout the book. Two others are shown in Figure 4.14. In a semiconductor manufacturer's manufacturing certification program, learners are given access to online labs and classroom courses to assist in completing their curricula. The core curricula is a long and highly involved web-based course, and these resources are provided as supplemental programs to be used when the learner has time. Although not specifically scheduled, they are required to be completed.

In many IT certification programs, such as Cisco and NCR's network certification, programs offer web-portal resources, online simulations, discussion rooms, and tests to assist learners in completing the certification. These programs typically have a rigorous certification exam the learner must pass, so all these resources are recommended in the program to prepare the user for the exam.

The fundamental difference between the core-and-spoke model and the content flow model is the latter supports highly

Figure 4.14.   Core-and-Spoke Model

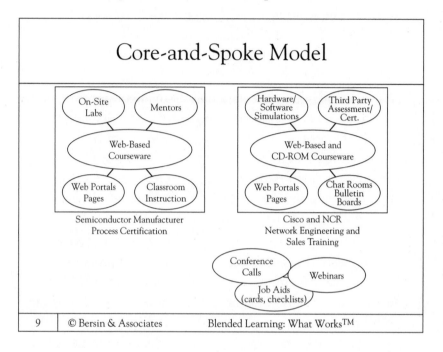

motivated learners who are working at their own pace to complete the program. Since there are no "scheduled events," the learner must have a strong incentive (for example, passing a certification exam) to complete. This approach is often used for technical training and higher education where the student has a fairly complex course to complete and many resources at their disposal. Some of the differences and benefits of this approach are listed below.

Benefits of the Core-and-Spoke Model

1. This approach is easier to build in stages. If you build the core curricula you can launch it immediately and add the supplemental materials over time. As we described earlier, you should specifically reference support materials within the curricula so that learners have a context for when to use the spoke resources.

2. This approach assumes you have a motivated self-study learner. The learners have to decide when to consult the supplemental materials, and you may direct them toward them but typically do not track or mandate their use.

3. You can make the spoke materials more important through exercises and events that encourage their use. In Digital-Think's IT content, for example, there are learning exercises that require the student to submit programming samples to a tutor. Although these exercises are not mandatory to completing the course, they are inserted as specific steps, and most students do undertake them.

4. The spoke learning activities can be very specialized for special needs. In NCR's network certification program, for example, the company uses online labs that enable learners to actually configure and manage routers through a web-browser interface. These labs have limited access and are expensive to manage, so they are available for many but not necessarily used by all students. Students who use the labs have a better understanding of the material, but because of their high cost and limited access NCR chose not to mandate them as part of completing the program. Not all students want them, but they are available for advanced learners.

5. The core-and-spoke model speeds the development process. The training organization can focus their resources on one major instructional activity (and outsource if needed) and then build the surrounding materials over time.

6. Flexibility. In this model, you can make some spoke modules mandatory and others optional. As you will see from the semiconductor process training example that follows, this enables you to tailor a rigorous program to learners' individual styles and interests.

Figure 4.15.   Semiconductor Manufacturing Engineer Program

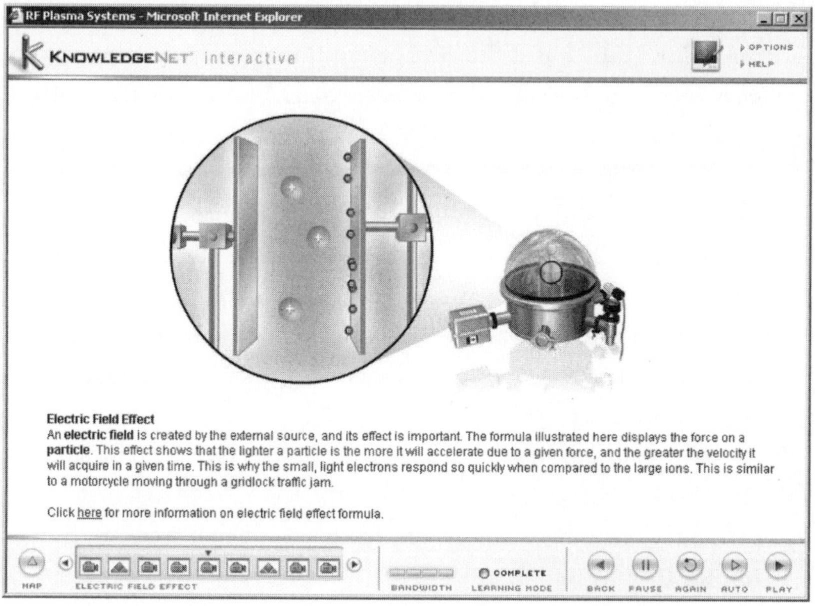

Example: Semiconductor Manufacturing Engineer Training

Figure 4.15 shows a very successful process manufacturing program for new engineers. It uses both a program flow and a core-and-spoke approach.

The curriculum is designed as a blended learning program that combines an online component with hands-on lab sessions. Using this approach, the original curriculum of nine in-class days was reduced to two ten-hour *self-paced online* courses followed by two eight-hour *lab sessions*. These modules are unscheduled, but must be completed before the final exam.

Throughout the web-based course there are exercises that must be performed in the lab, as well as many supporting materials. At several times in the curriculum the students attend a short instructor-led event to reinforce information, practice, and answer questions they may have had from prior steps.

Example: Company C—Retail Sales Training

Company C is a very large well-known retailer with 650 stores throughout the United States. Their online training program for sales representatives has dozens of modules in a wide variety of topics such as "how to sell HDTV," "understanding stereo components," and "fundamentals of making the sale." These are all self-study online modules in web-based courseware format.

To drive adoption and retention, the company found that online learning alone was not enough. They found that the most important step to add was a live intervention by the learners' manager where the manager asked them specific questions to probe and test their learning.

The result was an innovative core-and-spoke blended program. At various times in the online course, the learners are required to perform a "learning check," a printed checklist that requires the learner to walk through the store, identify items, and perform certain tasks. The learning check must then be submitted to the learner's manager for grading. The manager reviews the checklist (instructions are attached) and enters the grade into the learning management system. These on-the-job exercises are mandatory but not scheduled, so they are supplemental to the core training.

This simple approach has greatly improved Company C's return on investment in e-learning. Learners now have a real-life exercise to complete when they have time to reinforce and drive mastery and retention. Managers are intimately involved in the learning process and can assess their employees' progress directly.

Example: U.S. Navy Executive Education

Executive education often uses the core-and-spoke model. In executive education programs learners are given access to high-value seminars, group classes, and offsite programs complemented with outside resources such as books and articles.

The U.S. Navy's Flag University manages a seven-year executive education program for admirals and civilian executives (the top

six hundred executives in the Navy). The program is highly customized and references dozens of supporting materials available to
executives based on their individual needs. Each admiral has access
to a detailed self-assessment system to help him determine areas for
future work. He then customizes his own learning plan. The Flag
University team continuously reviews and offers new learning
programs as part of the ongoing curriculum.

As Figure 4.16 shows, the Navy's FLAG Executive Education
program itself is a linear program with very specific modules that
must occur at set times during this seven-year period. NFOTS, for
example, is a classroom course that introduces admirals to their
peers and brings in business executives for discussions.

At each step in the program the individual learner is given
hundreds of resources, courses, reference materials, and coaching
sessions to select. The FLAG University staff serve as coaches to

Figure 4.16.   U.S. Navy Executive Education Roadmap

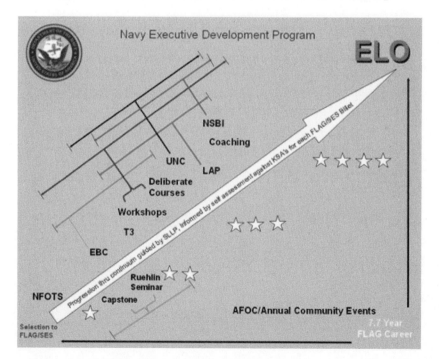

**Figure 4.17.   U.S. Navy Portal Provides
Core-and-Spoke Resources**

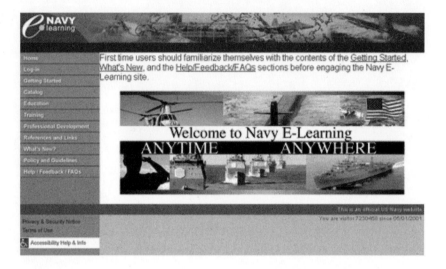

help each admiral get precisely the training needed. Outside of the defined events there is no blended learning curriculum per se, but rather a wide range of learning options that are custom fit for each learner.

If a learner feels that he needs help in financial accounting, for example, he can access courses through the U.S. Navy e-Learning Portal (Figure 4.17) or sign up for an outside class sponsored by Flag University.

This highly flexible core-and-spoke approach is an excellent model for executive and leadership education.

Lesson

The core-and-spoke model is effective when learners are motivated, experienced, and already experts. It gives them the choice of media and resources to succeed.

Summary: Program Flow vs. Core-and-Spoke

Most training managers have a lot of experience building linear curricula because it is the traditional approach to training. When

Table 4.2.   Summary of Program Flow vs. Core-and-Spoke Approaches

	Program Flow	Core-and-Spoke
Schedule	Linear flow of events, defined start and end of each event.	Core course is linear with optional supporting materials.
Flexibility	Rigid schedule to keep learners on track and synchronized in completion.	All resources and events around the core program are optional and self-scheduled.
Benefits for Training Organization	Highly structured and easy to assess progress, completion, and impact.	Easy to build and can easily be modified over time.
Challenges of This Approach	Requires scheduling logistics, instructor support, and demands that learners enroll and schedule time.	May not drive high levels of learning because many materials are optional. Hard to assess value of individual elements.
Learner Responsibilities	Learner has to "show up" and participate.	Learners have to take responsibility for their own learning and blending.
Examples	New hire training, major product or system rollouts.	IT training, executive education, sales training.

you consider any form of e-learning, you should make this decision quickly, because it will dramatically affect the media, cost, and complexity of the program. Table 4.2 summarizes the differences between the approaches.

Five Specific Blended Learning Models

Whenever I discuss the topic of blended learning among training and education professionals, someone always asks, "Where are the models I can use?" In an attempt to simplify this complex subject, I will take the large body of experience we have and give you some simple models to use. In reality, however, the "right" blend really varies depending on your specific learning needs and audience.

Let me use an analogy. Imagine you are a chef at a gourmet restaurant. On a given night for a given occasion, you will select from a wide variety of meats, vegetables, sauces, spices, fruits, bread, and pasta to create the best meal. Although no two dishes are identical, they do fall into categories. Imagine these are the basic categories: meat and potatoes, vegetarian, pasta, salads, desserts, and appetizers. The categories will not give you the precise dish, but you can decide what type of dish to prepare from them—and then determine the precise recipes.

Let's examine the five models described in Table 4.3.

Which Model Should You Choose?

After you decide which of the four program types you are building, the next important decision to make is which of the five models makes sense. Let us now compare the strengths and weaknesses of each.

1. e-Learning Self-Study

When do you use it? Self-study e-learning is an excellent fit for programs that require a broad reach and do not have cultural or socialization goals. It applies best to type 1 and type 2 problems where the material is not overly technical or "hands on." The self-study nature enables busy learners to complete whenever they have time.

Challenges: To drive utilization and completion you must create a series of launch, marketing, and support processes. People who are not computer savvy tend to find self-study web-based training impersonal and uninteresting unless you add complex

Table 4.3.   Five Blended Learning Models

Model	Defining Feature	Examples
1. **e-Learning self-study** with other blended media or events	A self-study course is the central learning program. No classroom training is offered. The learner accesses multiple media elements surrounding an online core-and-spoke course.	Retail sales training at PepBoys, Novell sales training, A Major Distributor of Industrial Products' SAP training, Intel's manufacturing engineer training, Kinko's sales training, Skillsoft/NETg's catalog courseware
2. **Instructor-led program** blended with self-study e-learning	The program is a blend of instructor-led events and self-study e-learning. e-Learning activities are used as prerequisites, activities during the class, and activities between classes. This is an excellent way to make classroom education more efficient.	Company F's bank call center training, Royal & Sun Insurance training, British Telecom product sales training, Verizon's new hire technician training
3. **Live e-learning** centered with other media added	Live e-learning events, or webinars, form the basis of the training. Self-study, exercises, and references are provided as surrounding activities.	Intuit's Quickbooks® training, Saba sales training, Peoplesoft product training, Grant Thornton employee training
4. **On-the-job training** (OJT) centered	The main components are on-the-job training with a manager or instructor. Largely used for programs where skills are complex and must be "shown."	IBM diversity training, U.S. Navy executive education, British Telecom's m-commerce training, Verizon's field training
5. **Simulation** and lab-centered	Simulations or labs are used. Often used for IT and application training where an entire environment can be simulated.	Roche SAP training, Verizon, Siemens financial and professional training, Cisco network certification

media. The higher the interactivity, the higher the cost, so the audience size must be large enough to amortize development costs. There are a wide variety of technical architectural issues to address to make sure that all learners can access the courseware.

Examples of where it is highly successful:	Type 1 and type 2 problems. IT training topics, update training for sales, channel, resellers, technical support training, and other specific areas where user needs to step through concepts at his or her own pace. As described earlier in this chapter, this approach is also very successful as a prerequisite to traditional classroom training.
Typical blending process:	Typically blended with online reference materials, audio or video (caveats discussed in Chapter 8), and manager intervention. Self-study programs themselves can be prerequisites to instructor-led programs.
Benefits:	No travel expenses, no scheduling needed, learners can advance at their own pace, very broad distribution and scalability to large audiences.

2. Instructor-Led Program Blended with Self-Study e-Learning

When do you use it?	The classroom is still the best way to develop new skills, awareness, and knowledge for small groups of people. When you are making cultural change, classroom training is vital. When you have "experts" to interact with, this is the best approach. Examples include new

employee training, new manager training, hands-on technical training, executive education, and workshops where groups of learners work through situations in their own work environment. It is best used for small groups (fifty or fewer) and typically e-learning is used as a prerequisite or co-requisite (see Royal & Sun and British Telcom examples presented earlier).

Challenges:
The biggest challenges are scheduling classes, assuring you have enough qualified instructors, and managing the process of enrollment. Typically, instructor-led programs are higher in cost due to travel expenses and instructor salaries. (We discuss this in Chapter 6.) Learners must devote a significant amount of personal and business time.

Examples where it is highly successful:
New hire training, product launches, major new company initiatives, ILT and workshops are often used for topics that require interaction with other learners, such as sales and customer service training where students can learn from one another. Whenever you have an outside expert or "celebrity," this is a valuable way to create excitement and drive retention. If you have a type 3 or type 4 problem, instructor-led training may be required to assess and certify skills development.

Typical blending process:
To save time and money "wrap" self-study and webinars around classroom events as prerequisites and post-class events.

Nearly every blended program we reviewed uses classroom training very sparingly and uses e-learning to get learners aligned and up-to-speed. Sometimes the classroom event itself is optional and remedial for learners who need extra assistance.

Benefits:

Rich cultural experiences are possible. Expert instructors can reach out to learners. Learners can interact with one another and ask lots of questions. ILT drives high levels of retention when the course is delivered effectively.

3. Live e-Learning-Centered with Other Media Added

When do you use it?

Live e-learning is essentially the electronic form of instructor-led training. It allows students to hear and even see (if video is used) the instructor online. Learners retain material because of the voice, interactivity, and motion included in the event. It is very effective for type 1 and type 2 training, such as new product launches, regulatory updates, organizational announcements, and so forth. Some companies (McKinsey and Grant-Thornton, for example) use webinars as their primary form of training and archive events as self-study. This media is often used as prerequisite training for classroom events.

Challenges:

One challenge of live e-learning is scheduling. Since learners are not physically attending a class, it is easy for them to either miss or ignore the event. The second biggest challenge is creating enough interactivity and excitement to make the program engaging. Techniques that increase learner involvement include the use of polling questions, interactive chats, and online video. Instructors developing these programs must become very familiar with the media, and build visually interesting slides. Webinars demand a high-energy interactive delivery style. Typically these events are limited to sixty to ninety minutes maximum. Often there are technical barriers, particularly for learners with low bandwidth connections. (See Chapter 7.)

Examples where it is highly successful:

Consider this approach to be similar to classroom instruction. Whenever you have an outside expert or "celebrity" this is a valuable way to create excitement and drive retention. "Update from the CEO," "Analysis of New Legislation by the Partner," and "Presentation by an Outside Expert" are all excellent applications of this technology. Typically, these are type 1 and 2 programs. You cannot drive competency and certification with webinars.

Typical blending process:

If the event is a type 1 or type 2 program, you should wrap supporting materials around the event—reference links, books, documents, and presentations. In order to drive skills and competencies, you must add exercises, which means adding either simulations (below) or assessments that force learners to study on their own. The webinar listening process is very passive, so learners often do not grasp or remember much of the material unless you have surrounding exercises and assessments included.

Benefits:

This medium is the easiest way to start with e-learning: costs are low, development is easy, and deployment is relatively simple. For topics in type 1 and 2, it is the preferred approach. Add assessments and simulations and exercises to drive toward type 3 and 4 programs.

4. On-the-Job Centered

When do you use it?

On-the-job training refers to exercises, coaching, discussions, and other activities that occur in the workplace and are typically led by an individual's manager.

We find in our research that this form of education and training is widely used in manufacturing and process education ("how to use the call center systems," "how to maintain a piece of equipment," "how to make a good sales call.")

The purpose of this approach is to bring the training directly to the work environment and simulate the real-world experience. Having a manager involved has many benefits: first, it increases the learner's motivation to succeed; second, the manager becomes intimately involved in the learning process and now understands the learner's needs; third, the manager is now obligated to engage with the training organization because they have a formal responsibility for the training process.

Verizon's new hire training for field service technicians, for example, is filled with on-the-job training in field locations. These exercises are designed to follow online courseware that gives learners background and basic prerequisite information.

Challenges:	In most organizations OTJ training already exists. If you are developing it from the beginning, you must focus training the managers in the field. e-Learning will help reduce the amount of time and effort in OTJ training by adding pre-work, references, and post-event assessments. In Verizon's case, for example, the "time to train" was reduced by 30 percent by adding self-study to their existing field training programs. Training throughout tripled without adding more instructors.
Examples where it is highly successful:	Type 3 and 4 problems such as field technician training, call center training, and process training. In retail sales training OTJ exercises can reinforce concepts presented on the web. DigitalThink, for example, inserts OTJ "learning checks"

into their web-based courseware for retail sales training. The learner must print out a checklist of in-store activities and take an assessment that must be delivered by the manager. The manager then enters the score into the LMS to validate that the on-the-job exercise was completed. This real-world assessment increases learning effectiveness by 200 percent and more, and drives the employee to complete the self-study courses.

Typical blending process:

As the examples show, OTJ can be inserted as steps in the overall program.

Benefits:

If mastery is your goal, you must include OTJ. OTJ improves motivation, it engages and involves line management, and it gives learners the confidence to learn material in a real-world environment. Only with this type of training will a student truly "master" a subject.

5. Simulation and Lab Centered

When do you use it?

Simulations and labs give learners the ability to learn by doing in a safe environment. The most common uses of simulations are in IT training, software application training, ERP application training, and scenario-based business skills training. The term "lab" refers to an environment in which the students can try different parts of their learning in the real world. In NCR's network repair certification program, for example, online virtual labs are used to configure and test routers. These online labs enable learners to configure, test, and maintain routers across the Internet without having to physically attend the lab.

Challenges:

Simulations, as we discuss in Chapter 8, can become complex and expensive to build. Business simulations, military simulations, and management simulations often take tens to hundreds of thousands of dollars to author. Companies find, however, that when the audience is large and diverse and the learning challenge requires a highly complex set of skills, simulation can pay off. The Siemens global accounting change used an expensive business simulation that paid for itself many times over. One category of simulations that has become very popular and easy to author is software application. Tools now enable you to build realistic simulations of software systems such as ERP rollouts or call center training at a modest cost.

Examples where it is highly successful:

Siemens used financial simulations to help more than 10,000 accounting professionals learn how to use U.S. generally accepted accounting principles; Company W and Roche Pharmaceuticals used application simulations to teach users of SAP how to use an upgraded order entry and sales processing system; Wells Fargo used application simulations to dramatically reduce the cost and time to train new call center agents; Dell Computer uses scenario-based simulations to train telesales representatives.

Typical blending process: Simulations are powerful learning exercises. Most simulation-based programs surround the learning with a kickoff meeting or webinar to establish learning objectives and follow the simulation with a series of assessments or discussion groups to help people share and learn from their experience in the simulation. In Siemens' case the program had five different simulations, each in stages, and the learners could not start the next chapter until they had successfully completed the prior chapter.

Benefits: Simulations drive mastery because the learner "learns by doing." Your learning problem has very high costs of error (military, call center agents, sales entry, airline pilots), then simulations are a good fit. Once developed, they scale tremendously and can touch thousands of learners at a fraction of the cost of traditional on-the-job training.

Lessons Learned in This Chapter

1. There are two broad approaches to blending: *content flow* and *core-and-spoke*. Content flow is the more traditional approach. Core-and-spoke is used for highly motivated and independent learners.

2. There are five basic blending models that use the sixteen different media types. If you familiarize yourself with these models in advance of program design, you will save time and money in selecting tools and infrastructure, and developing content.

3. There are no "perfect" models for any particular problem. By reviewing the examples here you can select a simple blended model then add more complexity as you learn what works.

4. As technology evolves, new models will develop. These models represent the basic five approaches, but as new tools become available the specific implementations of each will change.

5. In nearly every high-impact program, blending models use two or three approaches. Do not throw everything against the wall to see what sticks. Every media and learning activity should have a specific business purpose and learning objective.

Chapter Five

Eight Criteria for Selecting the Blending Model

Now that we have introduced the two flow models and the five fundamental models for building blended learning programs, you can start to see the options available (Figure 5.1). The next issue to address is that of "portfolio management," selecting the right combination of media and activities to solve your training problem.

One lesson I have learned in the design of training programs is the importance of asking the right questions. In this chapter

Figure 5.1. Where We Are

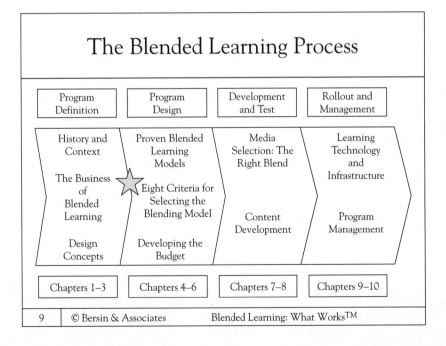

The Blended Learning Process

Program Definition	Program Design	Development and Test	Rollout and Management
History and Context	Proven Blended Learning Models	Media Selection: The Right Blend	Learning Technology and Infrastructure
The Business of Blended Learning	Eight Criteria for Selecting the Blending Model	Content Development	Program Management
Design Concepts	Developing the Budget		
Chapters 1–3	Chapters 4–6	Chapters 7–8	Chapters 9–10

9   © Bersin & Associates   Blended Learning: What Works™

we identify the eight questions you should ask (we call them the eight criteria) before you design your program. After we review these criteria, we will dive into program design in detail.

Criterion 1: Program Type

The first and most important criterion is the program type (types 1–4 are shown in Table 3.1 on page 46). Program type is driven by business need, not the content itself. The best way to identify the program type is to ask yourself a few pertinent questions:

- What is the revenue or cost impact of this particular training problem?
- How do we know that this is a training issue and not a management issue?
- Do we know whether mastery is needed to solve this problem? Or would access to information solve the problem?
- Is the problem big enough to justify a major strategic investment in training?
- How will line management measure impact? Do they want and need a measurable solution?

The program type will help you identify the level of mastery you are trying to achieve as well as the need to measure and certify the results. When we get into media selection in Chapter 7, you will see that certain media are good for tracking and others are not. In type 1 and 2 training, you can afford to develop a program that does not require completion or mandatory assessments. In type 3 it becomes important to assess learners, and in type 4 it is essential.

Criterion 2: Cultural Goals

The second criterion to consider is what I call "culture-building" goals. In our research we often find that a key subgoal of training is to build or reinforce a company culture. Culture means "the shared beliefs, values, and practices of a group."

In most organizations, culture has far more impact on behavior than skills and competencies. Culture affects the way that individuals behave when they are untrained, unmanaged, or unsupervised.

What role does culture-building play in training? Often a very large role. Many training programs have significant culture-building goals. Table 5.1 lists several examples.

In these programs a key goal is to introduce learners to each other—to create relationships, linkages, and shared values. These relationships are important to give employees a set of resources and peers to help them make decisions on an ongoing basis.

Typically, the two most popular ways to meet this goal are through face-to-face meetings and project-based learning. Case studies, group projects, and group presentations drive people to

Table 5.1. Culture-Building Examples

Program	Typical Culture-Building Goals
New Hire Training	Employees meeting each other
	Employees understanding company values
	Employees building network of new hires
	Employees meeting executives
	Employees developing a support network
New Manager Training	New managers meeting other new managers
	New managers meeting executives
	New managers developing a support network
	New managers working through common personnel issues
Executive Education	Executives learning how to work with one another
	Executives sharing their strengths and weaknesses
	Executives learning to problem solve together
	Executives creating new strategic directions
Leadership Training	Leaders learning from other leaders
	Leaders building a support network

work together and get to know one another. Although you may believe that these activities require face-to-face interaction, many programs accomplish such culture building through e-learning technologies.

Figure 5.2 shows an example of how Grant Thornton, a leading accounting, tax, and business advisory firm serving the middle-market, uses culture building in their criteria for blended learning. They built this model to help identify program types that compare online presence to face-to-face presence.

At Grant Thornton webcasting (live e-learning) is the core training medium. These programs fall on the left column of the chart and are either self-study (lower left) or live (upper left). Face-to-face

Figure 5.2. Culture-Building Goals vs. Performance Goals

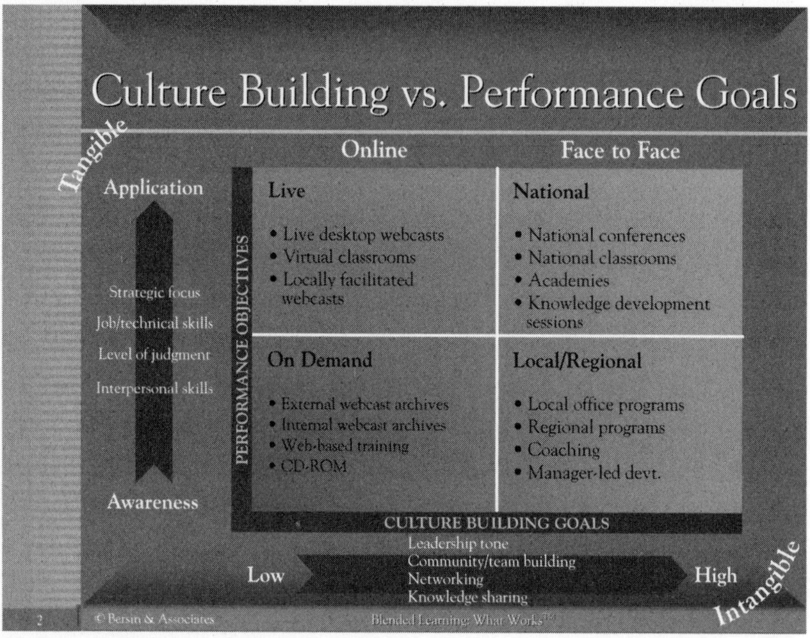

Compliments of Grant Thornton.

meetings and classes fall on the right. Here culture-building goals are high.

In 2002 Grant Thornton hired a large number of accountants from Arthur Andersen. These new employees needed to learn Grant Thornton processes and procedures but also needed to meet the partners, meet each other, and learn about the culture of the firm. To solve this training problem, Grant Thornton relied on the program elements shown on the right side of this chart.

One of the training activities Grant Thornton uses periodically is called a "National Conference." These events, typically conducted annually, bring together partners and many accountants for a few days of meetings and updates on important industry topics. These sessions build both application skills as well as culture and fit in to the upper-right quadrant of the chart. Although they are expensive, the payoff is well worth it.

Criterion 3: Audience

Audience analysis is the third area to explore. Many aspects of the audience are important. The most critical are described below.

Audience Size

How large is the audience? This will drive your decision about using a highly scalable medium versus a low scalability medium. (We will discuss this topic in Chapter 7.) A *large* audience is typically one measured in thousands. This size mandates some kind of electronic delivery, often self-study. A *small* audience is in the hundreds, which can often be handled by classroom or virtual classroom methods. Are they global? Or are they located in easy-to-convene locations. These are issues to think about up-front.

Job Role

What are the job roles of your target audience? Are they computer programmers? Entry-level service representatives? Senior engineers? Eighteen-year-old college freshmen?

The job role tells you their precise daily responsibilities and therefore their expectations, time constraints, and level of interaction with others. In Company W's SAP rollout, for example, the audience was telesales representatives in very busy jobs. These individuals are paid by the hour and have very little free time for training. The blended learning program must fit into their busy schedules and be available in a modular basis that can be taken during break times and staggered work interruptions.

Education Level

The educational background of your audience is important. How well can they read? Is a graphical or video-based program more appropriate? In Verizon's new hire training program, much of the online component consists of video and audio so that the audience can watch and listen instead of reading. These are individuals with a high school education who are training to be installation and repair technicians. The program must accommodate their vocabulary and reading level.

In Flag Executive Education at the U.S. Navy[1], by contrast, the executives are college educated so all program materials are designed to appeal to highly educated professionals.

Familiarity with Technology

Is your audience really ready for technology? In Giant Eagle Foods'[2] management training the company realized that many of the employees did not know how to use a mouse. Giant Eagle had to

---

[1]U.S. Navy Flag program.
[2]Giant Eagle Foods management training.

build a short introductory module to familiarize the learners with the use of the mouse.

For Cisco's Certified Network Engineer[3] program, the audience is typically very facile with technology. To satisfy their need for hands-on technology experience, these programs use virtual labs that enable learners to log in and configure real Cisco routers over the Internet. These learners want hands-on experience and feel very comfortable interacting with equipment over the Internet.

Motivation to Learn

The biggest challenge I see when reviewing e-learning programs is the problem of audience participation. In most corporate programs, attendance is somewhat voluntary, meaning that motivation is a key issue in program design.

There are broadly two types of corporate programs: *directed* (or mandatory) and *voluntary* (optional). Directed programs are typically driven through company mandate with first-line manager enforcement. If the business processes and culture supports these programs, you will typically find that 80 percent or more of your audience will enroll in these programs.

Voluntary programs, by contrast, are much harder to administer. You are now in the role of marketing, explaining, selling, and convincing people to take the program. We will devote much more time to this subject in Chapter 10.

"What's in It for Me?" It is important to ask, "Why would this individual want to enroll in and complete this program?" What is in it for them? Think about the motivation issues: Are they being paid for the time spent in training? Will they receive a raise as a result? Will this training be put on their performance appraisals? How does their manager feel about the value of the program?

---

[3]Cisco Certified Network Engineer program with labs.

Motivating the First-Line Manager. The most important person to consider in making a training program successful is the first-line manager. Motivating the first-line manager is your biggest challenge. How will managers feel about employees taking time away from their jobs? Why should a first-line manager make time for this program? What business value will they see? Increased sales? Happier employees? Lower turnover? Fewer errors?

Time Available to Learn

A simple but often overlooked problem in blended learning and e-learning programs is making time for people to interrupt their busy day for training. Corporate life has become a frantic set of e-mails, meetings, phone calls, and tasks to complete. Workers who are paid hourly often will not take time for classes unless they are paid. Workers in a production position rarely have time unless their managers give them time off.

At British Airways[4] the company found that e-learning was difficult to take because much of their audience is on planes or in transit. They did not have time or a quiet place to take the programs. The answer: airport learning labs. British Air set up a learning lab at Heathrow Airport for traveling workers to check in and take training before, between, and after long journeys.

Access to Network and PCs

Obviously, learners need the ability to access content. We find in our research that, despite the widespread use of the Internet and PCs in the United States, outside the U.S. Internet access can be problematic. In some countries Internet access is expensive or slow and erratic. In the case of NCR's global network certification[5] program, for example, workers in remote locations have to go to Internet cafés to access content. Many of the programs we reviewed

---

[4]British Airways e-learning program, with locations to study quietly.
[5]NCR global network certification program, Internet cafes.

also use CD-ROM versions of courseware so that learners can access content without the restriction of having to connect to the Internet. You need to understand what infrastructure is available before you make media decisions.

Manager Role in the Program

You must carefully consider the role of employees' first-line managers. These people have the biggest impact on completion rates. They will want to see the material in advance. If managers are heavily involved through learning checks or on-the-job exercises, you will need to train them.

Typically, for large programs you need a "change agent" to reach out to line managers. If managers are not "sold" or believe that the program is too complex or burdensome, you will have a hard time rolling the program out. Select the blend in a way that engages the first-line managers in the process, gives them regular feedback, and makes them feel confident that their employees will find the program easy, enjoyable, and effective.

Criterion 4: Budget

We will discuss budgeting in detail in the following chapter, but budget is one of your major constraints in a blended learning program. Your budget should have three parts:

1. Development Budget

The development budget covers the funds and resources needed to build the content. This is typically a capital outlay and is fixed. You can then divide it by the audience size to get a benchmark development cost per learner, which is a good way to benchmark different programs for cost effectiveness. If you build a business case, you may be able to set this budget yourself.

2. LMS and Infrastructure Budget

Do you have an LMS already? Will you need to build or buy one in order for this program to work? Do you need to pay an outsourced LMS provider for delivery fees or "hosting" fees?

3. Delivery or Deployment Budget

Do not overlook this. The delivery or deployment budget is the amount of money and resources you have to provide launch materials, marketing materials, promotional giveaways, and so forth. If you want your program to be successful, you should always allocate between 10 and 15 percent of your overall program budget to program management and delivery support.

Criterion 5: Resources

What resources do you have at your disposal to make this program successful? How easy will it be to access these skills? How much time and money will it cost to gain access to these people? Here are the typical resources that you will need to be successful, although in many programs these people will play a smaller role.

Program Manager

The program manager is the person who "owns" the overall success of the program. This person identifies the business need, creates the business case, develops a budget, obtains funding, and typically makes the final decisions on content blend, vendor partnerships, and the measure of success. This is a mandatory role and typically resides in the training department. The program manager makes the big decisions and manages the project.

Project Manager

In many organizations the program manager is given the title "project manager." For the purposes of this book, we will refer to the project manager as *a separate person who worries about schedules, resources, budget, and the project deadlines.*

One of the evolutionary steps most training organizations make is to create the project manager role. This person becomes an expert at the budget, time, and resource needs of various elements of the blended program—and also uses Microsoft Project® or another tool to make sure that the project stays on track. This person also typically manages weekly status meetings and holds different parties accountable when the schedule starts to slip.

I have seen that, for any project that is $75,000 or more in overall cost, this role is critical, and I highly recommend that you define this role.

Instructional Designer

The instructional designer is the person who owns the instructional architecture, content, and learning plan for the program. In blended learning program there is a business objective, a learning objective, an assessment strategy, and then a series of media elements and flow that create the entire program. The instructional designer takes responsibility for making sure that:

- The media elements fit together into an overall effective program;
- Each individual element has a reasonable objective and its content meets that objective; and
- Other developers use standard instructional design techniques and do not sway from the overall theme and flow of the program.

The biggest issue in blended learning is the relationship among the instructional designer, the subject-matter expert (SME), and the web developer (below). A variety of tools are used to manage this relationship: review processes, status meetings, check-points, design reviews, user testing, and check-in processes.

Web Developer

The web developer is the person who actually develops web-based content. These people must have intimate knowledge of HTML, Java® script, SQL, and other technologies. They typically also use DreamWeaver®, Flash, and other development tools to create content. This is often the role that is outsourced to a web design firm that specializes in e-learning content.

In some cases the instructional designer has developed the skills to take on this role. However, for a large program I strongly recommend that these roles be separated so that the technology limitations themselves do not limit the instructional design. In most cases an instructional designer can create a learning plan and assessment plan, and then the web developer works within this framework to build content. The two must interact continuously and often sit right next to each other or are joined together for the entire project.

A new category of e-learning we call "Rapid e-Learning" enables the development of web-based courseware directly from PowerPoint. If you are building this type of program, you may be able to avoid using a web developer. However, typically you still need technical skills for final editing, publishing, and deployment into your LMS.

Subject-Matter Experts (SMEs)

Working with SMEs is the trickiest part of all content development. In blended programs the challenges are magnified. In one of our recent surveys we found that "working with SMEs" was the second-most-cited challenge in e-learning development (after "it takes too long to build a course").

In any program you should think about how you will interact with SMEs. They are typically very busy people and they are often "on loan" to the training department. The team only has access to them for limited amounts of time. Most companies use an interviewing process to make the SME interaction efficient. Some examples of the types of interview questions to consider are

- What are the biggest challenges people face with this training problem?
- What background information do people need?
- What experiences do you think people should obtain?
- What are some of the exercises or interactivities you recommend?
- What are the technical skills required in this application?
- How do you measure proficiency?
- What are the "gotcha's" we should cover?

In the program design phase you must consider two questions:

1. How much access can you expect (hours, days, or weeks available) from the SME?
2. Can/will the SME author content for you (slides, documents, FAQs, and other materials)?

In some cases, if you are developing type 1 and type 2 programs, you can ask the SME to build much of the program in PowerPoint using Rapid e-Learning tools (PowerPoint to Flash tools such as Macromedia Breeze®) or live e-learning tools. Since PowerPoint is the tool of choice for SMEs, Rapid e-Learning and live e-learning appeal naturally to SMEs.

You must be careful here, however. If you choose to bypass the instructional designer, you run risks. Typically SMEs get into too much detail, use too much jargon, go too fast, or skip basic instructional background when they present material. Always use some instructional design principals before giving SMEs direct responsibility for content.

Example: Novell gives product managers an instructionally designed template in PowerPoint for every new product launch (Figure 5.3). The SME then creates a presentation based on this template, adds notes for narration, and turns it over to the training department. The training department then cleans up the content, adds professional narration to each slide, and publishes the slides into courseware using a Rapid e-Learning tool called Macromedia Breeze. They

**Figure 5.3.   Novell Instructional Templates
for SME-Authored Content**

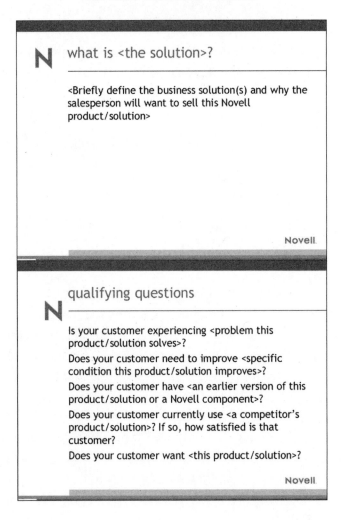

then wrap conference calls and a wide variety of other tools around these courses to train channel partners on new products.

Example: Grant Thornton, a leading mid-market accounting, tax, and business advisory organization, invests heavily in live e-learning for their blended learning programs. Subject-matter experts (often senior accountants) are coached by the strategic learning group to create interesting and easy-to-understand slides, and then deliver them from dedicated training rooms with excellent bandwidth, video facilities, and tools to make the experience easy for the SMEs (Figure 5.4).

Criterion 6: Time

Time issues can dramatically impact program design.

- How much time do you have before the program must be launched?

Figure 5.4. Grant Thornton Live E-Learning Meeting Room

- How much time do you have before the program must be completed?
- What is the duration of time learners can afford to spend in the program?

The timeline or lifecycle of a typical blended learning program is shown in Figure 5.5.

Development Time (Target Launch Date)

What is your total time to develop? When MUST the program be launched? Within the development time, you have to schedule time for content development, testing, and launch processes. If your time is short, some media may just be impossible to use.

Figure 5.5. Program Lifecycle—Time Issues

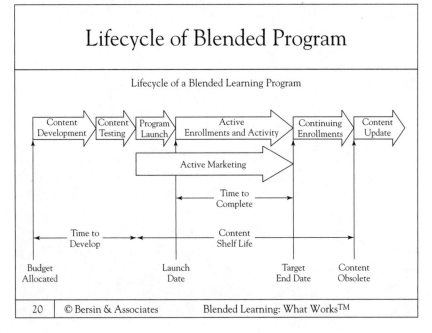

Time to Complete (Target End Date)

By when must the program be completed? In some cases this is an ongoing process and the program goes on for years. In some cases, however, a completion date is critical and the program must be "rolled out" by a certain date. This will limit the amount of time you have for launch and marketing and will set in place the processes you must build to ensure that the program is completed on time.

Content Shelf Life (When Is Content Obsolete?)

This is a critical time point. When will the content become out-of-date? Based on that information, how much money should be invested in the content itself? Should you build it in a form that can be easily updated? Or should you design content elements that can be thrown away? This time characteristic is an important one to consider long before you develop any content itself.

Criterion 7: Learning Content

Content-related issues are at the heart of any training program. To simplify the blending process, we break the content question down into two simple criteria, content complexity and content interactivity.

Content Complexity

"Complexity" is a simple term with many possible meanings. The question is, "How much time and thought-power will it take the learner to absorb the material." Understanding how to turn on a computer is simple. Understanding how to install a new application is complex. Understanding how to configure and customize the software is highly complex.

As an example, Kinko's developed a simple model (Figure 5.6) that requires the program manager to rank complexity into five

Figure 5.6. Kinko's Content Description Model

Analyst's Name: Kinko's		**Date:** 2/1/2003
Course/Module: Sample Course/Module		
Objective/Unit: Sample Objective		

Knowledge or Skill? | Knowledge / Skill | Kinko's Specific or Generic? | Kinko's Specific / Generic

Enter a rating from 1-5 for each instructional criterion listed below.

Criteria	Rating	Rating Definitions
Content Stability Estimated frequency that content must be updated.	5	1 = Needs updating weekly 2 = Needs updating monthly 3 = Needs updating quarterly 4 = Needs updating annually 5 = Needs updating less than once per year
Content Complexity Content complexity level.	2	1 = Highly advanced 2 = Advanced 3 = Intermediate 4 = Basic 5 = Simple information
Degree of Interaction Amount of interaction required during effective learning process.	1	1 = Total interaction 2 = Very frequent interaction 3 = Moderate interaction 4 = Some interaction 5 = No interaction
Frequency of Utilization Estimated frequency that learner will utilize behavior/skill.	2	1 = Daily 2 = Weekly 3 = Monthly 4 = Several times per year 5 = Once per year or less
Dissemination Speed Required timeframe for beginning content dissemination to target population.	3	1 = Within days 2 = Within weeks 3 = Within months (quarter) 4 = Within one year 5 = More than one year
Population Size Size and location(s) of target population.	5	1 = 0–50 people in one location 2 = 0–50 people in multiple locations 3 = 51–500 people in one location 4 = 51–500 people in multiple locations 5 = Over 500 people

levels. Complexity is defined subjectively as "simple, basic, intermediate, advanced, and highly advanced." Complexity will drive longer content, with more branching and more interactivity. You don't need to overwork this criterion, but as you develop more and more programs you should develop a framework for ranking programs from low to high in complexity.

Content Interactivity (Learning by Doing)

"Interactivity" connotes the amount of learner interaction required. There are many schools of thought on interactivity. Some believe that interactivity is the only way to learn. For some problems (type 1 and 2), reading and listening is enough.

We know from research that competency levels and retention levels are higher with more interactivity. As we discussed in Chapter 3, "mastery" requires learning by doing.

The question you must ask is, "How much interactivity is required for my particular problem?" For many training problems the term mastery is not appropriate. In type 1 and 2 problems, your primary goal is transferring information and knowledge—not creating skills and competencies. Therefore it is not worth the time and expense to develop interactive exercises in an e-learning or instructor-led format.

> **Example:** When Novell rolls out new sales training to their resellers, they are not trying to develop mastery of the skills of selling, but they are trying to drive awareness and knowledge about the new offerings and to fit this information into existing skills in selling. These programs use conference calls and audio-based PowerPoint media and are highly effective. No interactivity was needed.

> **Example:** When Company W and Roche roll out new versions of SAP, they must make sure that all users are fully proficient in these systems so that orders are processed quickly and accurately. In these programs interactivity must be built into the training—and in this case it was accomplished using an application simulation tool called InfoPak® from RWD Technologies. These interactivities gave users the confidence to "learn by doing" in a safe environment and then show their knowledge to their managers for validation.

> **Example:** When IBM decided to train all first-line managers on handling workplace diversity, they felt that competency was not only necessary but must be demonstrated. This required online interactivities as well as manager-led discussion groups that dealt with typical workplace diversity cases.

Criterion 8: Technology

Before you spend any money on development, you must understand the nature of your deployment environment. What type of computer, software, and network infrastructure will you demand? We discuss this in the content development section in more detail, but it may be a critical criterion when deciding what media you can use. If your organization has limited technology infrastructure, then clearly that limits your media choices.

Bandwidth Required

How much bandwidth can you expect a typical learner to have access to? Will learners need to access content from dial-up? If so, will your media accommodate this? Will they need to access content offline? What is your minimum bandwidth supported?

Plug-Ins Required

Does your company or organization have standards for PC plug-ins? Will everyone have Windows Media Player or Real Media? Will everyone have an Internet Explorer version with Flash? What about Netscape®? Will you need to support Unix client workstations that have limited plug-ins?

Tracking Standards

Will your content have to support AICC standards? Has your media been tested in your LMS?

Display Standards

What size and color depth will you require? Most PCs come with 800×600 pixel displays, but many older computers have lower resolution. What color standards make sense? 8-bit (older), 16-bit (newer), or 24-bit (newest)? Your content developer will need to know, because size and bit-depth can change content significantly.

Security Standards

Who will have access to the content? Do you mind if people copy it? Will offline versions (CD-ROM) be secure?

Other Risk Areas

Are there any vendor-specific technologies you are thinking about using? Simulation engines or live e-learning plug-ins? If so, these are deployment risks. They may not run or be available everywhere. Consider these as criteria for your media.

These eight criteria must be considered before you develop content or design a program. Consider all eight carefully before you start. Each of the eight can impact program design and the roll-out process. Spend several weeks reviewing these criteria before defining your budget, creating your blended model, or selecting development tools and infrastructure. A summary of the eight criteria is in Appendix E.

Lessons Learned in This Chapter

1. There are eight major criteria to consider when defining your blending mix: program type, cultural goals, audience, budget, resources, time, learning content, and technology.

2. The program type is the most important factor to consider because it drives decisions on measurement, tracking, and learning objectives.

3. Cultural goals are critically important to consider because they drive decisions for live versus self-study and group interaction versus individual learning.

4. There are several major aspects to audience analysis, including the size, job roles, education level, familiarity with technology, motivation to learn, time available to learn, access to networks and PCs, and the role of their first-line manager.

5. Resources are a "make-or-break" decision for certain programs. You must consider the availability of instructional designers, SMEs, web developers, project managers, and executive support for each program.

6. There is a typical lifecycle for a blended learning program. You should map out your timeline in advance because it will highlight constraints you have in content development, program management, launch, and completion.

7. Content itself is critically important, but you can categorize your content needs into easy, medium, and hard, which will make it easier to decide which media to use.

8. Technology enablement will drive decisions about what type of program you can roll out. Be realistic with your technology availability and build for the "lowest common denominator" so all learners can participate and complete your program.

Chapter Six

Developing the Budget

The cost of a blended learning program often drives many of the decisions about program design. In this chapter we discuss the economics of blended learning and how you can develop a reasonable budget that meets your program needs. Figure 6.1 shows where we are on our learning path.

Figure 6.1. Where We Are

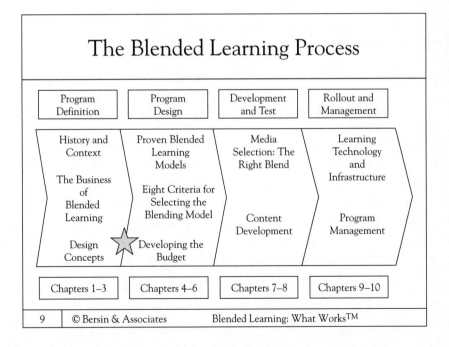

In some cases, the entire program is budget-driven: you have a certain amount of money to spend and you have to decide how to allocate these dollars for best results. In other cases you will be asked to develop the budget for a program with a key business goal. For both cases you must understand the cost components of the entire program and how you should allocate dollars to each of these different elements.

In nearly every corporate program, cost control is a key issue. One purpose of this chapter is to give you the perspective and tools to make sure that your program costs do not run out of control. As we discussed earlier, training is an expense item in most corporations, so any dollar saved is a dollar applied toward company profit.

As background to this topic, in 2002 and 2003 we conducted a major industry study of blended learning programs by investigating eighteen major corporate programs. (The study is entitled *Blended Learning: What Works*™[1]). At the end of this chapter we will review the cost models of these programs so you have a clear perspective on what drives program cost and what your overall budget should be.

Sizing the Budget: Define the Size of the Problem

In most organizations the program budget is fixed: "We have $75,000 to roll out this program. Go do it." In this case you have a simple problem: select the right media and program scope to stay within this fixed budget. The problem with this approach is that you have no way of scaling up the program design to meet the size of the potential business benefit.

The best way to budget is to start with the business problem. As we discussed in Chapter 1, all training programs are designed

---

[1]*Blended Learning: What Works*™ is updated regularly and is available for purchase by going to www.bersin.com or www.blendedlearning.com.

to either increase sales or reduce costs. One of your roles as a program manager is to work with line managers to estimate these potential benefits. This process should be your first step in program design.

If your company is launching a new product, for example, the product manager already has a revenue target. As part of the product launch a certain percentage of the total budget will be allocated to sales and channel training. This training budget may compete with R&D, support, marketing, advertising, and PR. In my life as a product manager, often the training budget was not even included in the launch plan. Find out what the product revenue targets are and convince yourself that the company is spending the right percentage of the total launch budget on sales training. A lesson here—skimping on sales training always results in higher costs later—costs of reduced sales, costs of poor support, and costs of errors in product implementation, installation, and delivery. If you are not allocating 10 to 15 percent of your product launch budget to training, you are spending too little.

Other business problems have different benefit models. If you are implementing a new safety training program, you can estimate the cost of an accident and, based on that cost, come up with a reasonable percentage of that cost you can and should spend on training to prevent or reduce such accidents.

If you work in a retail organization, one of the highest costs is turnover. What is the turnover rate today? What is a reasonable reduction you can expect from your new blended learning program? Can you get line managers to buy in to that reduction? (Typically we find that good retail sales training programs can reduce turnover by 30 percent or more.)

Lets revisit the Siemens example. Siemens understood that by being listed on the New York Stock Exchange they could generate many billions in market capital. This required a complete change in company accounting practices, which in turn required retraining more than 10,000 financial professionals throughout the organization. Given the very impact of the corporate program, a training budget of several million dollars seemed very reasonable.

Compute Cost Per Learner

An important concept in budgeting is to think about the program in terms of "total delivered cost per learner." This number measures the total delivered cost of a blended learning program, divided by the total number of learners served. The *total delivered cost* includes:

- Content development cost (cost to build the program elements);
- Infrastructure cost (cost to deploy and use the LMS and other infrastructure);
- Delivery cost (cost to deliver the classroom, on-the-job, physical, and electronic elements of the program);
- Program management costs (cost to launch, market, support, and measure the program); and
- Learner time and travel costs (cost of learners' time and travel to participate).

By computing total delivered cost per learner, you can compare each potential media element for its cost-effectiveness. You can also compare your total program against other programs and other models to make sure you are using the most cost-effective approach.

Let's look at Novell's reseller training program. The bulk of Novell's revenues come from resellers. This channel is made up of 6,500 resellers and consultants with a total learner audience of approximately 25,000 people. Novell rolls out nearly forty new products and services every year. Based on the size and potential revenue of the product, the company allocates a varying amount of money for reseller training.

Let's assume that a new Novell product is expected to generate $25 million in new revenue over the next three years. This translates into an average revenue of $1,000 per reseller. (We know that these numbers will be skewed toward certain high-volume resellers, but let's use the average anyway.)

If the company allocates 1 percent of the revenue toward sales training, the total program budget for training should be approximately $250,000 over this period of time. This translates into $10 per learner.

This $10 number gives us a "gut feel" for the value of the program. Is it worth $10 per sales representative to learn about this particular product? Would it have been worth $20? If we made the program more complex, and it cost $30, would that have been worth it?

In this simple example we are not including the cost of the learners' time or travel—the "non-training organization" expenses. We will explore this metric further in this chapter. These expenses become very important when comparing media and making blending decisions.

Economics of Blended Learning

There is a simple economic model that drives all blended learning investments. In any training program there are two types of costs: *fixed* costs and *variable* costs.

Fixed costs are fixed regardless of the number of learners (for example, the cost of content development, the cost of purchasing a tool). Variable costs go up with the number of participants.

- Fixed costs (development and infrastructure costs): content development, implementation of an LMS, purchasing tools.
- Variable costs (delivery costs): program management, marketing, license of software, support.

The fundamental difference between e-learning and traditional instructor-led training is that in e-learning (theoretically) the variable costs or delivery costs are far lower than for instructor-led training.

In instructor-led training you pay for instructor salaries, travel, facility expense, salary of students, and lost productivity. In e-learning there are no instructor costs and no travel costs, and the time away from the job is far shorter.

Therefore in e-learning or blended learning, you are willing to pay more in fixed costs (infrastructure and development costs) because you are saving so much money in delivery costs.

Hence, if you want blended learning to compete economically with traditional instructor-led training, you must keep your variable costs low enough to cover the fixed costs of e-learning content development, tools, and other technologies. In other words, *for blended learning to save money over traditional approaches, the cost of content development and infrastructure must not rise so high as to dwarf the cost savings in electronic delivery.*

The Five Components of the Budget

All e-learning and blended learning programs have five cost components. Let us now examine these components in detail. (A worksheet is included at the end of this chapter to use for future reference.)

Content Development Costs

Content development costs are the up-front costs of developing content itself. They are typically measured in development cost per student hour of content, meaning the cost to develop a single hour of content. These include:

- Content development expense (time and salary of employees or consultants);
- Cost of subject-matter experts' time (typically line employees who are already very busy with other projects);

- Web development (time and expense of IT-related personnel, typically twenty to thirty hours overall to publish or update content for your website, depending on your skills internally);
- Purchase of development tools, simulation tools, or assessment tools specific to this project (typically $5,000 to $20,000); and
- Cost of testing the content in a production environment to make sure that all the infrastructure and delivery technology works flawlessly (Do not ignore this step!).

In the next chapter we will show you how to estimate these costs based on the media you select. Typical development costs can range from $5,000 per delivered hour to more than $75,000 per delivered hour, depending on your media choices, internal resources, and experience. (A rule of thumb for web-based courseware: you should consider approximately twelve pages of dense content for one student hour.) In the next chapter we will give you guidelines for content development of different media.

Part of your content development costs will also be content maintenance. If your program is a type 1 or type 2 program, you will typically throw away the content or keep it unchanged once the program is complete. However, for type 3 and type 4 programs, you will need to modify and update the content every year or so to keep it current. This maintenance budget should include the cost of upgrading the content itself, the cost of subject-matter experts' time, and the cost of technology changes. In the first year of a program this will be negligible, but if you are budgeting for a several year rollout you should assume a major upgrade to the program every twelve to eighteen months.

Infrastructure Costs (LMS, Hardware, and Software)

Infrastructure costs cover the expense of technology and software used to deploy, manage, and maintain the program. These are typically amortized over many programs and in some cases are considered "free" if these services already exist. They include:

- Purchase and implementation of some LMS (or internal development);
- Purchase and implementation of content delivery servers;
- Purchase and implementation of assessment and measurement systems; and
- Purchase and implementation of hardware, databases, and other IT infrastructure.

If you do not already have such systems, you can estimate that a new LMS implementation will cost $30 to $100 per learner for software and implementation services. (Some very large ERP-like implementations can be two to three times this.) You must add an additional 30 to 50 percent to that for hardware, database, and other systems. The larger the audience, the smaller the cost will be per learner.

The operational cost of an LMS is typically 15 to 25 percent of its initial implementation cost, so if your LMS cost $1 million to implement, your organization will pay $150,000 to $250,000 per year for maintenance, support, and staff to keep the system running. *If you develop and deploy one hundred programs per year, each with the same audience size, the LMS alone is costing you nearly $2,000 per program for overhead.*

In most organizations, these infrastructure costs are embedded and not allocated on a program-by-program basis. If you are developing a program that requires a new LMS, however, you should use these costs in your budgeting. For a large program where cost per learner is low, the cost of the LMS will be a significant percentage of the total delivered cost.

Delivery Costs

For instructor-led training, delivery costs refer to the cost of instructor salaries, instructor travel, room rental, equipment rental, and other variable costs that are driven by the total size of the audience. In e-learning, however, there are significant delivery costs as well.

If you have a program with a large number of learners (5,000+), you will find that most electronic content must be stored and delivered through a set of computers (servers) and network bandwidth that support the workload of many users taking the content at the same time. For a very large audience, this cost can become significant because you will have to deploy multiple content servers to keep performance satisfactory.

Other delivery costs are dependent on the media mix. If you are delivering CD-ROM versions of the content, you will incur the costs of duplicating, packaging, and distributing the CD-ROM. If you use a proprietary player or plug-in, you will have delivery costs of supporting and distributing the necessary PC software to enable the program to operate. (We recommend strongly against a proprietary player, which most IT departments will veto.)

Program Management Costs

The fourth cost component (which most companies ignore) is the cost of program deployment and management. Program management includes launching the program, marketing the program, conducting meetings and conference calls to evangelize the program, staffing operational support to answer questions and resolve technical issues, and measuring results and effectiveness. *Our research has found that this step is the most critical in overall success.*

Without an ongoing program management team and launch process, many training programs die a fast death. A key part of this process is the time you spend convincing executives and line managers to support the program. Another key part is working with IT to make sure they support the software and content infrastructure.

You should also budget time for program measurement and reporting. Even if you have a mature, well-running LMS installed, you will need to spend weeks or months measuring and analyzing your program. This measurement process is needed to build executive support and to develop a process to improve the program over time. We will cover this in more detail in Chapter 10.

Some examples of these program management costs include:

- Salary and hourly expense for program manager;
- Developing and distributing marketing brochures or e-mails;
- Developing and maintaining a website for resources and Q&A;
- Purchasing measurement tools;
- Salary and hourly expense for reporting and analysis (sometimes requires writing new reports);
- Salary and hourly expense to prepare and deliver executive reviews;
- Salary and hourly expense to prepare and run program launch meetings;
- Cost to set up learning labs for learners who cannot access content through their own PCs; and
- Cost to upgrade computers so that all learners can run the required content.

Our research has found that these programmatic costs and deployment costs can be tens to hundreds of thousands of dollars. For example, when Verizon developed its blended program for new hire service technician training, they had to upgrade hundreds of PCs to run media-rich content. IT had to develop a new software utility that checked learners' PCs to make sure they had the required plug-ins before they could run the content. These costs were hundreds of thousands of dollars within a multi-million-dollar deployment.

A lesson here: Media selection will drive the cost of upgrading PCs and networks, so be very careful selecting rich media (video, audio, simulations).

Learner Time and Travel

The final component to any training program is the time and travel expense for the learners themselves. Most companies rarely compute this cost because it is not allocated to the training organization. If you want to truly rank programs for effectiveness and compute return on investment (ROI), however, you should compute this cost. *Programs that reduce the total amount of time in training typically have a large ROI*. In addition, if you want to get line managers to quickly adopt your program, convince them that it will significantly reduce learner time and travel expense.

Real Costs: The Blended Learning: What Works™ Study

Let's look at some real numbers. This study, which was conducted in 2002 and 2003, reviewed more than thirty different blended learning programs and developed detailed cost models for eighteen. The total number of learners covered by these programs was approximately 1.2 million. The participating companies included Siemens, Kinko's, Verizon, Bell Canada, Roche, a large enterprise software company, Peoplesoft, British Telecom, NCR, Royal & Sun Insurance, and others who did not want to be called by name.

The types of training programs in the study included:

- Call center training;
- SAP rollouts;
- New hire training;
- Process manufacturing certification;
- Sales training;
- Product introduction to sales and service;
- Channel training;
- Channel certification;

Table 6.1.   Blended Learning Study: Models Used

Company	Major Media	Secondary
Siemens	Simulations	On the job
Tellabs	Application Simulations	WBT
Roche	Application Simulations	WBT
Company W	Application Simulations	WBT
Ent Software Co	WBT	Classroom
British Telecom	WBT	Classroom
Royal and Sun	WBT	Classroom
Kinko's	WBT	Job Aids
Cisco	WBT	Internet Labs
EMC	WBT	Classroom
Verizon	WBT, Video	Classroom
NCR	WBT	Internet Labs
Chip Manufacturer	WBT	Classroom
Bell Canada	WBT	Classroom
Peoplesoft	WBT	Classroom

- Global accounting rollout;
- Retail product rollouts; and
- Retail process training.

Table 6.1 shows the variety of blending models encountered in this study. Each of the programs in this study included a major e-learning component and also had various combinations of instructor-led training, on-the-job interventions, and simulations.

Costs Vary Widely

In this study the cost per learner for a high-impact program ranged widely from $3.14 to more than $500. The biggest factor in cost per learner was audience size. A few of the very small audience programs generated very high costs per learner. As Table 6.2

Table 6.2.   Blended Learning: What Works™ Study Metrics

Total Program Costs

Highest Program Cost	$5,800,000
Lowest Program Cost	$ 130,000
Average Program Cost	$1,308,571

Cost Per Learner

Total # of learners in study	1,072,000
Highest cost per learner	$ 1,400
Lowest cost per learner	$ 3.14
Average cost per learner	$ 79
Standard deviation of cost per learner	$ 340
For companies with >10,000 learners	$ 58
Standard deviation of this number	$ 32
For companies with <10,000 learners	$ 257
Standard deviation of this number	$ 400

© Bersin & Associates 2003.

shows, as the number of learners goes up, the variance in cost goes down—so you can predict the delivered cost much better for large audiences than for small audiences.

Lesson

If you are going to go to the trouble of developing a blended program, make sure you are applying this effort to a problem with a relatively large audience.

Table 6.2 further shows the effect of audience size. As the audience size grows beyond 5,000, the cost per learner starts to follow a simple curve downward. The reason for this is that every one of these programs used web-based training as one of its major media elements. The cost of developing this training (a fixed cost) was significant and similar from company to company.

What Affects Program Cost?

The study found three major factors in program cost per learner:

1. *Total audience size:* Larger audiences justify a larger total program budget but should drive a lower cost per learner. This illustrates the "scale effect" of handling large audiences with Internet technologies.

2. *Media selection:* Programs that used complex web-based content (simulations, for example) were much more expensive to build than simpler web-based programs. Programs that used application simulations were at least 20 to 30 percent higher in cost than those that used more traditional linear media. Programs that used labs and business simulations had as much as two to three times the development cost of those that used traditional web-based training.

3. *In-house vs. outsourced:* Programs that were built in-house were nearly an order of magnitude less expensive than those outsourced to full-service content providers. Outsourced web development, although easier, increased development costs by two to three times—and in some cases more.

Example: Blended Learning Economics at a Major Bank

Let's look at the economics of new hire training at a major bank. This bank has five call centers and 2,000 employees spread across these centers (four hundred in each). These call centers generate more than 50 percent of the bank's retail revenue, so productivity has a large impact on revenue and profitability.

Due to high turnover, the bank needs to train nearly half these employees every year (approximately 1,000 employees per year). Before blended learning, the company allocated three weeks per student to new hire training. This training covered all aspects of customer service: sales techniques, handling a variety of customer requests, problem resolution, and using the bank's complex IT systems.

The new hire training program has with several goals:

- It gives employees the basic skills in selling, dealing with customers, and handling customer complaints ("soft" skills);
- It teaches agents how to enter a large number of complex IT transactions (application training);
- It gives workers the self-confidence to get on the phones and maintain a positive, service-oriented attitude; and
- It introduces new hires to the bank's sales culture and gives them the connections so they can ask questions and learn on the job (culture building).

Due to the high volume of people in this program, the bank was suffering from training backlog, high training costs, and a lack of qualified instructors. Let's look at the economics of this program. The current program is approximately one hundred hours in length.

Current Program Costs: Delivery and Learner Time and Travel

- Cost of Instructor Time: Each instructor costs the company $90,000 in salary and benefits, and each instructor teaches approximately eight classes per year. The instructor cost translates to $11,000 per class.
- Student Time: Each student receives salary and benefits of $60,000. Since their training time is approximately 100 hours (1/12 of the year), this costs the company $5,000 per student or $100,000 for a twenty-person class.
- Student Travel: If we assume that half of the students must travel to the class, the cost of travel is approximately $20,000 per class ($2,000 per student for ten students).
- Instructor Travel (assume the instructors travel to the students): $2,000 per class.
- Facility Rental: $10,000 facility cost per class.
- Materials Cost: $5,000 materials cost per class.
- Delivered Cost Per Class: $11,000 for instructor salary; $100,000 for student salary; $20,000 for student travel; $2,000 for instructor travel; $15,000 for facility and materials.

- Total: $148,000 per class or $74 per student hour ($7,400 per student).

The total audience size is approximately 2,000 and 1,000 are trained each year. This means that on an ongoing basis the entire program costs the bank *$7.4 million per year.* To reach this audience with a class size of twenty, the bank must schedule fifty classes per year, which means they need at least seven instructors. This is a very costly program, and we are not even including the lost time and productivity for call center agents who are waiting to get into class.

A Blended Learning Approach

Now let's look at the transition to blended learning. This is a complex program with goals in soft skills, culture building, and application training.

Under the existing approach, each individual class breaks down into the following cost components:

Total Class Cost:	$147,000 (100 percent)
Student Salary:	$100,000 (68 percent)
Instructor Salary:	$11,000 (8 percent)
Facility/Materials:	$15,000 (10 percent)
Travel:	$22,000 (14 percent)

By far the biggest cost is student salary. If we want to reduce delivery costs, our goal should be to reduce the total time spent in training. How do we do this? Today the program is one hundred student hours in length. We should create a blended learning program, perhaps using some application simulations, to interweave some self-study into the curriculum so that students spend less time in training. This reduces the number of classes, clears out the backlog, and reduces overall training time.

How much can we afford to spend? Let's assume that we can reduce the time in training from one hundred hours to eighty hours by inserting application simulations and self-study exercises. We keep instructor-led training but reduce its length.

The savings from learner time alone will be more than *$1.4 million per year* (20% of $7.4 million). This means that we can afford to spend $1 million to develop and deploy this program and still see a positive ROI from cost reduction within the first twelve months.

This "budget" can easily be established. We still have to make sure that by accomplishing this transition, you have had no reduction in the actual learning that takes place. If we reduce the training impact, the financial effect could be disastrous. When 2,000 call center agents become unproductive and start producing errors, the effect on sales and customer satisfaction can be tens to hundreds of millions.

This case study is real. It was implemented by a large bank. They used application simulations to enable learners to "try" and "practice" on real call center problems online before attending any classroom exercises. The classroom events were used to introduce concepts and offer special help while students performed most of their call center training online.

Exhibit 6.1 is a worksheet you can use to develop your own budget. Figure 6.2 is an application of this worksheet to a low-cost program that builds a call center product update course for five hundred learners in two locations. This example program is a "content flow" program with a pre-class application simulation exercise, a brief instructor-led program, and then a final online assessment. You can see how easy it is to compute the total delivered cost per learner and total cost per delivered course hour.

This is a very inexpensive program and, as you can see, if it has any return at all it will pay for itself very quickly. (For simplicity we have left out learner salary and travel expense.) As you can see from this simple example, this analysis will be very useful for budgeting and benchmarking the cost of this particular (small)

Exhibit 6.1. Budget Worksheet

Program Segment	Item	Typical Cost
Development Costs		
Capital	Purchase of tools	$2,000–3,000 per developer
		$15,000–25,000 for LCMS (Learning Content Management Systems)
		$10,000+ for end-to-end development system
		Application simulation, assessment rich media tools
		$20,000–30,000 for live e-learning server, plus more for large audiences
	Content development costs/Media mix	Total up by module, depending on media type per module
		Module 1: Estimated # of hours and cost per hour (from table)
		Module 2: Estimated # of hours and cost per hour (from table)
		Module 3: Estimated # of hours and cost per hour (from table)
	Testing cost	Typical testing two–three weeks for total e-learning portions
		Include time to install in LMS and test performance across the network
		Cost: three weeks × $3,000 per week of developer/IT time.
	Outside contractors	SME: Estimated # of hours per module. Are they billable?
		Editor: $10/hour for copy editing and text editing.
		Web developer: any extra time to create AICC or SCORM wrappers to make sure course materials are trackable, bookmarks, etc.

Infrastructure Costs	LMS (most costs are allocated over many programs)	
	If already installed	If already installed, estimate $3–5 per enrollment as operational costs if they are recharged.
	If hosted	If a hosted LMS from third party, estimate $5–10 per enrollment; you can get this from the vendor.
	If new licensed product	If you need a NEW LMS for this program, the cost will be capitalized; likely license cost will be $30–$100 per learner to purchase and equal amount to implement.
	Software and hardware maintenance	Maintenance cost: for internal LMS is typically 20 percent of initial license cost for software maintenance, and at one–three people to handle administration and catalog maintenance.
	IT hardware and software	$2–4 per learner for IT hardware and software.
Program Deployment and Management	Program manager	Need a full-time program manager to handle launch and rollon for some period of time. Estimate cost based on salary.
	Marketing plan and launch process	Estimate 5–10 percent of total cost for marketing expenses. These include e-mails, conference calls, promotional items, trips to regional locations, etc., if the program or curricula is strategic. Do not expect people to flock to your program without marketing!

(Continued)

Exhibit 6.1. Budget Worksheet (Continued)

Program Segment	Item	Typical Cost
	Learner Infrastructure Upgrades (PC software, networking, labs)	Could be low or could be very high. If you develop content that requires streaming media, for example, you need streaming capability on all learner PC's and bandwidth to handle it. This is why establishing a technology standard and the testing phase is critical. Verizon, for example, spent millions here to support local streaming video.
	Reporting and analysis	If you need to build custom reports to monitor and manage the program, this will cost $5K or more per report, and you likely will need to wait for your IT department to handle it. You should always assume that there will be some custom reporting and analysis.
	Three-four-week reporting checkpoint	Estimate three to four weeks or longer if you want to measure the program, once to measure initially after launch, and once to measure ninety days after launch to determine business impact. Depending on salary of program manager, this could be an additional expense for a consultant. Do not ignore this step—without measurements you cannot determine impact or how to improve.
	Classroom components	Instructor salary Instructor travel expenses Facility rental and food Printed materials and printing charges Student salary lost Student travel

Other media delivery costs		Conference call costs to convene managers and kick off program Production and distribution of job aids, workbooks, and other materials Rental or license of a survey tool for Level 1 or Level 2 assessments (if not built into LMS)
Maintenance		Estimate some percentage of the content becomes "obsolete" and then needs revision/content development

Summary	Type of Cost	How to Compute
Content Development Tools	Capital cost	One-time cost
Content Development Expenses	Expense cost (could be capitalized)	Compute these costs and divide by number of course hours to arrive at content development for the total program and cost per course hour.
Audience Size	Used for computation of total costs	Number of learners
Program Length	Use for computation of total costs	Number of hours
Content Development Per Student Hour		Take content development expenses and divide by total number of students and course hours to arrive at cost per "student hour."

Figure 6.2.   Sample Application

Program	Tele-service center product update course
Length	8 course hours
Audience	500 learners in 2 locations
Development Tools	$21,000 (web development tools, app sims)
Content Development	Module 1: $45,000 (application simulation)/ 2 hours
	Module 2: $25,000 (ILT materials)/3 hours
	Module 3: $50,000 (final simulation and assessment)/3 hours
	Testing: 4 weeks: $20,000
	Total: $140,000 or $17,500 per course hour (a bit high)
LMS/Infrastructure	Company already has an LMS, assume $5 per enrollment
	Or $10,000 for LMS infrastructure
	Ongoing support from IT: $20,000
	Total: $30,000
Program Management	Launch: $15,000 for launch materials
	Job Aids: $10,000
	New PCs for learning labs: $30,000
	Reporting project at end: $20,000
	Instructor salary/travel: $25,000
	Kick off conference calls: $3,000
	(learner salary will not be included)
	Total: $103,000
Program Cost	$273,000 + $21,000 for development tools
Delivered Cost	$5.46 per learner, or <$1 per course hour

program. As you can also see, program management is a significant percentage of the overall cost.

Table 6.3 will help you select media based on its development cost and deployment cost. These costs are "rules of thumb" you can use to make broad decisions about when to use which medium. Use

Table 6.3. Media Costs—Development and Deployment

Medium	Live or Self-Study	Network Requirements	PC Configuration Requirements	Training Type	Ability to Track Completion and Results	Development Costs (per student hour)	Deployment Costs (per student hour)	Instructional Value (interactivity)
Instructor-Led Training	Live	None	None	Type 3, 4	High	$5,000–$25,000	Very High	Very High
Webinars (Live e-Learning)	Live	Medium Bandwidth	Plug-ins and setup required	Type 1, 2	Low	$1,000–$5,000	Medium	Medium
Courseware (Web-Based)	Self-Study	Low to Medium Bandwidth	Plug-ins and setup may be required	Type 3	Medium	$5,000–$50,000	Low	Medium-High
Simulations	Self-Study	None	Plug-ins and setup may be required	Type 3, 4	Medium to High	$15,000–$100,000	Medium	High
CD-ROM-Based Courseware	Self-Study	None	Plug-ins and setup required	Type 3, 4	Medium	$10,000–$50,000	Medium	Medium
"Rapid e-Learning" Courseware	Self-Study	Low Bandwidth	Plug-ins and setup rarely required	Type 2	Low	$2,000–$15,000	Low	Medium-Low
Internet-Delivered Video	Self-Study	Medium to High Bandwidth	Plug-ins and setup required	Type 1, 2	None	$10,000–$50,000	Medium-High	Medium-Low
EPSS (Electronic Performance	Self-Study	Low to Medium	None	Type 2, 3	Low	$20,000+	Low	Low
Offline Video (Videotapes)	Self-Study	None	None	Type 1, 2, 3	None	$10,000–$20,000	Medium	Low
Video Conferencing	Self-Study	High	Plug-ins and setup required	Type 2, 3	Low	$10,000–$20,000	Medium-High	High
Collaboration Systems	Self-Study and Live	Low to Medium	None	Type 2, 3	None	$2,000–$5,000	Low	Medium
Conference Calls	Live	None	None	Type 1, 2	None	$100–$2,000	Low	Low
Job Aids	Self-Study	None	None	Type 2, 3	None	$100–$1,000	Low	Low
Workbooks	Self-Study	None	None	Type 2, 3	None	$100–$10,000	Low	Medium
Books	Self-Study	None	None	Type 1, 2, 3	None	$100–$500	Low	Low-Medium
On-the-Job Coaching	Live	None	None	Type 3, 4	High	$500–$5,000	Very High	Very High

it as a guideline as you build your module-by-module budget. In the next chapter we will dive into media selection in detail.

Lessons Learned in This Chapter

1. Budgets should be set based on the size of the business impact, not the size of the learning problem.

2. The simple economics of blended learning are as follows: to keep costs under control you must amortize the cost of e-learning content development across the audience size. Larger audiences can cost-justify higher investments in content.

3. You must factor shelf life and maintenance costs into decisions about content development and budget.

4. Use delivered cost per learner as your benchmark cost to compare different alternatives within a single program and to compare programs to each other.

5. When you are computing your budget, you should include program management and program administrative costs.

6. For large audiences (more than 1,000 people) you can predict the total delivered costs. For smaller audiences, costs will vary widely depending on the media you select.

7. Outsourcing development usually drives up costs significantly.

Chapter Seven

Media Selection

The Right Blend

At this point you have a business problem well defined, you have a good idea of the program strategy, you have developed an appropriate budget, and it is time to design and develop the program. (See Figure 7.1.) In this chapter we will give you all the tools you need to identify the right media for your particular problem, audience, and budget.

Figure 7.1. Where We Are

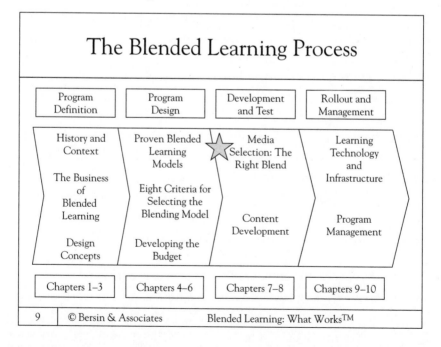

143

Review of the Selection Criteria

Appendix E provides a brief review of the eight criteria outlined in Chapter 5 so you can apply them toward your content decisions. This exhibit is designed so that you can copy it and post it on your bulletin-board for future programs.

The Sixteen Media Types

Early in the book we introduced the sixteen different types of blended learning media. In this chapter we will discuss them in detail. For reference, Appendix F provides an overview of each.

When to Use Instructor-Led Training

First we must address an important topic, the $64,000 question: when is it appropriate to use traditional instructor-led training (ILT)? Although there is no single right answer, there are some proven rules to follow.

A training program is a business investment designed to produce a business outcome or return. Instructor-led training (ILT) is the most expensive, time-consuming, and difficult-to-schedule form of training today. ILT demands that you schedule a scarce resource (instructors) across a large audience. This scheduling process makes program rollouts long (months to years) and often makes "fast deployment" training problems impossible to solve. ILT is expensive for learners because it demands that they travel and spend many hours away from their work.

On the other hand, there are well-proven benefits of ILT that justify these expenses. As our research has found, ILT is often the only solution in the following situations:

- *Learners are being introduced to brand new material and have no prior experience with the topics.* When learners are very new to the organization, topic, or material, they often cannot "teach themselves" through self-study. ILT is an excellent way to get people up-to-speed on a complex set of new skills. If you want to teach a C programmer how to use Java, for example, a week of ILT is probably the best way to start.

- *Culture building needs are high.* When the program must create relationships and introduce company culture, ILT is often the best way to go. A good example is new hire training. In all new-hire training learners are being introduced to the company, their jobs, specific work procedures, business processes, management procedures, and much more. Because this information is so new, it may be well worth the investment in ILT to make sure that people have time to meet their peers, ask questions, and interact directly with an expert.

- *Experts and celebrities are available.* ILT is very valuable when you have a celebrity or world-class expert available. Even though the audience size may be large, people remember appearances by experts and celebrities. Take executive education for example. In the Navy's executive education process for admirals (which is a 7.7-year program), many of the steps involve meetings with business executives to share ideas and strategies. Some of these meetings are held offsite at company locations. Although these could be conducted via webinar, the experience of meeting and visiting with these experts is some of the most valuable learning these Navy executives receive.

- *Direct interaction and discussion with peers and discussion is primary to the learning process.* In many programs, the need to interact with other learners is part of the learning experience itself. Case studies and sample sales team building are good examples. For example, in British Telecom's rollout of "M-commerce," a new set of technologies for mobile professionals, the amount of new material was so great that the company decided to use small meetings with sales representatives to reinforce material after the students took a web-based course. In sales training, interaction between sales representatives and field support personnel delivers powerful anecdotal information that is difficult to teach online. In CNA's program to teach performance management, for example, team members share sample performance plans with peers to get ideas and feedback. In many sales training programs, learners perform practice sales calls and are critiqued by their peers. Team activities such as these create mastery and proficiency as well as high levels of retention by connecting people with others who share the same work challenges.

When to Use On-the-Job Exercises

A second form of real-world training is an on-the-job exercise. This type of learning intervention can take many forms. In the most common approach the learners are asked to perform an exercise, quiz, or demonstration to their manager as part of their learning experience. By doing this work "on the job," the learners experience the real-world environment (equipment, processes, people) that they will experience after training is completed.

These types of exercises are extremely valuable because (A) they force the learner to learn by doing, and (B) they incent the learner to excel because they are being evaluated by their first-line manager.

> One of the lessons drilled into us at IBM was well-known research that shows that the single most important factor in an individual's job performance and satisfaction is the relationship with his or her direct manager. Whenever you can introduce on-the-job training, it will add this manager dimension to the learning and retention process.

The challenge to on-the-job exercises is the need to engage and train the learner's manager as an active and knowledgeable instructor. The manager must clearly understand what to do, when to do it, and how to use the results. Typically, first-line managers do not want to take the time for these programs, so you may need to recruit higher-level executives to help persuade and require first-line managers to participate.

Many programs I have reviewed use on-the-job interventions to turn a "low-impact" program into a "high-impact" one. Let me give you two examples that illustrate when and how to use this approach.

OTJ Exercises: Retail Sales Training

Retail new hire sales training is difficult, expensive, and business-critical. In most retail organizations the audience is made up of young employees with limited experience with the company. Let's use an example from a large retail electronics chain.

> Company C's retail sales representatives must stay current on a dizzying array of electronics, stereo, TV, computer, and mobile equipment. In Company C's retail e-learning program students are assigned to take many e-learning courses describing new products, promotions, and selling techniques. Initially, workers found that the e-learning experience was fun, interesting, and useful. Over time, however, store managers found that this approach did not drive measurable skills on the job. To make the training more relevant and applied, the company added a new element that they called the "learning check."
>
> The "learning check" is a randomized set of instructions with questions about real products on the floor. The students must print out the worksheet and walk the floor with their manager while coming up with the answers. The printed learning check form has a management version that includes the correct answers, hints for coaching, and a place to record scores. Managers deliver the "learning check," score the answers, and enter them into the LMS. These scores are then reported back to regional and executive management.
>
> This process has many benefits. It forces the manager to coach and evaluate the employee. It makes managers aware of the training problems on their teams. It improves morale. It drives retention. And at an executive level, it gives executives a good view of the real results of the training.

OTJ Exercises: Diversity Training

In another example, described below, on-the-job exercises are used to reinforce diversity training in small work groups. This program was developed at IBM.

> IBM has a program in several locations called "Generation X Diversity Training," which is designed to sensitize employees to the issues of working in a diverse work group that may include young "genX" employees. This program is e-learning based. It walks the students through the issues and principles of diversity and shows them how Generation X people think differently from other generations.
>
> The e-learning material serves as introductory training material for a diversity meeting with the first-line manager. After the e-learning program, the first-line manager schedules a group meeting and walks through a series of exercises with the team. These exercises are built around real-life management problems (someone wants to quit, someone is a low-impact worker, someone is difficult to work with) and lets the team discuss how best to handle them. The discussion forms the basis of the training, and both managers and employees practice the material they have learned. The process builds teamwork and drives a common understanding of the issues that face the entire team.

The benefits of on-the-job (OTJ) exercises such as these are numerous:

- You can cover topics which are complex and require direct interaction;
- Learner motivation and completion rates are high because managers are involved;
- The program trains managers as well as line workers;
- The program has long-lasting impact because management is now directly involved in coaching and assisting employees; and

- The program gives you direct feedback on business impact because managers will tell you how well the program works.

For any program that has critical business impact, I strongly urge you to consider some kind of management intervention. Although it requires buy-in and involvement from upper management, the results will go up exponentially. *The single biggest factor in making a training program succeed is direct engagement of the learner's first-line manager.*

When to Use Live vs. Self-Study

Another important question is when to use live events and when to use self-study. Table 7.1 shows which of the sixteen media types are live and which are self-study.

Live events (also called "synchronous") require an instructor or mentor to be available in real time with students. Webinars are a form of live event. Although live events are often the most interesting, they required scheduling and are usually the most expensive to deliver. When the number of instructors is limited, class size gets large and it becomes difficult to create an interactive experience.

Self-study events are called "asynchronous" because they do not require synchronization with anyone. Reading a book is

Table 7.1.   Live Media vs. Self-Study Media

Live (Synchronous)	Self-Study (Asynchronous)
Instructor-Led Training	Simulations
Webinars	WBT or CD-ROM Courseware
EPSS	Rapid e-Learning
Video Conferencing	Offline Video
Collaboration Systems	Job Aids
Conference Calls	Workbooks
On-the-Job Exercises	Books

self-study, for example. Web-based courseware is asynchronous or self-study.

Table 7.2 is a review of the pros and cons of classroom live events, web-based live events, and self-study activities.

Blend Live and Self-Study in Every Program

The most successful approach is to try to blend both live and self-study activities in each program. A simple content-flow model is a live kickoff event (a meeting, conference call, or webinar) followed by a series of self-study activities, followed by a final live class. The reverse is also very powerful: self-study as a prerequisite to an online or instructor-led class.

Example: Best Practices in Live e-Learning

Grant Thornton is an excellent example of an organization that uses live e-learning for many parts of their blended programs. They see webinars (or webcasts) as a primary learning channel. They use this approach for all types of programs including new hire training, general accounting, case studies, and special topics on new laws and new accounting applications. Their success has been astounding—learning satisfaction rates are excellent.

Grant Thornton's success comes from a focus on process. First, they have refined the methodology for producing and delivering webinars so that each event is closely managed like a live production. A production schedule, crew, and special delivery room is used. Every event has a facilitator, speaker, and support person who handles the online chat session that takes place simultaneously with the webcast. Second, all of Grant Thornton's employees have high bandwidth so they can see slides, hear voice, and see online video easily through their computers. Third, Grant Thornton uses IP-telephony so that webcasts deliver voice through the PC, leaving employees free to use their telephones if a client calls.

Table 7.2.   Pros and Cons of Live vs. Self-Study Media

	Pros	*Cons*
Live Events in a Classroom	Highly interactive, excellent feedback, students gain the benefit of class interactivity and discussion, easy to gauge learner absorption, easy to build culture, connections, and relationships. Needed for team learning experiences.	Very expensive to deliver, not scalable to large audiences, difficult to schedule, and may take many events to reach a large audience. You will never get 100 percent of the audience in a single event. Reserve live events for "kickoff events" or "special topics" in blended learning programs.
Live Events Online (Live e-Learning or Webinars)	Speaker's tone and style come through well, very scalable, easy to deliver, but lack interactivity unless delivered in small groups. Usually best used for "broadcast" events, such as lectures with limited feedback, and then breakout sessions for interactivity. Some companies, however, have turned webinars into a highly interactive experience through careful design and constant interactivities.	Require scheduling and use of scarce resources (instructors). Again, you must schedule multiple events to reach everyone. Many learners have problems with bandwidth, plug-ins, and use of the technology the first time. Often companies avoid this technology simply because of the complexity of scheduling instructors. Limited tracking available for certification programs.
Self-Study	Very scalable and easy to distribute to large audiences. Learners can work when and where they want; high degree of tracking, assessment, and certification possible.	Does not connote the tone or interactivity of a live event and can therefore have a high dropout rate if there are not incentives and events wrapped around the courseware or object. Although this modality was the biggest focus in the early days, the industry realizes that self-study alone often does not generate enough interest without an external mandate.

Interactivity is strongly woven into every program through several approaches:

- Presenters ask questions that are answered by chat session during the event;
- Quizzes are presented continuously during the program;
- Presenters ask questions that require learners to "raise their hands" online to concur (this tells the presenter that the audience is listening); and
- Events have breakout exercises that require learners to go into small groups and then re-enter after a brief period.

Grant Thornton's model requires that all subject-matter experts have a coach from the strategic learning group to show them how to develop a compelling program. Subject-matter experts are given strict guidelines on how to develop content that is instructionally sound, graphically rich, and easy to understand. Rehearsals are mandatory. During the event the moderator introduces the speaker, makes sure that the pace is appropriate, handles interactivities and online questions, and serves as the audience's "advocate" to make sure the program stays on-time and on-track.

Figure 7.2 shows Grant Thornton's webinar design and development process.

As powerful as live e-learning is, it still fits into an overall blended learning paradigm. Grant Thornton realizes that many learners cannot attend the live events and may need to use self-study. Every webcast is archived and then becomes a self-study program for review and replay on the company's learning portal. Over time, Grant Thornton has built a large library of these events, and they are mixed with online self-study courseware to give their professionals a rich set of resources and blended learning opportunities to stay abreast of new laws, principles, and approaches in accounting (the core-and-spoke model).

"Live e-learning can be one of the most powerful parts of our blended learning strategy. During the last two years we have

**Figure 7.2.   Grant Thornton's Webcast Design
and Development Process**

Webcast design and development process

	1 Establish Business Case	**2** Design Session	**3** Develop Storyboard
Activity	**Determine:** • Business strategy • Business and performance outcomes • Audience • Content scope • Measurements of success • Delivery strategy **Create communications plan**	**Establish:** • Performance and learning objectives • Technology options **Draft:** • Storyline • Content • Visuals • Interactions • Enrollment and communication	**Develop:** • Content development and review • Performance support resources • Pilot with target audience **Finalize scope:** • Timing • CPE
	Business case	**Draft storyboard**	**Complete storyboard**
	Deliverable Result		

Webcast design and development process

	4 Prepare Presenters	**5** Deliver Webcast	**6** Assess Impact
Activity	**Practice:** • Using Centra interface • Communicate storyboard with impact • Managing webcast interactions **Iterate storyboard based on practice**	**Send logistics** **Conduct:** • Communicate content • Focus on performance outcomes • Engage learners • Solicit interaction and feedback	**Track:** • Reaction • CPE processing • Application of new knowledge and skills • Business results **Identify:** • Other initiatives required to achieve business goals **Archive & re-purpose content**
	Compelling presenters	**New learning and insight**	**Application of business results**
	Deliverable Result		

refined our process to an art. We now deliver compelling high-impact training through our online portal and live events that can be every bit as powerful as classroom training." (Bob Dean, CLO, Grant Thornton)

Let's look at the four program types and see which media best applies to each.

Program Type 1: Information Broadcast Programs

These are typically rapidly developed programs that must reach a large audience quickly. The goal is to impart information as broadly and quickly as possible. An example of such a program is a new product introduction.

In a new product introduction many types of training are needed: sales training, support training, field service, order processing, and customer support. The first goal is to inform sales, support, and other functions about the product launch and show them how it will affect their jobs. Later they may need detailed training about the product or service itself and how to use it, support it, price it, or order it.

The learning objective for a type 1 program is not very detailed. The objective is to inform the learners, teach them a few things that they must know immediately, and show them what they must or should do to learn more.

For a product launch, for example, the learning objectives may be

- Tell learners that a new product has been introduced and when;
- Teach learners to name and describe the product and how it fits into the current product set;
- Have learners identify three ways this new product affects the company and their current job; and/or
- Teach learners what additional training is available and why they need it.

Typically, type 1 programs are not tracked, so media such as web-based courseware or instructor-led training is not used. The best media for such programs are conference calls, webinars, booklets, and PowerPoint-based Rapid e-Learning programs. Follow-up training typically falls into the category of type 3 and type 4 programs.

Program Type 2: Critical Knowledge Transfer Programs

Type 2 programs focus on transferring critical new knowledge to people who already have basic skills in a particular area. The learning objectives in type 2 programs are typically to take existing skills and competencies and update them based on a change in the company, business, or environment (often called "delta training"). There are many examples of these programs:

- *Sales training on a new product.* Learning objective: teach all sales representatives how to position, price, and sell the new product in the context of the existing sales strategies of other products. We are not teaching them how to sell, but rather how to take their existing skills and apply them to this new area. Training is urgent, strongly recommended, but not mandatory.

- *New operational procedures.* Learning objective: teach all field service technicians how to fill out the new job-scheduling worksheets. We are not teaching people how to fill out worksheets, but rather how this process has changed and what they should do differently. Training is urgent, but not mandatory.

- *Updates to a production software application.* Learning objective: teach all sales order entry personnel how to handle credit card transactions and returns in our new module of SAP. We are not teaching them how to use the system, but rather how to handle the changes. Training is urgent and may be mandatory.

In these types of programs, you are primarily updating people with important new information that affects their work, not training them on entirely new areas. Typically, these programs can be handled well with live e-learning, recorded live events, Rapid e-Learning, recorded video clips, conference calls, and job aids.

Sometimes these programs are both urgent and critical, so tracking is required. If you need to track completion, rapid e-learning may be the best bet. We believe that in corporate training as much as one-third of the training needs fall into this category. We will discuss Rapid e-Learning as a solution for these programs a bit later.

Program Type 3: Skills and Competency Programs

Type 3 programs make up the core of most training portfolios. In these programs the goal is to develop new skills and competencies in a critical area. To develop these skills the training should include introductory material, demonstrations, practice, assessment, and coaching. In the past, these programs were taught in multi-day classroom sessions with labs, hands-on exercises, discussion sessions, and class projects.

To select media for these programs, consider your program as of multiple parts: *introductions to material, context setting,* and *hands-on learning.* Introductions and context setting (or theory and concepts) can be taught using broadcast media such as live e-learning, conference calls, books and job aids, and web pages. The problem with such media is that they may not motivate learners to pay attention. You can force learners to read the introductory material through good program management and launch processes (see Chapter 10).

The skills development and hands-on learning part of your program demands different media depending on the audience. In IT training, for example, it is very common for web-based courseware to include programming samples and even tutor-submitted exercises. In DigitalThink courses a set of tutors read students' sample programs and grade them via e-mail within twenty-four hours. This works well for a technical audience, which is comfortable communicating via e-mail.

In Company W's bank teller training, the goal was to teach agents how to handle different types of incoming calls and the subsequent online transactions. These skills require knowledge of IT systems that open accounts, change account options, transfer funds, look up individual checks, cancel checks, and other processes.

The medium selected for this problem was a series of *application simulations*. These simulations ask the learner to walk through each transaction in a simulated online environment. The program uses different customer *scenarios* that require the student to select the right transactions and complete them before moving on to the next scenario.

In a follow-up session, the students get direct time feedback on their performance by an instructor. The results: new tellers develop real-world skills before they take calls and work on the line system.

Program Type 4: Certified Skills and Competencies

As we have described earlier, in this category the key issue is not only developing the right skills but, more importantly, *certifying* that the learner has reached this level of proficiency. In certification programs the most important issues are assessment, tracking, and documentation. Learning objectives are similar to Type 3 programs, but in this case you must *assess learners* and establish a criterion for "pass" or "fail."

In many certification programs the "pass" criterion is simply completion of the course. The reason for this is the difficulty in determining what a "passing score" should be. If a student gets 50 percent of the questions right, for example, does that mean he or she does not understand 50 percent of the material? Is 50 percent enough to demonstrate proficiency? If you are going to use assessment-based certifications, you must test the assessments on a set of proficient workers to see what a passing score should be.

In the Siemens global accounting rollout the company developed a series of *business simulation modules* to teach and evaluate students' proficiency in new accounting practices. Each module was part of a long case study, which asked the student to actively "close the books" for this department.

To certify that students were learning the material, each student had to submit his or her results to the central finance organization. Only after this submission would he or she receive the next module. The simulation itself embedded an assessment engine that scored each phase of the exercise and told the students whether or not they passed.

Some of the media and design issues to consider in certification programs include:

- How do you define certified? Completion? By score?
- Is time a factor in certification? Must the learner complete by a certain date? Must the learner complete within a certain number of months of being on the job? Must the learner complete within a period of time after starting the course?
- How often does the learner have to recertify? Do the certifications expire every year?
- Does a work group need to be certified? If so, how would that be defined? Is everyone in the group being certified or some percentage?
- What levels of reporting will you need for external certification programs? What levels of tracking will be required to generate these reports?
- If the certification is mandatory, how will you ensure that the learners themselves took the test?

As you can see, certification programs (type 4) are the most complex of all because they add issues of assessment, tracking, and reporting to the learning objectives of type 3.

Media Selection

Scalability

One of the critical issues in selecting the right media for a blended learning program is the issue of *scalability:* how many learners are there and how do you reach them? The scalability goal of a blended learning program is

> To reach a large audience in a short period of time for the lowest possible cost per learner without requiring major upgrades to technology.

We have found through research that total audience size is one of the biggest factors in designing a program. A large audience gives you the flexibility to amortize the cost of developing more complex media over a large number of learners.

Large audience sizes also limit the amount of instructor-led or live media you can use because of the difficulties in scheduling so many learners' time. In Figure 7.3, we have plotted scalability versus program type so you can see which media fit into different scalability quadrants.

As you can see from the figure, different media types fall easily into different categories. We have shaded the figure by different costs to develop—darker being the lowest cost and lighter being the most expensive. The chart illustrates that, for certain problems (type 4 high scalability problems), you have to use high-cost media to solve them.

In a large audience program you must think about deployment technology. Across a broad audience learners will have many different configurations of PCs, networks, and accessibility to the Internet.

In NCR's global network certification program, for example, the company decided to distribute all the materials in CD-ROM format because so many learners were either on the road or in low-bandwidth geographies. Some individuals in remote countries had to go to Internet cafes to access assessments and only had modem dial-up access at 24k bits per second.

Figure 7.3.   Media Scalability

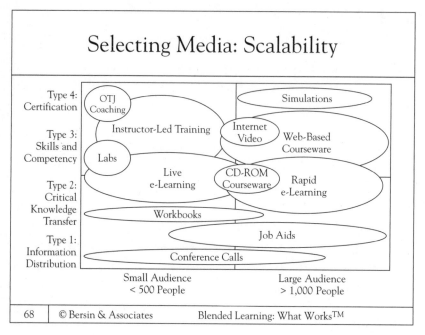

In Verizon's national service training program all the PCs were located in training facilities. But as the company found, the program used high-bandwidth video and audio and many of these facilities did not have the bandwidth or PC horsepower to run the content. This forced Verizon to upgrade many of these systems before the program could be rolled out. For learners who take the content at other locations, Verizon had to develop a small plug-in program that checked the network bandwidth and PC configuration before a learner could start the courseware.

Content Durability

An issue you will face over time (and you should consider up-front) is the issue of content shelf life or "durability." Your biggest investment over time will be in the content itself, and if the content is changing rapidly you should invest differently than if the content is static for months or years.

> The simplest rule is this: if the content will be out-of-date in a few months, do not invest in any medium that takes more than a few weeks to develop. The reason for this is that your time to develop will be close to your time to expire for the content—putting you at risk of developing a program that is out-of-date soon after you launch it.

Example: In Novell's channel sales training and certification programs, the company uses Rapid e-Learning PowerPoint-based development tools because they can release training topics within weeks after a product is launched. The product development process must be nearly complete before training can be developed, and that only gives the training function one or two months' time beforehand to develop training. The launch materials are appropriate for up to nine months after launch, but are then frequently out-of-date. If the company spent six to eight weeks to develop the content, not only would they miss the product launch window but they would lose 10 to 20 percent of the total time available for the content to stay current.

For more long-lasting topics (for example, how to administer and configure Novell products), the company uses more traditional web-based training, which takes many months to complete but has a shelf life of two years and more.

Figure 7.4 shows you how to map the durability of different media against program type.

Urgency

"Urgency" refers to the issue of how much time you have before you must launch the program. Highly urgent programs must be launched within a week or two. An example of an urgent program

Figure 7.4.   Media Types Mapped Against Durability or Shelf Life

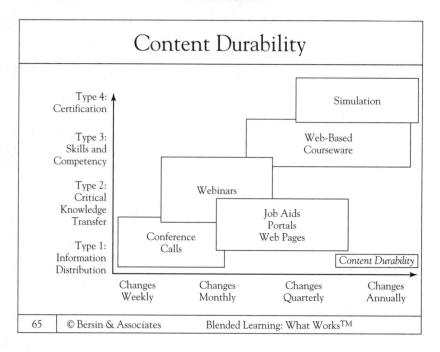

is a company merger, major regulatory change, or a natural disaster. These programs tend to be event-driven and you do not have much time to develop content.

Most training programs are less urgent. Product launches, price changes, new hire training programs, and executive education programs are typically planned months or quarters in advance. Programs that are ongoing can be developed over years. As Figure 7.5 shows, urgency and durability tend to go together. If a program is urgent, the content usually has a short shelf life and should not be developed in a medium that requires heavy up-front investment.

> Simply put: the more urgent the program, the less time you have for development and testing. Urgent programs require media that can be authored rapidly.

Figure 7.5.   Durability vs. Urgency

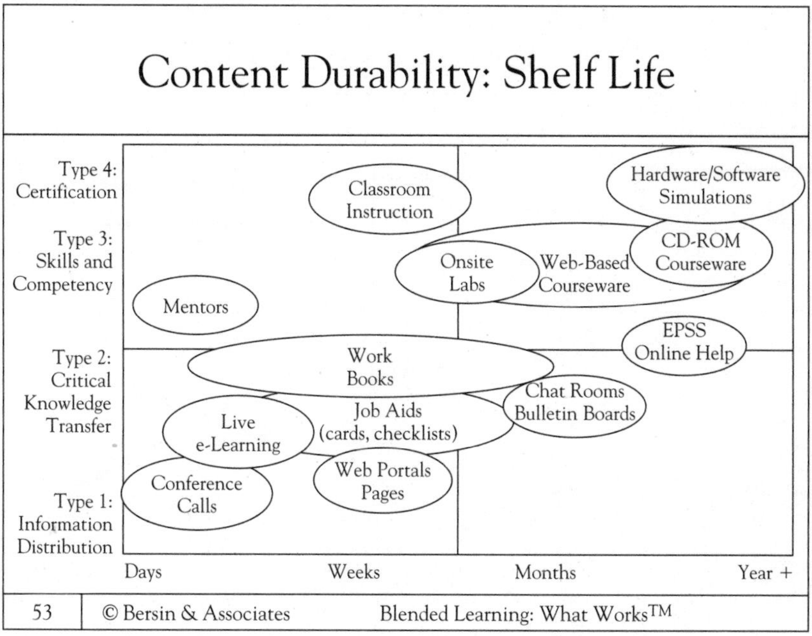

Content Durability: Shelf Life

53	© Bersin & Associates

Blended Learning: What Works™

Time to Build

One of the most important issues all blended learning managers face is the time it takes to develop a given piece of content. In a typical program, you will have some web-based content, some instructor-led content, and perhaps some simulations, animations, or even video. Each of these individual media elements has a time to build.

You must be very careful about matching the time to build against the durability or shelf life. If the shelf life is short, you can rarely afford to build content with a long time to build. Figure 7.6 illustrates these tradeoffs.

In the lower left quadrant are the problems that require rapid development and have a short shelf life. These are problems that may be addressed by e-mail, conference calls, live e-learning, and Rapid e-Learning (PowerPoint-based). Which you select depends on whether it is a type 1, 2, 3, or 4 problem.

Figure 7.6.   Time to Build vs. Shelf Life

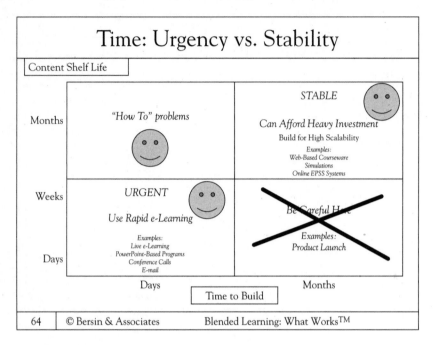

In the upper right quadrant are the "stable" training problems. These are programs like new hire training, IT training, process training, management and other soft-skills, and software application training. In these programs the content lasts for months to years, and you can afford to spend months in development. In these programs the media you choose can be web-based courseware, simulations, or even video-based demonstrations. If the problem is one where learners may need on-the-job assistance and training, you can spend the time to build an EPSS (Electronic Performance Support System) solution, which functions more as an online help or online directory of assistance. EPSS solutions are costly to build but form the basis of a long-term solution.

If you find yourself in the upper left quadrant, you are lucky. These are the easiest and most cost-effective programs to build and they last a long time. We call these the "how-to" problems. Believe it or not, there are many problems like this. Examples include: "How to fill out a time sheet," "how to handle objections," or "how to report an error." These problems can be solved with short, small learning objects and exercises that explain ongoing operational procedures. They are good modules to build using web-based media because they are used often and often linked from other programs. They become "reference" items in your corporate website. You can start your e-learning development here.

The final quadrant, the bottom right, is tricky. In this quadrant you have a problem that demands a long development cycle but has a short shelf life. An example of this may be a product launch. The learning needs of a product launch may be complex, but may also be obsolete within six to nine months. Your risk here is to avoid over-spending on a program that needs regular maintenance or may become obsolete.

There are two ways to deal with these problems. First, avoid spending large sums of money on problems that go out-of-date quickly. You should essentially view these as problems in another quadrant and convince your constituents that they are not worthy of complex blended programs.

The second way to deal with these programs is to architect them carefully and thoughtfully for ongoing maintenance. Content development companies frequently do this. For example, if you are building product-related training, you can build the content in small chapters that separate concepts and processes from product-specific information. As the product information changes, you can update these chapters without modifying the general business process chapters.

Avoiding Long Development Cycles

Although you can never avoid the need to deal with time pressures, long development cycles almost always lead to problems. The longer the development cycle, the more likely the content itself will change (as will the constituents, SMEs, and executive sponsors). Remember that for any blended program, the time to test, launch, enroll, and complete may also be long—so after you complete your development you still have many months (or years) that the content must be maintained.

The solution here is to stay away from media that are expensive and complex to build, and modularize the content into two types: one that is stable (upper right) and can be reused over time (such as general selling strategies or a general organizational overview) and another type that goes stale quickly. These two types of content can both be launched at the same time, but you can throw away the unstable content after a few months and keep the stable content for the next event.

There are many new tools and techniques to reduce development cycles, including tools that empower SMEs to author content and Rapid e-Learning tools (PowerPoint to Flash) that make development simple.

Tracking and Reporting

Tracking and reporting are important dimensions in selecting media. Some media (web-based courseware, for example) provide detailed tracking information. Others (webinars, for example) provide much less.

In our research[1] we find that most training programs are not tracked in detail. Figure 7.7 charts the percentage of programs that measured each particular item: enrollments, completions, satisfaction, learning (scores), job impact, and business impact. You will recognize the latter four items as Kirkpatrick's levels 1 through 4.

Although there is a trend toward more analysis and reporting, our findings show that most companies rarely measure ROI or job impact. The most common tracking measure is enrollments and completions: "Did the learner take the course?" and "Did the learner complete the course." The term "complete" can be defined in different ways. Did the person attend? Did he or she complete an end-of-course exam? Did he or she complete more than half? Did he or she attend the final session?

---

[1]Survey of 7,000 training professionals, March 2004.

Figure 7.7.   Measurement and Tracking in Use

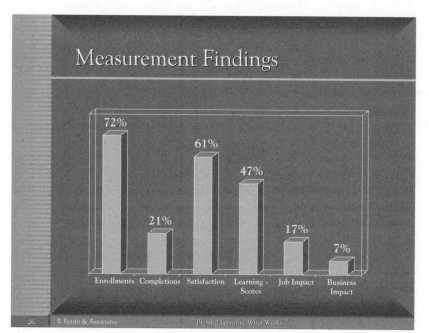

We will discuss measurement strategies in Chapter 10. For the purposes of this chapter, the media you select will drive what tracking is available.

First, you must decide how much tracking and measurement is important. Typically, there are cultural issues at play. Some organizations are very metric driven and others are not. We find that airlines, for example, have a tendency to measure training in detail. This is because the airline industry runs on statistics: on-time percentage, percentage of lost bags, and so on.

Type 4 programs demand a high level of tracking and reporting. We call these "compliance" or "certification" programs. In these programs, companies specify a criteria for completion, for passing, and for annual recertification. They are usually tied to government, industry, or external certification standards. Examples of these include HIPAA compliance, Sarbanes Oxley compliance, financial sales certification, Microsoft or Cisco certification, IT Security certification, and many more. When you have a true certification program such as these, you need media that are trackable.

Some of the media that are excellent for tracking include web-based courseware, simulations, and classroom instruction. Media that provide enrollment information are live e-learning, Rapid e-Learning (PowerPoint-based), online video, and—to a lesser extent—conference calls. The remaining media types are self-study and provide little or no tracking technology that can allow you to identify when and whether a person completed the material. At the end of this chapter you will find a media selection matrix (Table 7.3), which will help you prioritize blended learning media based on its tracking capabilities.

Tracking: Industry Standards

If tracking and reporting are critical to your program, you must be aware of the role of industry standards. In the e-learning industry, two major technology standards are in use: AICC (Aviation Industry CBT Committee) and SCORM (Sharable Content Object Reference Model). Each of these standards uses a similar approach to tracking electronic content. In both cases, if the content is developed using tools that meet the standard, then your learning management system (LMS) can capture detailed information about the learner's interaction with the content. The types of information these standards specify include:

- Date and time of enrollment;
- Last chapter completed;
- Scores achieved on each assessment;
- Total score on the entire program;
- "Mastery percentage" (score divided by a "passing" score);
- Time spent in a chapter, time spent in the entire media/course;
- Percent completion to date;

- Completion date; and
- Much more.

With all this data, you will be able to track almost anything you need to create a certification or compliance-related program.

The tricky issue, which we will further explain in Chapter 9 (Learning Technology and Infrastructure), is that the standards are not "specifications" and therefore the interface between tools, content, and LMS (which captures the data) is not always complete. Tools and content providers must decide which parts of the specification they want to implement. LMS providers decide which parts of the standard they want to implement. The only way you know what precise data you are getting is to perform a test or ask your vendors to give you a specific demonstration.

For example, if you want to track "percent complete" through a web-based course, your tools and content must capture completion status at each course chapter (or "assignable unit," in AICC terms). The LMS must be able to understand the course structure so it knows how to compute percent completion. Many LMSs today will not allow this—hence the content may produce the right set of data but your LMS may not be able to report on it. Added to this complexity is a final issue: even if the data is in your LMS, you may need a custom report to get the data out in a usable format.

Bottom line: tracking is an issue in content development and media selection. For the purposes of media selection, you should decide what tracking you need and specify it in your selection of media, tools, consultants, and LMS providers. We always recommend that you test content in your LMS to make sure it launches, bookmarks, and tracks correctly.

Rapid e-Learning

One of the most exciting new areas of blended learning is the emergence of a new category we call Rapid e-Learning, a whole new approach to training that puts the power of web-based training into the hands of subject-matter experts. It has several important characteristics:

- Typically builds on PowerPoint as its base;
- Enables development of courses in weeks not months;
- Can be authored by SMEs; and
- Is typically used for type 1 and type 2 problems.

In our research into the content development market, we found that, for a typical course development project, there are three or four subject-matter experts involved at various points in time. If you can give these individuals authoring capability, you can dramatically reduce the cost and time of developing a blended learning activity.

The technology used generally converts PowerPoint to Flash format, so it plays easily in a browser without any plug-ins.

Some of the more advanced features available in most Power-Point publishing tools include:

- The ability to record audio on a slide-by-slide basis, which plays through the Flash plug-in without any need for Real Audio or Windows' Media Player;
- The ability to view animations on the web by converting animations to Flash;
- The ability to insert assessments between slides and capture results of these assessments;
- The ability to track page-by-page progress through the course and compute completion rates;
- Bookmarking, which lets a learner return to where he or she left off easily;
- Searching, which lets learners search for slides and courses based on words and phrases; and

- Indexing, which reduces the size of the material and enables easy searching.

These new tools include products like Macromedia Breeze, Articulate®, Trivantis®, Impatica®, and others. Live e-learning tools also fit into this category.

Example: Rapid e-Learning in Action at Novell

Novell's channel training team created instructionally sound PowerPoint templates for product managers to use when creating sales training for a new product launch. The templates use instructional design principles and force the product manager or subject-matter expert (SME) to use a standard format and standard fonts and graphics (see Figure 7.8). The SME also types notes into each

Figure 7.8.   Novell's Rapid e-Learning

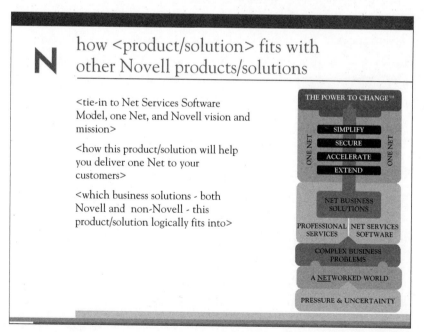

slide describing the audio that goes with the slide. SMEs can prepare this material in a week or less.

Novell's training group then takes the SME-authored material and cleans it up and gives it to a professional narrator. The narrator records the text and makes sure that all the slide materials make sense. Novell then publishes the material onto their channel training website using Macromedia Breeze and Novell's 6500+ channel partners can obtain new product training within days or weeks of a product launch. Novell tracks completion rates and sometimes scores students to make sure that resellers are staying certified on new products and services. This approach has reduced Novell's development time from three months down to three or four weeks per course.

The downside to these tools, and the risk you take by embarking on this approach, is that you skip the instructional design process needed to make courseware work. These tools do not let you add interactivities and other more complex animations without the use of a web developer. Many people think this approach will be the death of e-learning because it bypasses the instructional design process. My belief is quite the opposite—most SMEs understand the training process well and can easily author instructionally sound materials for type 1 and type 2 programs that can be published quickly. This frees your instructional designers to focus on the type 3 and type 4 training programs.

Keep It Simple

Simplicity is important. Since each medium has its own special content development issues and its own technology issues, you will need time to become familiar with each. If you choose to use one or more of the technology-based mediums, stick with it for some time so you can become familiar with its strengths, weaknesses, and limitations. We find that most large programs use only two or three media types at most. As we described in the previous chapter,

Table 7.3. Media Selection Matrix Summary

Medium	Live or Self-Study	Network Requirements	PC Configuration Requirements	Training Type	Ability to Track Completion and Results	Development Costs (per student hour)	Deployment Costs (per student hour)	Instructional Value (interactivity)
Instructor-Led Training	Live	None	None	Type 3, 4	High	$5,000–$25,000	Very High	Very High
Webinars (Live e-Learning)	Live	Medium Bandwidth	Plug-ins and setup required	Type 1, 2	Low	$1,000–$5,000	Medium	Medium
Courseware (Web-Based)	Self-Study	Low to Medium Bandwidth	Plug-ins and setup may be required	Type 3	Medium	$5,000–$50,000	Low	Medium-High
Simulations	Self-Study	None	Plug-ins and setup may be required	Type 3, 4	Medium to High	$15,000–$100,000	Medium	High
CD-ROM-Based Courseware	Self-Study	None	Plug-ins and setup required	Type 3, 4	Medium	$10,000–$50,000	Medium	Medium
"Rapid e-Learning" Courseware	Self-Study	Low Bandwidth	Plug-ins and setup rarely required	Type 2	Low	$2,000–$15,000	Low	Medium-Low
Internet-Delivered Video	Self-Study	Medium to High Bandwidth	Plug-ins and setup required	Type 1, 2	None	$10,000–$50,000	Medium-High	Medium-Low
EPSS (Electronic Performance)	Self-Study	Low to Medium	None	Type 2, 3	Low	$20,000+	Low	Low
Offline Video (Videotapes)	Self-Study	None	None	Type 1, 2, 3	None	$10,000–$20,000	Medium	Low
Video Conferencing	Self-Study	High	Plug-ins and setup required	Type 2, 3	Low	$10,000–$20,000	Medium-High	High
Collaboration Systems	Self-Study and Live	Low to Medium	None	Type 2, 3	None	$2,000–$5,000	Low	Medium
Conference Calls	Live	None	None	Type 1, 2	None	$100–$2,000	Low	Low
Job Aids	Self-Study	None	None	Type 2, 3	None	$100–$1,000	Low	Low
Workbooks	Self-Study	None	None	Type 2, 3	None	$100–$10,000	Low	Medium
Books	Self-Study	None	None	Type 1, 2, 3	None	$100–$500	Low	Low-Medium
On-the-Job Coaching	Live	None	None	Type 3, 4	High	$500–$5,000	Very High	Very High

consider a simple approach that uses one live medium and one self-study medium as a way to start. After you understand the dynamics of these two media, you can evolve to more complex blended learning programs.

Table 7.3 presents a brief summary of each of the media types and a summary of its characteristics. Keep this grid in mind during the program design phase and use it as a reference.

———

Lessons Learned in This Chapter

1. Familiarize yourself with the pros and cons of each of the media types before making decisions about which to use.

2. Instructor-led training is still the most common form of training and should be considered whenever you have culture-building and collaboration goals in your program. Short ILT events can be blended with other media easily to create a highly scalable program.

3. On-the-job exercises have proven to be one of the best way to engage first-line managers and reinforce mastery in field-oriented programs.

4. Live events (web-based or in-person) have many benefits over self-study. Wherever possible you should try to use live events in various parts of your program. Grant Thornton's methodologies give an excellent example of how to use webcasting as a key component of all live programs.

5. One key issue in media selection is the "durability" or "shelf life" of the content. You should carefully consider this issue when selecting media because some media are easy to maintain and update and others are not.

6. "Time to build" will drive media decisions in many programs. Review the Time to Build vs. Shelf Life matrix in Figure 7.6 to get perspective on this critical time issue.

7. Tracking and reporting features vary widely across the media types. If tracking and reporting are required, you must carefully select a medium that delivers enrollment, completion, scores, or certification information. Industry standards affect what information is available and you should check for interoperability between your content and your LMS to make sure you receive the data you need.

8. Consider SME-authored Rapid e-Learning content for short shelf-life urgent problems.

Chapter Eight

Content Development

Once you have developed a media strategy, it is time for the nuts and bolts of building learning program content. In this chapter we review many of the strategies, processes, tools, and techniques for content development (Figure 8.1).

Figure 8.1.   Where We Are

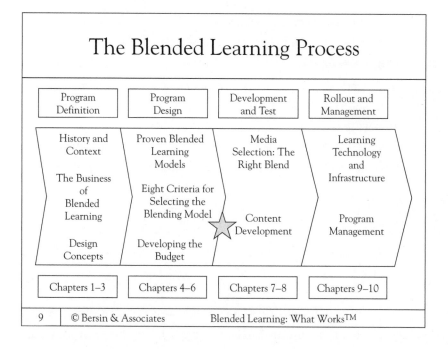

The Instructional Design Team

We discussed the issue of resources in Chapter 5. In any blended learning program there will be a team with four different roles:

- *Program manager:* the person who develops the budget, worries about launch and management, and takes overall responsibility for the program success. *Key skills:* budgeting, planning, executive interaction, business planning, partnering with line of business managers, launching, marketing, promoting, and measuring the program.

- *Project manager:* the person who reviews project plans, timelines, and critical paths to make sure the project stays on track—this is often the program manager. *Key skills:* project management and resource management, experience managing teams.

- *Instructional designer:* the person who creates the learning objectives, the instructional plan, the content outline, and who owns the blending decision. In many cases this is the same person as the program manager. *Key skills:* instructional design and familiarity with technology.

- *Subject-matter expert (SME):* the person or people who truly understand the content well and can author or assist in authoring the training. *Key skills:* deep knowledge and experience in the area of the program itself, understanding of the issues that make people truly effective, and masters of the topic.

- *Web developer:* the person or people who understand how to build content using the technologies you choose. *Key skills:* HTML, ASP/Java, Dreamweaver, database, and other web technologies.

Each of these functions requires different types of skills, experience, and commitment. SMEs typically have the least amount of time to participate; often they are "borrowed" from a line position to assist in the development of a particular program. The program manager and instructional designer must have experience in developing, launching, and managing training programs. The web developer should have some experience with learning technologies and may have very specialized skills in the tools you choose. The project manager may come from IT or another discipline.

Depending on the program type, you will spend more or less time on the instructional design part of the program. Designers of urgent type 1 and 2 programs tend to skip many instructional design processes and go directly from SME to authoring. Type 3 and 4 programs require much more lengthy instructional design.

Typical Content Development Challenges

In a large study we finished in early 2003, we asked more than 9,000 e-learning professionals what their single biggest challenge was. Their single most common answer is shown below.

"It takes too long to build courses."

In almost every program I have reviewed, time is the critical missing ingredient.

> "Most instructional designers would rather get it RIGHT than get it DONE." (unknown)

Because the e-learning process is still unknown to many developers, there is a tendency for many programs to become overly complex and take months and months to build—pushing up costs and missing deadlines. There is no substitute for finding people who have built courseware before, as they will be familiar with the issues of "overdesigning" content.

Developing a Program Plan

The most important lesson we have learned through our research is to maintain a laser-like focus on the *business objectives* of the program. Exhibit 8.1 presents a very simple hierarchy you must consistently revisit during the development process. Exhibit 8.2 presents an example.

This simple but powerful approach to breaking down the business strategy, learning objectives, and instructional strategy will help you develop the content and select the media for blended learning.

The Instructional Plan

The instructional plan is your detailed outline of the entire program. It describes each instructional element, its learning objective, what media it will use, how it will be delivered, how long it is, and how it will be developed. In most blended learning programs the different elements will be developed by different people, so the master plan is your blueprint to make sure that the whole program comes together.

The plan is typically developed by the instructional designer working hand in glove with the SME. If you are developing Rapid

Exhibit 8.1. Business Strategy for Content Development

The *business problem or objective* is _____ (stated in business terms):

The *learning objective* that drives the business objective is _____ (stated in learning terms: what will the learner specifically know at the end of this program?):

The *instructional strategy* is _____ (methods of teaching we will use: case studies? scenarios? dialogue? examples? interactivities? on-the-job exercises?):

We will *track results and completion by measuring* _____ (completions? how long it took to complete? whether they enrolled? whether managers see value?):

We must *develop* this program by _____ [date], *launch* it by _____ [date], and drive *completion* by _____ [date].

Exhibit 8.2.   Sample Business Strategy

The *business problem or objective* is to drive sales volumes of our new product in the first quarter of its availability at a rate higher than the last product launch. The target sales volume in Q1 is $300,000.

The *learning objective* that drives the business objective is to create awareness of the product and proficiency in positioning and objection handling for the product in North American sales force, building on their existing skills in sales, strategy, and closing deals. People should be able to identify, promote, differentiate, and price this new product. They should be able to handle simple objections that we will outline.

The *instructional strategy* is to roll out a three-hour blended learning program that trains sales representatives in how to position, sell, and handle objections using webinars and a one-hour online module that tests their positioning skills through a short assessment. The program will use lectures and a case study to reinforce learning. Learners will have a homework assignment between lesson 1 and lesson 2

We will *track results and completion by measuring* enrollments and scores on the final assessment. All sales managers must have at least 80 percent completion within ninety days of program launch.

We must *develop* this program by September 30, 2004, *launch* it by October 31, 2004, and drive *completion* by January 31, 2005.

e-Learning, you may in fact allow the SME to build the plan and much of the content. Even in this mode, however, we recommend that the instructional designer develop a template and review the content with the SME regularly.

An example of an instructional plan is illustrated in Figure 8.2. This plan was developed for a project management course and was provided compliments of DigitalThink.

Developing Standards

When developing blended programs it is important to have standards—standards for terminology, standards for the tone and tense of the content, standards for the target educational level of the audience, and standards for colors, fonts, graphics, and navigation.

Figure 8.2.   Sample Instructional Plan

Project Management Foundations
A Practitioner's Guide to the Art and Science of Project Management

curriculum map

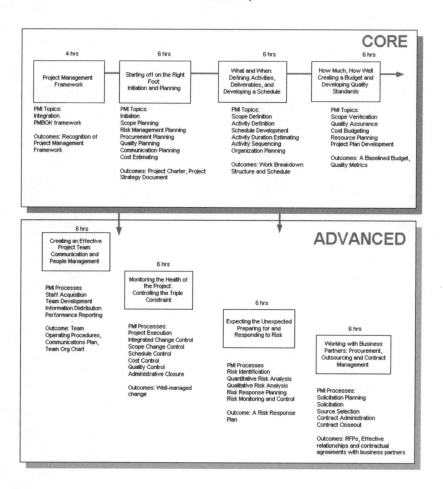

Since your program will include different types of media, the learner should see consistent messages, images, words, and concepts throughout the program. If you have content coming from multiple sources, maintaining consistency can be difficult so you must create a process to make sure there is a common glossary, vocabulary, and set of graphic standards for each author. Some examples of things you may want to standardize include:

- Course name;
- Program name;
- Learning objectives;
- Grammar for titles and descriptions;
- Reading level of copy;
- Color scheme;
- Logos; and
- Fonts.

Use a single artist for all graphics to help with this.

Making Content Reusable

As you start developing electronic content, you will find the need to share modules or chapters from course to course—making content reusable. The biggest benefit to reusable content is that when you need to update or maintain that module, every course that uses it is also updated automatically. The key issues in creating reusable content are as follows:

- Make sure that you have established the graphics and usage standards that truly make it reusable;
- Separate the content from its context. When Verizon was building a blended learning program on "Aerial Wire Safety Techniques," for example, there was a module on basic electricity concepts. This module could also be used in the course on "Inside Home Wire Safety Techniques." In order to make it reusable, however, it could not have any references to aerial wires; in other words, "context" must be separated. In fact, Verizon did accomplish this and has saved hundreds of thousands of dollars in maintenance.

- Establish "metadata" standards. Metadata refers to descriptive information, such as chapter name, chapter topics, length, author, and so forth. This information that describes each module of your program should be standardized so that when you pick up and select a reusable module, you have all the descriptive information you need to manage it within the second program.

- Learning content management systems (LCMS) help to manage the development and use of reusable content. If you are building many courses, you should strongly consider purchasing an LCMS.

If you are new to e-learning content development, it is important to understand the overall process you will face. Similar to the development of any other material, content development requires regular checks and feedback. One of the best overall process pictures we have seen is shown in Figure 8.3 and described below. In this approach the content development process is broken into four parts: analysis (outline and learning plan development), technology (building the content itself), SME (interacting with subject-matter experts), and editor (reviewing content for clarity, appropriate language, and errors).

e-Learning Content Development Process

Content development is not a task, but a process. One of our study companies, Roche Pharmaceuticals, shared their development process for SAP training. As you can see from Figure 8.3, there are a variety of phases, each of which requires reviews by various stakeholders. In the Roche environment there are four roles: analyst, technologist, SME, and editor. The analyst is the instructional designer. The technologist is the courseware developer. The editor is actually an external editor who makes sure that all copy, graphics, and usage are consistent. The editor is not a subject-matter expert.

Figure 8.3.   e-Learning Content Development Process

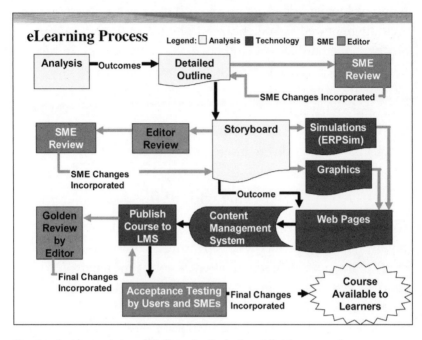

You see the iterative nature of this process. There are several stages of review before the course makes it into the hands of learners:

- SME review of course outline;
- SME review of the storyboard;
- Editor review of the storyboard;
- Editor review of the course; and
- Acceptance testing by users and SMEs.

Each of these review steps takes time. The biggest bottleneck in these projects is usually the SME review. SMEs are busy people and often take weeks to give feedback on course outlines, chapters, and detailed text.

The second thing you can see in this figure is that software content development does not begin until the outline and storyboard are fully reviewed by stakeholders. The technology development process is the hardest part to change, so you want to push them off until as many reviews as possible have been completed.

Finally, note that there is a final step to publish courses to the LMS and review again. This final review is necessary to make sure that the delivered course performs and behaves precisely as designed in the final production environment.

Working with SMEs

Working with subject-matter experts is a way of life in training departments. In our surveys of e-learning developers, the second most common problem stated (after the long time required to build courses) was *difficulty in working with subject-matter experts*. You should expect this to be a challenge.

Subject-matter experts are by nature busy people. They are individuals (line workers, managers, sales reps, engineers, IT programmers) who spend much of their time in their subject of interest and have very high levels of productivity in that task. They are proud of their expertise. When asked to teach someone else how to do what they know, they may find the task difficult or burdensome. They have spent years developing their skills and experience and may not easily understand how to translate that into an easy-to-use course that will help novices get started.

Your role as a program manager or instructional designer is to coach the SME and ask him or her the right questions so his or her deep level of knowledge comes out in the form that you need. Do not expect an SME to author a course—you may end up with a detailed book. Ask questions relating to your learning strategy such as:

- What are the most important things someone must understand in order to do this job right?
- What is the first step you take to make sure you save time?

- What background do you think people need to do this correctly?
- What are the typical mistakes people make when doing this task?
- What tips do you regularly give your peers or subordinates in this work?

The most important process issue for working with SMEs is protecting their time. You must carefully decide what information you need and what level of involvement they must provide—and then carefully schedule their time. Most SMEs cannot be "loaned" to content development projects for very long. Schedule a limited and well-organized set of meetings and send the SME information in advance.

Developing Webinar or Live e-Learning Content

Two of our media types, live e-learning and Rapid e-Learning, are typically developed and delivered by SMEs. These forms of content require a unique type of content development process.

A good example of such a process is the one developed by Grant Thornton. Grant Thornton uses webinars as their core blended media, then stores webinar replays for self-study use. Bob Dean, the CLO, believes that webinars are a "content creation engine" that creates a large library of subject-matter expert content that can be reused over time.

As you can see from Figure 8.4, even live events need learning objectives and a storyboard. The storyboard is developed by the subject-matter expert with help from Grant Thornton's training consultants. Similar to Novell's approach to Rapid e-Learning for product training, Grant Thornton's approach gives SMEs a detailed timeline, templates, and ongoing coaching during the development of slides. The Grant Thornton training organization reviews all slides to make sure they are graphically interesting, simple, easy to

Figure 8.4.   Live e-Learning Methodology

Webcast design and development process

1 Establish Business Case ◎	**2** Design Session	**3** Develop Storyboard
Determine: • Business strategy • Business and performance outcomes • Audience • Content scope • Measurements of success • Delivery strategy **Create communications plan**	**Establish:** • Performance and learning objectives • Technology options **Draft:** • Storyline • Content • Visuals • Interactions • Enrollment and communication	**Develop:** • Content development and review • Performance support resources • Pilot with target audience **Finalize scope:** • Timing • CPE
Business case	**Draft storyboard**	**Complete storyboard**

Deliverable Result

Courtesy of Grant Thornton.

understand, and jargon-free. One of the challenges they found is that SMEs often use terms and jargon familiar to them, but not well explained to the audience. In a webinar there is limited ability to "raise your hand" if you don't understand, so the Grant Thornton process requires the SME to remove as much jargon and to simplify content as much as possible.

During the delivery process, Grant Thornton recommends that the SMEs rehearse at least once. The rehearsal gives the presenter the confidence to be comfortable with the technology, flow, and material. As you can see in step 5 (Figure 8.5), the Grant Thornton methodology encourages the use of learner feedback and interactivity during the webinar and always has a survey at the end to track satisfaction and learning.

This six-step process, while simple, was developed over more than a year of experience and is implemented by training personnel on every webinar developed. The result is that Grant Thornton

Figure 8.5. Live e-Learning Methodology

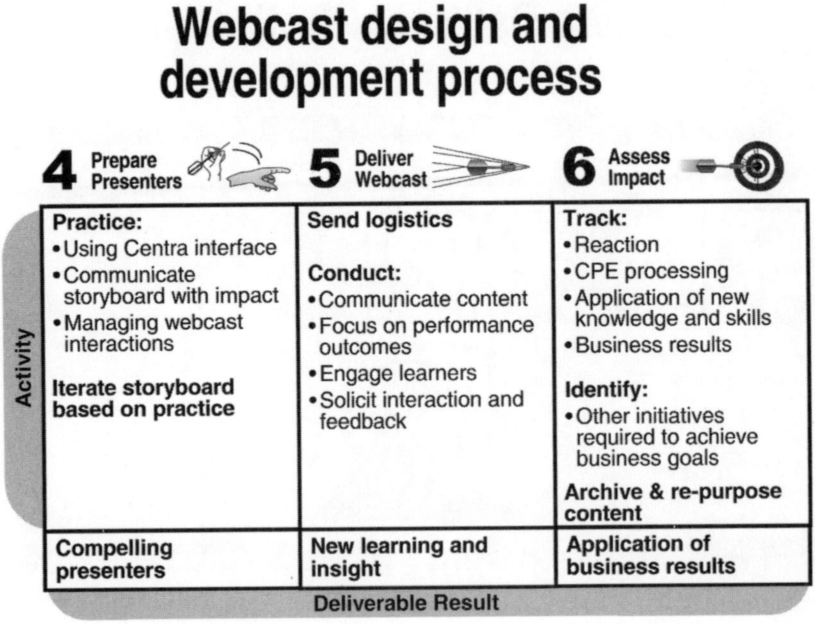

Webcast design and development process

4 Prepare Presenters	**5** Deliver Webcast	**6** Assess Impact
Practice: • Using Centra interface • Communicate storyboard with impact • Managing webcast interactions **Iterate storyboard based on practice**	**Send logistics** **Conduct:** • Communicate content • Focus on performance outcomes • Engage learners • Solicit interaction and feedback	**Track:** • Reaction • CPE processing • Application of new knowledge and skills • Business results **Identify:** • Other initiatives required to achieve business goals **Archive & re-purpose content**
Compelling presenters	**New learning and insight**	**Application of business results**

Activity (left axis label), **Deliverable Result** (bottom label)

Courtesy Grant Thornton.

webinars are highly valued and replayed again and again by their busy audience.

Grant Thornton webcasts as a key channel in their learning continuum (Figure 8.6). They are used for foundation training in nearly every basic accounting practice. These events are combined with local coaching sessions for foundation training on new concepts and practices and then for community building. Web-based courseware and other documents are provided as supporting materials for performance support.

Development Tools

There are dozens (maybe hundreds) of development tools for developing electronic content. Since this book is not intended as a review of tools in detail, we will highlight the different categories of tools and give you some basic examples of each.

Figure 8.6.   Webinars as Foundation for Learning Continuum

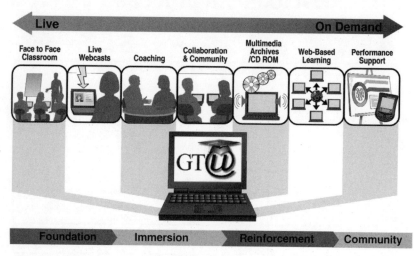

Courtesy Grant Thornton, University-GT.

First, you must realize that the e-learning market is flooded with specialized tools. Be prepared to invest in at least four to prepare yourself for content development. (Our research shows that the average corporate e-learning content development group has 3.7 tools!)

Examples of Tools

Instructor-led training tools	PowerPoint, Word
HTML web development	Dreamweaver, FrontPage®, GoLive®, HTML
Dynamic animation and graphics	Flash, Authorware, Quicktime®
Static graphics	Photoshop®, PowerPoint
Complete courseware development tools	Lectora®, Trainersoft®

Assessment tools	Questionmark®, Knowledge Advisors Metrics that Matter®
Survey tools	Zoomerang®, WebSurveyor®, and tools built into LMS systems
Audio and video streaming tools	Real™ Audio/Video, Windows Media Player
Live e-learning tools	Centra®, Placeware®, Webex®, Interwise®, iLinc®
Web-based application simulation tools	Robodemo®, Robohelp®, Firefly®, Softsim®, and many more
Instructional design tools	Designer's Edge®, Authorware
SME and Rapid E-Learning Tools	Macromedia Breeze, Articulate, iCanvas®

Selecting a Tool Set

Your biggest challenge will be to find the right tool to build the media you want without becoming locked into this tool for all future development. Each tool has its own learning curve and its own focus area. Remember that the *largest investment you will make is in the content itself,* so do not try to save money on the tool. The time and effort you invest will be ten to a hundred times larger than the money spent on the tool, so purchase the tools you need.

e-Learning tools are like building tools. You need a tool belt of hammers, screwdrivers, drills, and some sandpaper to build a great course. (Hopefully not too much sandpaper.) As I mentioned above, e-learning developers on average use more than four different tools for a typical e-learning project. You will certainly need some HTML development tool (for example, Dreamweaver) and then specialized tools to build interactivities, animations, graphics, and simulations.

Today most companies rely on Flash as the technology to deliver courseware and try to stay away from players such as Real Player, Windows Media, and Quicktime. The main reason is that nearly 98 percent of all Internet browsers now have the Flash player built in. Flash supports graphics, animation, audio, and even video. We strongly recommend that you set Flash as your deployment standard and try to select tools that can create Flash-based output.

Examples of Different Tools

Figure 8.7 and Figure 8.8 show examples of some of the more popular tools in use today.

Figure 8.7.   Trainersoft Tool from Outstart

Figure 8.8.   Lectora from Trivantis: An Integrated e-Learning Content Development Tool

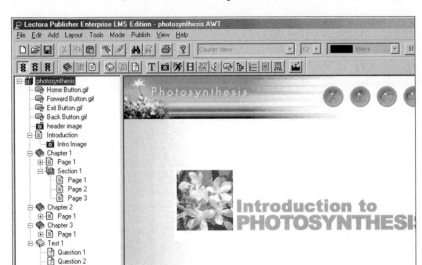

Lectora is a trademark of the Trivantis Corporation.

Simulations

Simulations are a hot new topic in e-learning. The term essentially means creating a learning environment that "simulates" the real world, enabling the learner to learn by doing. Simulation is widely used throughout industry and typically applied to jobs where the impact of failure is very high. Simulations enable workers like pilots, military, and flight controllers to make mistakes without ever crashing a real plane, shooting a real bullet, or putting two flights on the same flight path.

In the business world, the advent of faster computers is making simulation easier and easier for white collar training. The benefits of simulation are clear: it creates high levels of mastery and performance by enabling learners to learn by failure. See Figure 8.9 for other benefits.

Your challenge in blended learning is to decide when and where to apply this approach. Since simulations are a costly

Figure 8.9. Simulation Benefits

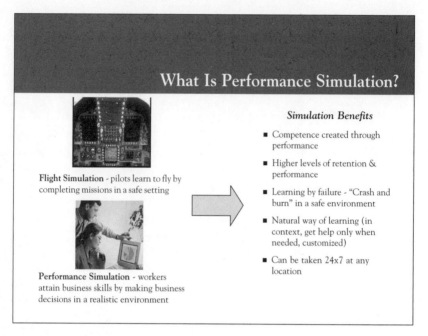

Courtesy of Accenture.

and time-consuming way to build content, I recommend that you go carefully. Make sure that your investment in a simulation approach is justified by a large audience and a high-ROI business problem.

There are three basic categories of online simulations in use today:

Software Application Simulations

Software application simulations are the most mature and easy to implement of any simulation approach. If you are training someone how to enter an order into SAP or add a new sales entry into a PDA, you are essentially training someone how to use a piece of software. The cost of errors can be high and the cost of using the real application for training may also be high. This is a perfect case for simulation.

Luckily for program managers, this problem area is filled with excellent tools, approaches, and examples. Some of the most popular tools in this area include Softsim from Outstart, RoboDemo from eHelp, Producer® from Camtasia (Figure 8.10), and Firefly from Knowledge Impact. As in any market, the tools range from easy to use to very powerful and complete.

The tools provide many capabilities, ranging from simple product demonstrations to actual prototyping tools that enable you to simulate actual menus and screens to tools that actually test and coach users through an entire application. Typically, these tools let you add screen tips, branching, and a wide range of assessments and other instructional interactivities (see Figure 8.10 for an example).

As a blended learning medium, application simulations are typically embedded within a content flow program. *You must always*

Figure 8.10.   Application Simulation Tool—Camtasia Producer

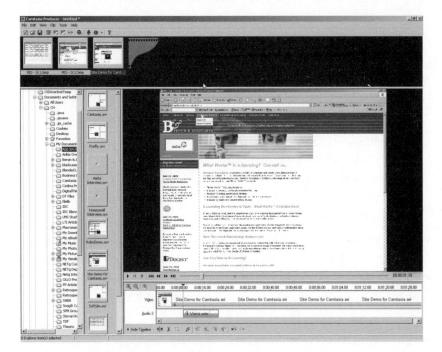

introduce learners to the business process from a high-level viewpoint before diving into an application. Typically, an introduction is used to give users the context and understanding of the business flow; then the simulation is used to give the learner the ability to learn and practice the application; and then follow-up exercises, tests, or discussions are used to assess learners and answer questions. In many of the programs we reviewed, the final step is a lab-based exercise where learners get on the real system and show an instructor what they have learned.

> **Example:** Hertz recently rolled out an entirely new reservation system to more than six hundred field offices. The program is a blended learning program that uses application simulation as its core. The program works as follows:

- First, users take an *online course* comprised of simulation-based tutorials on how to use the system. Hertz uses the RoboDemo FrameHelp to create simulations on using the application. Learners begin the process of learning the new application using these tutorials.
- Learners next move to a *live system* that is used specifically for training in order to get a feel for using the real application. The training system is a replica of the production system, although learners feel less pressure since they can make mistakes without recourse. The training system also provides online help (which contains the same simulations as the training course) so that users can get help when they need it. RoboHelp is used to create the online help.
- Learners participate in regularly scheduled *virtual classrooms sessions* with a live instructor to go through questions and also cover region-specific nuances of how the system works (for example, procedures for dealing with local tax rates). Instructors are stationed locally and are equipped to deal with rules and regulations for the various localities.
- Learners can also rely on local management staff to provide onsite mentoring throughout the training process.

Scenario-Based Simulations

The second type of simulation is a category we call "scenario-based." Some of the more complex performance-based training problems (such as leadership training, management training, negotiation, and some sales training) are best solved with scenarios. Such scenario-based e-learning typically uses videos or animation to show the learner a real-world situation and then asks the learner "What would you do in this situation?" These simulations are most often used for leadership and sales training.

There are many ways to build scenario-based simulations. Some of the most powerful (and expensive) are the video-based leadership programs developed by Ninth House. These video-based scenarios show real-world business situations and force the learner to decide what action to take in a difficult situation. Ninth House's programs are available in a complete blended format for both web-based and CD-ROM delivery.

Many companies build scenario-based simulations themselves using easy-to-use tools such as EEDO's Force10® platform. These tools enable you to create a "branching story," which gives learners consequences from each decision, resulting in a final "pass" or "failure." Some screen shots of scenario-based simulations are shown in Figures 8.11, 8.12, 8.13, and 8.14.

Many of these simulations look and feel like games, but in fact are asking the learners to test their judgment and knowledge. In the case of Ninth House content, often these programs are used in conjunction with facilitated meetings, discussion groups, and workbooks to create a complete blended program.

Business and Financial Numeric Simulations

The third type of simulations is financial and business simulations. These simulations are essentially "live spreadsheets" that enable learners to enter numbers and assumptions and see what happens. Typically, these programs require the learner to optimize a range of inputs (for example, budget projections, sales targets, resource allocations) and then, over a period of simulated cycles

Figure 8.11.   Branching Story Simulation from Cognitive Arts

Figure 8.12.   Branching Story Simulation
for Military Applications

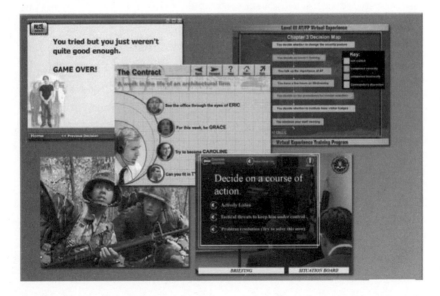

Figure 8.13.   Soft Skills Simulation: "Supportive Confrontation" by Ninth House

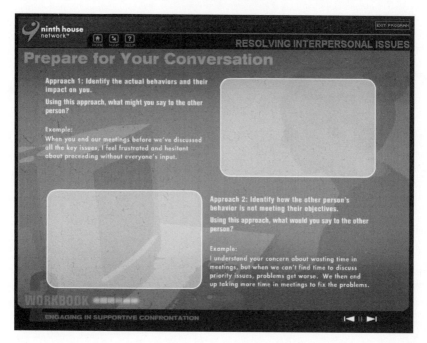

Reprinted with permission from Ninth House, Inc.

(months, quarters, or years), the learners see the impact of their actions.

Because these simulations often mimic a real business, they can be complex to build. One example, the Siemens global accounting change simulation, took months and millions of dollars to build. It was used in conjunction with a series of meetings and conference calls to certify more than 10,000 financial professionals throughout Siemens worldwide on new general accounting practices. The impact of this program was tremendous. It enabled Siemens to become listed on the New York Stock Exchange.

Figure 8.15 presents a screenshot from a business simulation from PowerSim that shows how product pricing and discount affects demand, total revenue, and profit.

Figure 8.14.   Ninth House Business Scenario
Simulation Features

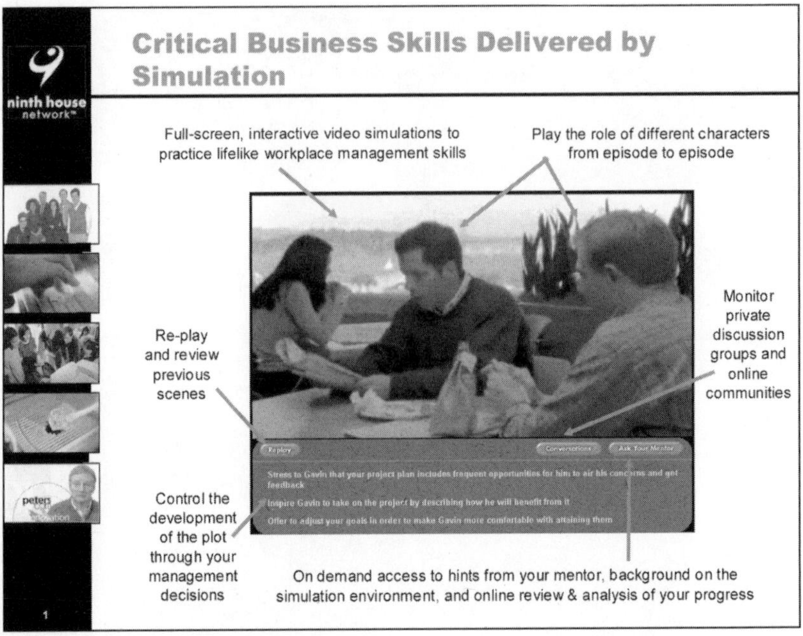

Reprinted with permission from Ninth House, Inc.

If you are searching around for simulation solutions, there are a wide variety of small companies now offering tools. The http://www.bersin.com website is filled with indexes and reviews of these tools.

Content Development Tips and Techniques

Many books have been written on content development processes, techniques, and tools. Our goal here is to introduce you to the issues with content development and give you enough information to decide which media elements make sense for your particular problem. Some of the biggest things we have learned follow.

Carefully Manage the SME Interaction Process. Make sure you have a process for regular reviews of content with SMEs. Many blended learning programs go into the development phase and

Figure 8.15.   Business Simulation from PowerSim

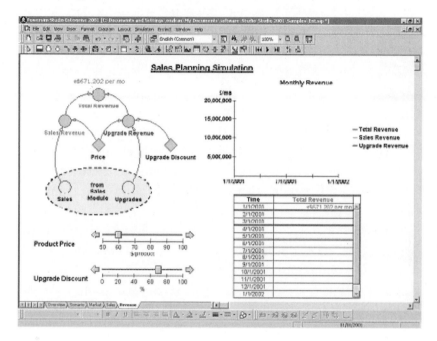

then need major revision near the launch because the content development team misinterpreted or modified some of the content. SMEs should be checking off on your work throughout the process, as the Roche process described earlier shows.

Buy the Right Tools, and Enough of Them. As the old saying goes, if all you have is a hammer, everything looks like a nail. If you have a limited set of tools, you will find that your content suffers as a result. Consider integrated tools like Trivantis' Lectora and Outstart's Trainersoft, which have many of these functions built in.

Outsource Specialized Skills. If you are building simulations for the first time, don't be afraid to hire a consultant. Make sure, however, that your consulting agreement has two important features: First, consultants must develop to your technology standards. You tell them what PC configuration, network configuration, and plug-ins you can tolerate. Second, make sure your contract specifies that they will teach your team how to use the tool and edit the content. Over time, the cost of maintenance will dwarf the content of initial development—and you want the consultants to work themselves out of a job. Otherwise you will have tremendous headaches maintaining the content and building the next set of courses.

Develop a Team or Committee for Review. Training content in general should be reviewed by subject-matter experts, managers, and executives. Blended learning programs, because of their expense, typically need reviews as well. Your program committee should consist of a few users, subject-matter experts, IT personnel, and one or more executives. This committee will help you with content issues, rollout issues, and decisions about how complex and expensive the content should be. Content development is a never-ending sink hole for resources, and the hardest part is often deciding when to stop developing and launch!

Use Editors and Outside Assistants. All text copy and graphics should be reviewed by some outsider for clarity, readability, and language. If your organization is global, you will need a translator to translate certain chapters or components into multiple languages. This small investment pays for itself many times over in quality and consistency.

Outsourcing Content Development

After reading all the issues in content development, you may decide to outsource this particular function. Many companies choose to outsource the development of content—sometimes web-based as well as instructor-led content. The benefit to outsourcing is that you will often get an excellent product and you do not have to invest in tools, training, and specialized skills in courseware, simulations, video production, and assessment. However, our research has found that in the last year more and more companies have brought content development in-house. Here are the pros and cons of outsourcing.

Benefits of Outsourcing Content Development

1. *Faster development.* An outsourced team will have all the skills and resources available immediately and can typically start and finish quickly.

2. *Higher quality.* If you select the right vendor (one with experience in your particular problem area), you will benefit from their learning curve. Always select a content developer who has proven experience building content of the type you need. Ask to see demonstrations and talk with references.

3. *Lower costs.* If you are building a large library of content, some content developers have low-cost programmers (in India and other low-wage countries) who can dramatically reduce the cost of basic graphics and HTML development.

Risks of Outsourcing Content Development

1. *Loss of control.* If you outsource the content development process, you have to carefully specify your content and specify your standards so that the product you receive fits seamlessly into your long-term strategy. This means specifying the technology standards, the graphics and usage standards, and the deployment technology.

2. *Maintenance difficulties.* The biggest issue with outsourcing is maintenance. If you do not develop the skills to edit and modify this content, you will be dependent on your provider for maintenance. Make sure you negotiate this process up-front.

3. *High cost.* In most cases, the cost of outsourced content development is far higher than doing it in-house. This may vary depending on the amount of content you are building, of course, but overall, companies are bringing this function in-house to reduce costs.

4. *Lack of internal expertise*. As e-learning and blended learning grows, you should be developing some expertise in-house. It is important to think about your long-term strategy before you outsource a function that may eventually be part of your core competency as a business. I frequently recommend that clients ask developers to include a component in their bid to train their team in how to modify or maintain the content they provide.

Lessons Learned in This Chapter

1. Assemble a complete team that includes a program manager, project manager, instructional designer, SME, and web developer.

2. Develop a process that includes SME reviews of content outline, storyboard, and final product before launch.

3. Consider hiring an external editor to make sure that copy and graphics are consistent, clear, and easy to understand.

4. Set up a process to manage live e-learning events. Do not just turn them over to SMEs or instructors without assistance.

5. Take the time to develop your own internal standards for metadata, graphics, fonts, audience analysis, and other content-related issues. Make sure you consider reusability whenever you take the time to build a module, chapter, or course.

6. Manage your SME interactions carefully to save their time and energy. They are critical resources and should be used carefully.

7. Be prepared to purchase a wide set of development tools. These tools should be easy to use and built to deploy content in industry standard formats. Try to use Flash for your deployment technology. Buy enough tools to simplify the process—your big investment is in the content itself.

8. Consider using simulations if the problem has a high impact of failure. Application simulations are the most mature form of simulations, but scenarios and business simulations are also growing rapidly in usage.

9. Think about outsourcing large projects or high-value programs to get started, but make sure that your outsourcing agreements include terms for maintenance and training of your staff.

Chapter Nine

Learning Technology and Infrastructure

"In e-learning, content is king, but infrastructure
is God"

Tom Kelly, Cisco, Circa 2000

No book on blended learning is complete without discussing the important role of technology and infrastructure.

"Technology is the most important enabler you have
in blended learning. A sound technology plan will
make your program work. A poor technology plan
will make your program impossible."

Josh Bersin, 2004

In our research we consistently find that, although infrastructure alone is not enough to make blended learning work, it is the enabler that makes blended learning effective. This chapter will give you a basic understanding of what infrastructure you need and how to avoid problems (Figure 9.1).

Review of Blended Learning Infrastructure

Let's review the basic building blocks of a learning technology infrastructure (Figure 9.2). Those of you who are technologists can browse through this section quickly.

As Figure 9.2 shows, there are seven basic components in your infrastructure.

Figure 9.1.   Where We Are

The Blended Learning Process			
Program Definition	Program Design	Development and Test	Rollout and Management
History and Context The Business of Blended Learning Design Concepts	Proven Blended Learning Models Eight Criteria for Selecting the Blending Model Developing the Budget	Media Selection: The Right Blend Content Development	Learning Technology and Infrastructure Program Management
Chapters 1–3	Chapters 4–6	Chapters 7–8	Chapters 9–10

9 | © Bersin & Associates | Blended Learning: What Works™

Figure 9.2.   Learning Technology Infrastructure

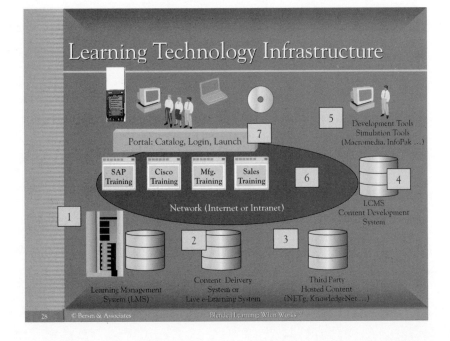

1. Learning Management System

The LMS is the central administrative system to manage blended learning. Its role is to create a course catalog, enable learners to register and enroll, track their progress and scores, and implement the business processes around learning. It is the data repository for all administrative learning information.

LMS vendors typically position their products as an entire platform, but in reality the main function of the LMS is to handle *administration*. Many companies manage programs without LMS systems. But once you have multiple programs, multiple audiences, and lots of business processes to manage (fee-based training, certification programs, different learning paths, prerequisites, skills-based programs), an LMS is required.

Many issues exist when selecting the right LMS. A very wide variety of business processes are associated with training. From a blended learning standpoint, you need an LMS that can manage:

- Scheduled events (classroom as well as live e-learning);
- Self-study programs (web-based courses);
- Reference objects (web pages); and
- Offline materials (books).

Most commercial LMS systems have this functionality. Within each of these four areas are many features and workflow issues you should explore. For example, do you want learners to automatically order a book when they take a course? Would you like the LMS to automatically order the books? Would you like the LMS to track progress through a single program that includes a live event, a web-based course, and a book? Would you like the LMS to give you reports on learners, showing their progress on each step?

These are the types of blended learning features some LMS systems do not yet manage. If you want your LMS to truly manage the mixed media of blended programs, you will have to review these features in detail.

2. Content Delivery System

An important but often overlooked part of a blended learning or e-learning system is the content delivery system. In any e-learning implementation, you will be building many pages and files of content. This content will be arranged into course chapters or reference materials. When a user starts a piece of electronic content, the following steps take place:

- The learner identifies the course or course step in the LMS course catalog;
- The learner enrolls and clicks on an URL link to start the course or chapter, and the LMS tracks this enrollment;
- This link launches the URL of the first page of content in that media object, and if it is a live webinar, the content opens up in a window and streams to the user;
- The user then clicks through the content, going from chapter to chapter, completing exercises and assessments;
- While the content is playing, a stream of "tracking data" flows back to the LMS to store bookmarks, progress, scores, and completion; and
- When the user is finished, he or she interrupts or completes the content, and a bookmark is set in the LMS.

The role of the content delivery system is to store, deliver, and manage that content. If you purchase a learning content management system (LCMS), this functionality is built in. However, most companies do not have LCMS systems today so you will have one or more content delivery systems of your own. If you use live e-learning, you will have a server handling the delivery of live events (for example, Centra, Interwise) or this will be outsourced (for example, Webex).

The key issues in this component are making sure that you have the capacity and performance to handle the workload. If you have thousands of people using the content, your IT department must be prepared for the workload of thousands of people streaming content or hitting pages.

The second issue in content delivery is security. Your IT department must make sure that this content is protected from unauthorized access, either by hiding it from view or using the LMS as the only way to link to and access this content. The LMS can hide access to the course catalog, but not the content itself. If a user finds the URL to launch the content, he or she could bypass the LMS.

3. Hosted Third-Party Content

A frequent component in most companies is the use of third-party content from a hosted provider such as NETg or Skillsoft or ElementK. These are courses or other electronic media that run in the same fashion as above but do not reside within your organization's network. These courses function similar to the example above with a few major differences: the content is sitting behind someone else's LMS and must inter-operate over an insecure network. When you launch these courses, data is stored in your content provider's LMS as well as your own. Often the amount of data available to your LMS is less than it would be if the content ran in your own systems. Your IT department must typically be involved to set up these interfaces.

As we discussed in Chapter 1, many hosted content providers require proprietary players that download and run in your local browser. Although these work, they sometimes create problems downloading and running correctly in your corporate intranet.

The most important thing to do when you select these courses is to *test the launch and play process across your corporate network*. It is also important to *test interoperability with your LMS,* as often the content does not send precisely the correct data to the LMS for tracking.

4 and 5. LCMS Content Development System and Development Tools

The content development infrastructure has two components—the development tools themselves, used by content developers and instructional designers, and the content management system, which houses their work during the development process. The latter, typically called an LCMS (learning content management system), is a relatively new part of the e-learning infrastructure that helps you manage large numbers of courses and teams of content developers. We see a trend toward more and more usage of LCMS technology over time.

The development tools are clearly critical; they give you the power and capability to build the media objects you select. The LCMS functions as a repository for work in process so that you can have one developer working on a graphic object while another works on an assessment, for example. It also makes sure that all the components of a course are integrated and versioned so you can modify and maintain the course easily over time.

We will not get into tool selection in this book; however, the main issue to consider is the format for the final course that is delivered. Some tools require proprietary players or proprietary streaming servers. You should try to avoid using these because they will make deployment difficult and they lock you into a particular vendor's technology. The key standards here are HTML and Flash and streaming media standards such as Microsoft Media Player, Real Player, and Quicktime.

6. The Network Itself

Your network itself is a critical piece of infrastructure. All electronic content takes some amount of bandwidth to run. Some has been designed for very low bandwidth; some requires high bandwidth. You will find that within your network some locations have more bandwidth than others. We have found that for you to have a seamless deployment, you should test your content at various places in your network. If you know that users will be dialing in from home on 56K modems or lower, you have to design your content to perform well under these conditions.

British Air, for example, found that within the Heathrow area bandwidth was high, but that in outlying areas in the UK bandwidth was much lower. As a result, in their blended learning and e-learning programs they avoid any content that requires greater than 56Kbps to run effectively.

Many companies we talked with have users in remote geographies across the globe where Internet access is either slow or very expensive. In some cases (NCR, for example), service technicians had to go to Internet cafés to get sufficient bandwidth to take their network certification curriculum.

7. Learning Portal

The final component in the infrastructure is the learning portal—the interface from which the learner takes courses. The portal has an important role—to simplify the process of learners finding and enrolling in the appropriate content. Although this may sound easy, in many cases it is not. Most LMS systems have some capability of creating a learning portal, but often they are not flexible enough to give you the corporate look and feel you need.

You must work with your IT department to integrate your program into the appropriate internal portal. The portal must give learners information about why, when, and how to enroll in your blended program and provide supporting information such as what PC standard software they need, how to schedule the live events, and so forth.

One of the biggest challenges you will face is recruiting learners to enroll in and complete the network-based parts of your program. The portal plays a critical role in attracting learners and easing their transition into your events. Some examples of learning portals are shown in Figure 9.3 and Figure 9.4.

Figure 9.3.   British Airways Learning Portal

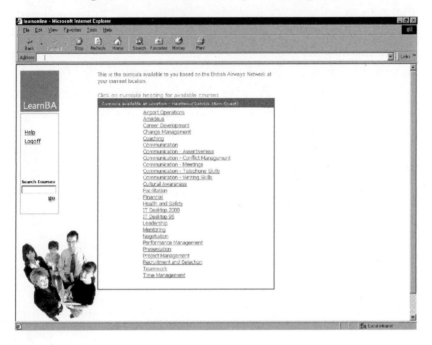

Figure 9.4.   Sabre Learning Portal

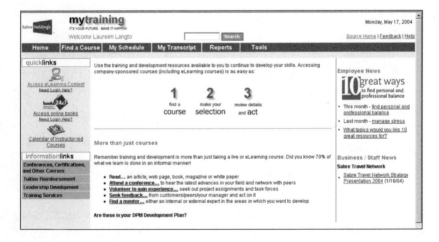

Using and Setting Standards

One of the critical lessons we have learned is this market is the need to set technology standards. Despite the broad awareness and adoption of industry standards (AICC and SCORM), these standards are not implemented uniformly in all products. You must develop your own internal standards.

PC Deployment Standards

Most corporations have a wide variety of PC software and hardware distributed throughout the company. How, then, can you guarantee that your e-learning courseware will run? The answer is to set a technology standard. The standards you set should specify:

- Amount of memory and CPU speed needed (500 Meg. or higher?);
- Version of Windows or MAC OS required (Win 98? XP?);
- Screen size and resolution (800 × 600 is the standard on most PCs today);
- Bandwidth needed (56Kb, 256Kb, T-1?);
- Version of Internet Explorer or Netscape (many Java script programs run differently in Netscape, for example);
- Player technologies needed (Flash? Which version? Quicktime? Real Audio/Video? Windows Media Player? Proprietary player?);
- Languages supported (Will your courseware run in multiple languages and need character sets?);
- Audio card needed and, if so, what audio codecs; and
- Video card or video codec needed.

The purpose of these standards is not to force people to upgrade their PCs but rather to set a minimum configuration that you can use to test your e-learning content. In some cases your standard may make it impossible for large parts of the audience to participate in the program. To avoid this situation, you must work with your IT department to make sure that your content meets their standards for corporate PCs.

In addition, these standards serve as specifications for your third-party developers to develop content that meets your needs precisely.

> As we have seen again and again, when a piece of courseware does not run correctly, learners will often leave and never come back. If the learner's first experience is negative, you may lose him or her forever.

Verizon Example

When Verizon rolled out their video-based training (Figure 9.5) for new service representatives (which drove tremendous improvements in productivity), they found that many of the PCs in the training locations needed to be upgraded. As a result Verizon wrote a small utility that tested the PC for the right plug-ins and bandwidth and refused to run the content until the system was upgraded.

How Much Learning Infrastructure You Need

Many companies have a tendency to buy too much. LMS vendors have created a flurry of interest in buying LMS software that has more and more features every year. Most LMS implementations use less than 20 percent of the total feature set of the LMS. The most important features for you to drive an effective program are

- A flexible, easy-to-use course catalog;
- An easy user interface to locate, enroll in, and launch a course;
- The ability to group courses together into learning paths and curricula;

Figure 9.5.   Verizon Content Sample

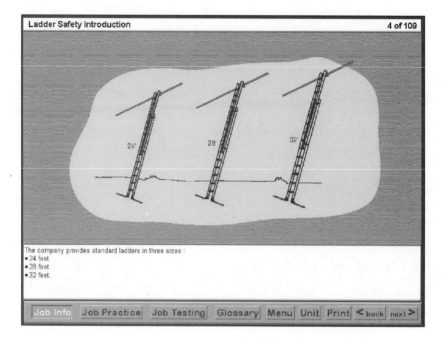

- The ability to schedule and integrate classroom and live e-learning events into a single program with self-study content;
- The ability to attach resources (web pages, documents) to a course;
- Some kind of assessment tool (built-in or purchased separately);
- The ability to track via AICC standards; and
- A fantastic reporting and analysis system (often the most overlooked part of the system, yet the one you will use the most once you get into deployment).

Do You Need an LMS at All?

Many of the most exciting and effective programs do not use an LMS at all. Remember that the role of an LMS is to manage, track, and organize multiple learning programs. If your job is to develop and roll out a single program of blended learning with two or three media elements and some supporting documentation, you can implement this without an LMS.

How would you do this? Have your IT group develop a single web portal that outlines each step of your program and has easy-to-understand links to each part of the program. You can track registrations in a simple registration database. This approach may not give you the tracking you need, but if your budget is small you can track enrollments and completions and scores, and that will likely be enough.

Low-Cost LMS Approaches

If your budget is small and your organization does not already have an LMS, you have several choices:

1. You can select a "built-in" or "hosted" LMS from a variety of companies that have full-function LMS systems that are easy to implement and do not require any software installation on your part. Companies that offer this include Blackboard (for secondary and higher education), Vuepoint, GeoLearning, Edcor, DK Systems, Thomson NETg, Intellinex, and more. These systems will cost you only a few dollars per learner to implement and will save you the expense of implementing complex software internally. Examples of companies that have used such solutions include Cisco's global channel certification program, which uses Intellinex's LMS, and NCR's global certification program, which uses EDCOR.

2. You can purchase an integrated tool set that has LMS features built in, such as DigitalThink's e-briefings and Macromedia's Breeze (Figure 9.6). These tools include built-in technology for developing content and a built-in registration, tracking, and reporting system to roll out electronic content. Breeze

Figure 9.6. Macromedia Breeze Rapid e-Learning Solution with Embedded LMS

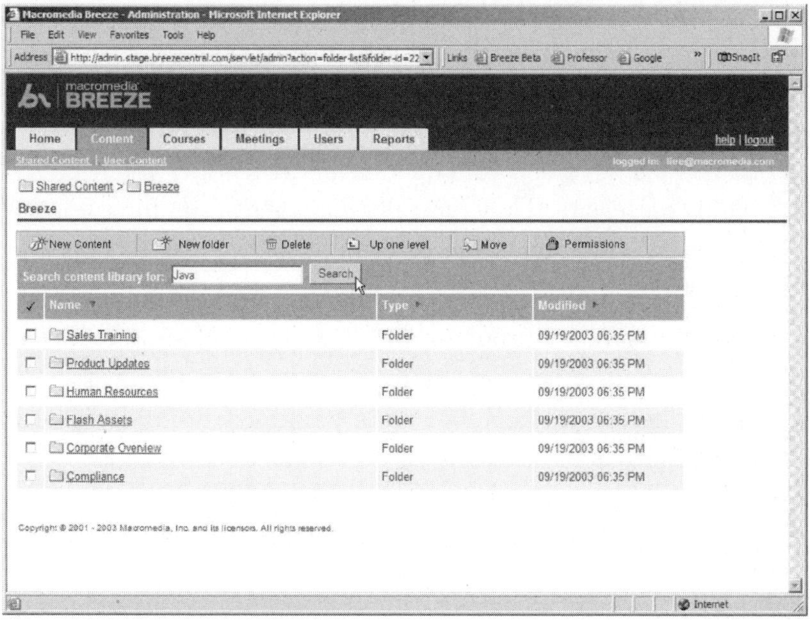

includes features for both live e-learning as well as self-study, PowerPoint-based content.

LCMS and Development Tools

When you look at the development tools market, you will find a dizzying array of vendors, each with its own particular slant toward blended learning. They tend to fall into five categories:

- HTML web-development tools such as Macromedia Dreamweaver and Microsoft FrontPage that help you to develop pages, portals, and general web-design objects. These tools cost $200 to $500 per developer. Associated with these are the graphic design tools such as Fireworks® and Photoshop, which you need in order to build graphics and edit images. Macromedia Flash, which enables you to build "movies" and animations, is often included in this category.

- e-Learning specific tools such as Trivantis Lectora, Trainersoft, Authorware, and others that give you a complete tool set for building courseware. These tools typically cost $1,000 to $2,000 per developer and include all the features you need to build courseware. They typically include features for assessments and some simulation capabilities.

- Simulation tools that help you build application simulations and other types of simulations. Macromedia Flash is the most commonly used generic tool for simulations, but many specialized tools such as RoboDemo, Camtasia®, InfoPack®, Firefly, and others focus exclusively on different simulation models. These tools range in price from $200 to $10,000, depending on the complexity of your needs. If you are training people on SAP, for example, a powerful simulation tool will be very valuable.

- Assessment tools, such as Questionmark, that enable you to build complex assessments, store and reuse questions, analyze results, and so on.

- Live e-learning tools, such as Centra, Interwise, Webex, and Placeware, which help you to build live events and distribute, track, and manage them.

If you are building a single program, you should consider using e-learning specific tools such as Lectora or Trainersoft. They are designed to be easy to use and have everything you need to build courseware. As your sophistication grows, you will have to purchase and use standard HTML tools to embellish your content and add animations. Simulation tools are most widely used for application simulation problems (training in how to use software). Some more specialized tools are excellent for building scenario-based training, including Knowledgeware®.

Lessons Learned in This Chapter

There is no perfect platform. Blended learning is still a relatively new field, and despite the hype of platform providers, there is no "complete solution" for blended learning. A blended learning platform should be able to launch, track, and report on each element of the program. Few platforms I have seen can manage the entire end-to-end process from a single interface, so you will have to manually track progress through each of the steps.

Our recommendations on infrastructure is that "less is better." Most LMS companies have far more features than you will need, so you should focus on the key business process functions you need to be successful (that is, prerequisites, enrollment process, reporting tools) and the user interface. In most LMS systems, the biggest problem companies face is inability to customize the user interface to meet different learner populations. Test the user interface with real learners and make sure they understand how to interact with the system well before you buy.

If you choose to purchase software and bring it in-house, your IT department will need to be involved. Our most recent research found that, for a typical LMS implementation, the cost of implementation, customization, and support is more than double the cost of the initial software purchase. Make sure IT has "bought in" to the infrastructure you select, because they will play a major role in your success.

1. Buy "just enough" technology to meet your needs. Try not to become entranced by dozens of features you do not need.

2. Make sure your IT department is helping you with software purchases and standards.

Chapter Ten

Program Management

Launch, Rollout, Support

This chapter could easily be a book in itself. Throughout my research I have continually found that the launch, marketing, support, and operational aspects of e-learning are the areas that have the greatest impact on success. You can develop great content, deploy great technology, and still end up with e-learning that no one takes. This chapter shows you how to manage program rollouts to drive excitement, high levels of participation, completion, and overall satisfaction (Figure 10.1).

Figure 10.1. Where We Are

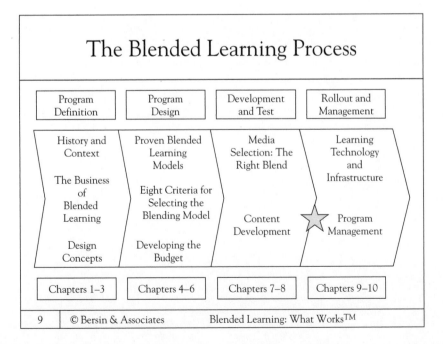

The Challenge of Utilizing e-Learning

Let us first examine why utilization can be a challenge (Figure 10.2). In traditional instructor-led training, certain "perks" and "privileges" are included. Students have a chance to get away from work, go to a special location, drink coffee and eat donuts, chat with peers, and take a step back and reflect on their jobs. This process itself is therapeutic and educational for most employees.

In a purely web-based program, most of these factors do not exist. Workers are typically asked to squeeze web-based training into their already overscheduled day. Learners take courses at their desks, where they are already flooded with e-mails and phone calls. Interaction with peers may be minimal.

Finally, many organizations do not have a learning culture. Many line managers do not encourage and support workers to take time away from work and attend training. *Your job in program management is to avoid or overcome these challenges.*

Figure 10.2. The Challenge of Utilization

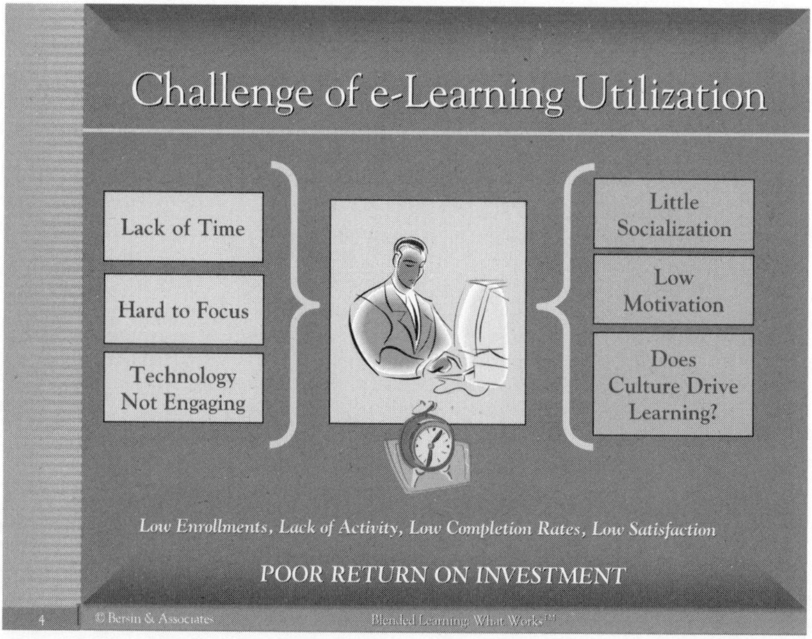
Challenge of e-Learning Utilization
Lack of Time
Hard to Focus
Technology Not Engaging
Little Socialization
Low Motivation
Does Culture Drive Learning?
Low Enrollments, Lack of Activity, Low Completion Rates, Low Satisfaction
POOR RETURN ON INVESTMENT
4
© Bersin & Associates
Blended Learning: What Works™

Review the Program Schedule

Every blended learning program has a timeline. Let us review the lifecycle discussed in Chapter 5 (Figure 10.3). You have developed an interesting, compelling program that meets your business goals. You have clearly defined business goals that are quantifiable and measurable. You are ready to launch.

As the timeline (seen in Figure 10.3) shows, you typically have a limited amount of time for this program to roll out. You must quickly drive enrollments early in the process so that learners get through the self-study parts of your program in time to meet the target end date. Once learners enroll, you must take actions to make sure that they complete in time to meet the target end date or attend the next live scheduled event. Finally, you are probably working with content that will soon become obsolete, so you must make sure that learners complete the program before the material becomes out-of-date.

For self-study events, activity levels typically looks something like the curve presented in Figure 10.4. Initially, people enroll and

Figure 10.3.   Program Lifecycle

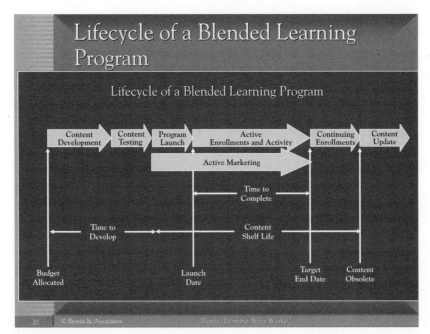

Figure 10.4.   Typical Learning Activity in Self-Study Events

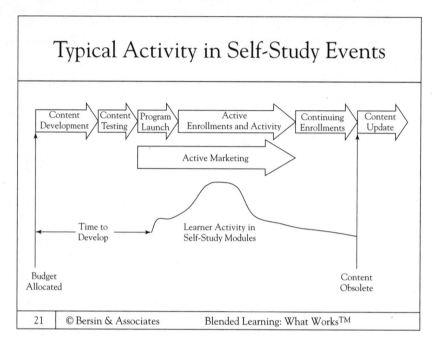

jump into the program. Once the initial awareness fades, however, activity diminishes. Perhaps people find that the work is harder or more time-consuming than they originally anticipated. The activity then fades and learners postpone completion until some scheduled event demands completion of self-study as a prerequisite.

In your program design, as we stressed in Chapter 4, you should include a mixture of self-study and live events. This design encourages activity because it gives learners a fixed date by which they must complete certain modules. Nevertheless, remember that you must provide ongoing program management to make sure that learners engage and complete your content.

Program Launch

The first part of program management is the *program launch*. The word "launch" implies the beginning of the marketing process. Marketing? Yes. Marketing is a critical issue in every major program. The word simply means clearly communicating the program's value to your audience, their management, and the executive team. This process starts at the launch and continues throughout the program.

A program launch also creates awareness, excitement, and a buzz about your program. The launch has several purposes:

- It tells line management that the program exists and convinces them why they should spend time making sure their employees participate;

- It tells line management their role in making this program a success;

- It tells executives that the program is underway so that they can communicate and evangelize the program across the organization;

- It informs learners about the availability of the program, why this program is important to them, and how to register, enroll, and begin; and

- It tells support people (IT, operations, trainers, instructors) that the program has started and that their support is now needed.

One of your most important audiences in the launch is first-line managers. Their motivation and participation are critical to success. Your biggest job during the launch is to convince line managers that the program is critical to them and that they should support it completely.

Executive and Management Support

Executives should be well aware of this program far before the launch. Executives in line operations as well as HR and training will want to know what the program is about, why the company is investing in it, and what role they should play. Present the program to them in advance and ask for their advice and coaching. If you planned well, at launch time these individuals will be some of your most important advocates.

In this set of meetings you should be prepared with a slide set that answers the following questions:

- What is the business problem being addressed by this program?
- How does the program work? Is it a certification? A course? A series of manager-led interactions?
- What are its components? How much time will it take from employees?
- What role do first-line managers play? Coaching? Specific activities?
- What role do second-line managers play?
- How will you be reporting back to line management on activity? How can they monitor the progress of their organization? Will there be a contest or competition among employees for scores or completion? Will people see each other's results?
- How should they be supporting their employees? Should they give them time away from work to complete? Should they be paid overtime? Will they need to travel?
- Where do learners go for help? (Typically managers do not want to become the point of contact for support.)
- What specifically do you want them to do during the launch? (Give you a quote for a newsletter? Participate in a conference call? Send employees an e-mail?)

During these meetings you will hear valuable feedback on issues to address in completion. Write these down. There may be a big project coming that will interrupt the program. There may be a misunderstanding from line management about the problem being solved. There may not be funding for the time and resources to complete.

These are all issues that should have been addressed well before the launch—but after the launch you must listen again. These objections will typically resurface when the program rolls out and could be land mines to the success of your carefully designed blended learning program.

Remember also that this process will continue throughout the program lifecycle. Line managers have many more important things to think about than your training program, so you should communicate with them regularly to see how new events may slow down or speed up your program success.

Specific Launch Events

When the program is ready to launch, you should consider a series of events and communications. There are many possible techniques to use here. A few of the most common ways to roll out the program include:

- Conference calls to managers and executives;
- Regional coordinators in each line organization;
- E-mail blasts and updates to the corporate website; and
- Kickoff meetings in regional locations.

Some of the important things to include in launch materials include:

- The purpose of the program;
- The logistics for registration and enrollment;
- The technology platform standards;
- How learners will be measured and how results will be reported;
- How much time the program will take (how many hours of their time);

- What executive or business mandates this program supports;
- The business goal of the program; and
- Who they can work with to get help and support.

Ongoing Marketing

One of the issues companies face with any technology-based training program is the need to continuously remind people to complete their assignments. In your blended learning program you will have several self-study elements. You must continuously remind people to enroll and complete these activities.

The best techniques for these reminders are

- E-mail newsletters (Figure 10.5);
- Direct e-mails to people enrolled in the course;
- Surveys to request feedback;
- Visits to field locations; and
- Conference calls with managers.

In many of the application rollout programs we studied, we found that students did not complete their assignments between real-world interventions. This problem is very frustrating to trainers and it forces the instructor to revisit topics that students should have covered during self-study. Your job as a program manager is to reinforce and motivate learners to complete their self-study assignments. One way is through contests, as seen in Figure 10.6.

One of the best marketing tools you can use is an online survey. Surveys give learners the sense that they are being listened to.

Training people are not typically trained in the art of marketing. When you embark on e-learning and blended learning, however, you should think of yourself as a marketer. Most audiences are volunteer learners. If they are busy, they may choose to skip much

Figure 10.5.   Newsletters Drive Awareness and Enrollments

From: Devaughn, Tarra
Sent: Thursday, February 13, 2003 10:53 AM
To: !SEA IT Broadcast Announcements
Subject: NETg Xtremelearning Training Tips for February!
Importance: High

NETg Xtremelearning Skill Builder DX Training Tips for

FEB

Microsoft Outlook - Proficient

Tracking Activities with Contacts
A contact can be the focus of different actions originating from the various components of Outlook 2000. The same contact can be sent a message from inbox, a memo from notes and a meeting request from your calendar. You can keep track of all these various activities by using the Activities feature. For example, you can review all recent messages you have exchanged with a contact without having to search for each Outlook component. Sound difficult? Not at all. If you are not using this time saving feature, learn how by going to *Tracking Activities with Contacts, located in Unit 1, Lesson 3, Topic 2.*

Adding a vCard to a Message
The business community is a system of interactions. A colleague may ask you to recommend a reliable service provider or the name of a hotel to use on a business trip. Did you know that the Outlook Contacts component could also be used to share information about yourself or a contact? It's called vCard, the electronic equivalent of a business card. This handy feature is explained in *Adding a vCard to a Message, located in Unit 1, Lesson 3, Topic 3.*

To access Outlook 2000 Proficient and other courses, go to the TRAINING link on SEAport and follow the directions on how to get started. If you already have an account, you can go directly to NETg Xtremelearning.

If you have questions, need to have an account created, or encounter difficulty logging on, e-mail your NETg Administrator, Jacqueline Matthews.

**Want to take a class without any distractions?
Try the new Corporate Learning Center located in Room 241!**

---

of your content if they can. You must continually reinforce the value of your program to your audience throughout the rollout cycle in order to drive enrollments, activity, and completion. This means a combination of activities.

Figure 10.6.   Contests Can Drive Awareness and Enrollments

Here is an easy way to help yourself, learn a thing or two and maybe even net some cool gear!

Learning & Development is pleased to sponsor the **NETg Catch of the Month** contest. Each month, Learning & Development will publish the course for the month. At the end of the month, we will collect the names of everyone that has **completed** the course during that month and randomly select one winner. The winner will receive their choice from the *Ceridian Clothing Catalog*. We will announce the winner and let you know the next course at the beginning of the new month. The contest will run from March 2002 through October 2002.

So, are you ready to get started?

The course for **October** is:

Stress Management - Fundamentals for Employees #43006

First Time Users
If this is the first time you have used a NETg course, please read the attached material on how to log in and get started:
<<NETgGettingStarted.ppt>>

Below are the links to access NETg from Ceridian or from Home:

Via **CeridiaNET** (Recommended for First Time Users):

http://ceridianet.ceridian.net/cnet/section/0,1159,295,00.html

Via your **home PC**:

https://www.xtremelearning.com/formsloginsecure.asp

Click here to see the fabulous choices in Ceridian Clothing:

http://170.153.28.80/cnet/ceridian/clothing/1,1843,1060,00.html

We are collecting the results from the September contest and will announce the winner no later than Monday, October 14.

Good luck!

Example: At Siemens Energy and Automation, the training program manager periodically calls up line managers and visits plant and sales locations to give a short presentation on their blended learning offerings. These visits help drive awareness and also give the training group direct feedback on the quality of their content and impact of their programs.

Support and Operations

It is critically important to have a support infrastructure for questions and problems. In scheduled live events (web-based or classroom), there will always be learners who cannot enroll, need a new time scheduled, or want to attend a make-up session. They need someone to call.

For self-study modules be prepared to address a wide variety of issues. Learners will need help with PC software, performance issues, and questions about material. They may actually need to talk with an SME to get help. Let's hope you have built in enough help or have a set of supporting people assigned to provide this assistance. Two typical approaches are to provide learning labs and to assign regional coordinators (discussed in the next section).

For technical questions, you will need an IT person or technical support person available. For example, when Giant Eagle Foods rolled out their internal manager training in their retail stores, they used a combination of off-the-shelf content from NETg and manager meetings with employees. One discovery was that many of the store employees did not have computers at home and therefore did not know how to use a mouse. The Giant Eagle training department needed to develop a short "how to use a mouse" program to go with the blended learning program to deal with this issue.

If you do not have any support available, you risk creating a poor impression on learners, which creates rumors and poor public relations for your program. If the word spreads that the program is hard to use or does not work, you will find it very hard to change this impression. *In marketing, first impressions are often last impressions.* You must make every interaction with a learner a positive, helpful one.

Learning Labs

One of the program management techniques we continue to see in large organizations is the traditional learning lab. Although e-learning is intended to let people learn "anytime, anywhere," many workers have limited access to computers, networking, or space to learn at their work locations. Learning labs solve this problem.

United Airlines, for example, uses blended learning to certify and train 35,000 field personnel throughout the United States. These individuals include baggage handlers, gate agents, and operations personnel—people who do not have regular access to computers at work. Much of their programs are type 4: certification based and therefore require end-of-course assessments to validate completion and learning.

They accomplish this by setting up learning labs in secure locations at each airport. These learning labs are sometimes staffed by part-time training managers who are available to assist learners gaining access to the program they need.

Giant Eagle Foods and many retailers set up a small cluster of PCs in the back room of the stores. These workstations are available for shared use and typically have access to a higher-speed intranet than would typically be available throughout the store. They give learners the ability to control the environment by carefully configuring the PCs to make sure they can run the online content.

As we described in Chapter 6, you must budget for this equipment, space, and support. In some cases this infrastructure will cost millions of dollars. It can be leveraged across dozens and dozens of programs, but is a sound investment in making blended learning a workable, ongoing investment in your organization.

Field Coordinators

In nearly every major program I study, companies find that some type of field coordinator is needed. These people are typically workers in the line organization who are specially trained to help roll out, support, and coach learners through the program. In a large SAP application rollout, for example, the company recruited local telesales people as field coordinators. The coordinators scheduled conference calls, answered questions, and made sure that the program manager received regular feedback on the progress of the program. In the case of this SAP rollout, the program had a very short timeline to complete so the coordinators met regularly with managers and learners to make sure they had completed training before the switchover. One of the other big roles these coordinators played was meeting with local managers to make sure that they were giving employees the time they needed to complete the training program.

If you see a need for such coordinators, you should include their time and travel in the budget. Without such a field presence, you may be forced to get on an airplane yourself to go out and meet with learners and resolve problems.

Measuring and Reporting Progress

A critical role you play in program management is measuring and reporting progress and success. People will come to you and ask, "How is the program going?" You should prepare for this question in advance and make sure you have the reports and statistics to answer these questions and identify problems.

There are many ways to measure training, and my upcoming book on Training Analytics will cover this in detail. In the hierarchy of measures (Figure 10.7), the six measures you can strive for are enrollments, activity, completion, satisfaction, scores or learning, and job and business impact (ROI).

Figure 10.7.   Measurement Points in the Program Lifecycle

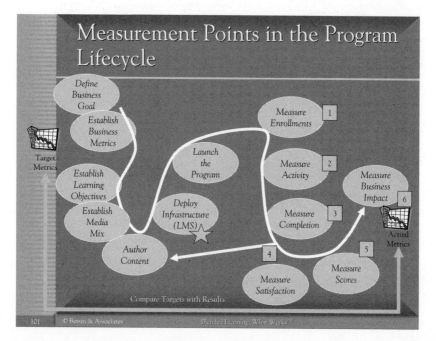

The last measure, business impact, is the topic of many books and we will not cover it in detail here. I will cover the process in detail in my upcoming book.

The other measures, however, should be planned in advance. If you need to measure scores, one hopes you built the content in a way that scores are captured. If you need to measure completion, define "completion" and have a technology architecture that can capture completion data.

Remember here that you will be very dependent on your LMS. If you adequately tested your content in your LMS, you should be able to easily obtain this information. You should meet with IT or your LMS coordinator in advance to design the reports you want that will best display the enrollment, activity, and completion data for your organization.

> **Example:** In a major retailer's large sales-focused e-learning program, which consists of many modules supported by manager intervention, the concept of "completion" is not important. The target audience for this program is sales associates in one of the company's more than six hundred retail locations. These individuals are very busy and typically take training during their breaks, lunch, or when business is slow. The company does not expect them to complete each and every course, but rather to take the ones they feel they need based on their own needs and their managers' direction. Enrollments are the barometer of success. Completion measurements are used to analyze some specific target programs, but not expected on a general basis. Scores are rarely used. Satisfaction is measured continuously. Business impact is measured through measurement of store volumes, product volumes, and regular interviews with line managers and employees.
>
> In Siemens' global accounting rollout, however, completion was critical. Since the target program was designed to create completely proficient financial managers (type 3 and 4), the company felt that it was critical to measure completion and scores for every learner. In fact, the program (which used a business simulation to actually force the learners to apply the information they learned) was designed in

a way that each module was shipped to the learner independently. People could not receive module 2 until they successfully completed and passed module 1. This gave the program sponsors (the CFO's office, in this case) the ability to carefully monitor and measure activity, completion, and scores.

It is important to understand that the simplest and easiest way to measure progress is to measure enrollments, activity, and completion. Before you can declare victory and call your program a success, you must have a level of enrollment, activity, and completion that meets your plan.

Communication with Upper Management

In any blended learning (or e-learning) program, you have made a significant investment in content development, tools, and program management. You must communicate progress, lessons learned, successes, and action items needed to your executive sponsors. Sponsors fall into two types: executives in HR and training and those in the line of business you are serving.

The reason for this communication is not to advance your career. Rather, it is important to enlist executives as your allies in driving program success. As we have continuously stated, one of the biggest challenges program managers face is enrollment and completion. Executive support is one of the best ways to drive awareness and usage. If you are rolling out a program that is "mandatory"—a type 4 certification, for example—management will be keenly interested in enrollment and completion rates.

How do you best communicate with upper management? The best way is to prepare a "program review" process, which gives you the opportunity to update management during content development, right before launch, after launch, and some time after the program is complete. These reviews will force you to assess your schedule and success to date at each step. These reviews do not need to be long; typically, HR and training managers are not keenly interested in the details of each program (unless it is a very critical program). You should be prepared to ask the executive for help in some way. This gets him or her involved and makes sure that he or she is aware of the issues you face.

Communication with Line Management

If you are in corporate training, you know that serving your "clients" in line operations is the most important part of your job. In a blended learning program, you must regularly communicate with line management to make sure that you are hearing feedback on "what works" and "what is not working."

How do you tell managers what is working and what is not? How do you communicate success? How do you communicate problem areas? You need measurements and reports. Figures 10.8 through 10.14 show some of the more interesting examples of how training organizations use metrics to create interesting management reports.

Enrollment Reports

Figure 10.8.   Measurement of Enrollments (BCE)

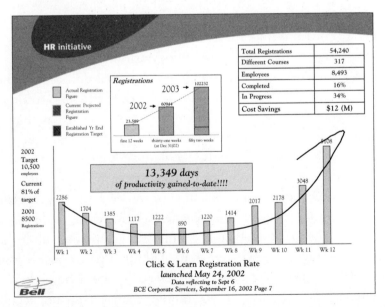

Activity Reports

Figure 10.9.   Measurement of Activity (Accesses)

Top 10 most used courses (time spent)

Course Name	Language	Accesses	Duration	Average Access Time (mins)
MS Excel 97 Proficient User	English	224	226:55	61
MS Word 97 Proficient User	English	221	224:54	61
MS PowerPoint 97	English	177	194:10	66
MS Word 2000 Fundamentals	English	141	172:13	73
MS Excel 2000 Fundamentals	English	136	135:42	60
MS Access 2000 Fundamentals	English	109	122:09	67
MS Access 97 Fundamentals - Part 1	English	107	107:47	60
Lotus Notes R5 Messg and Remote	English	72	102:33	85
MS Excel 97 Expert User	English	69	90:48	79
MS PowerPoint 2000 Proficient User	English	64	79:45	75

As of Apr 1st 2003

Figure 10.10.   Measurement of Activity: Hours (Rockwell)

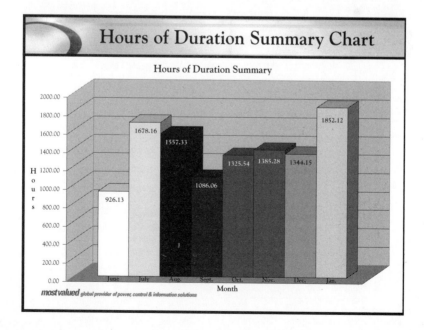

Delivery Mode Reports

Figure 10.11.   Measurement of Delivery Mix (BCE)

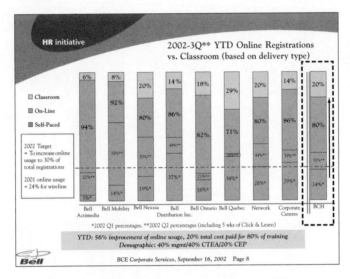

Survey/Satisfaction Reports

Figure 10.12.   Measurement of Level 1—Satisfaction (Roche)

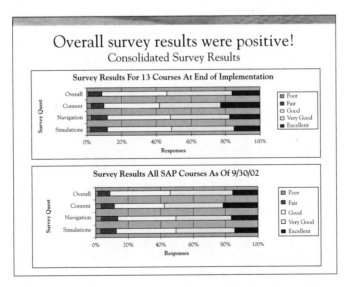

Score and Learning Results Reports

Figure 10.13.   Measurement of Level 2—Scores (Rockwell)

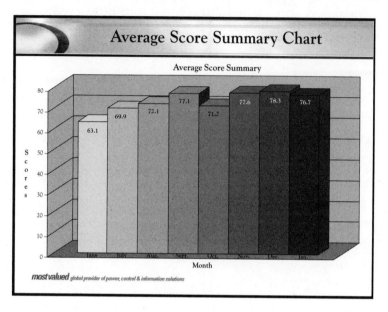

Executive Summary Reports

Figure 10.14.   Insurance Company Impact Report

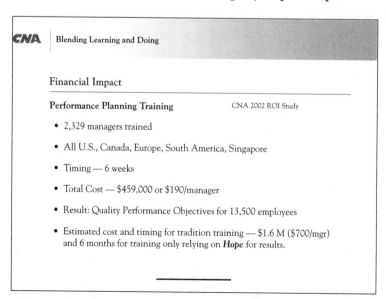

Lessons Learned in This Chapter

1. Program management will make or break your program. The best design, media, and content cannot succeed if you do not adequately plan, launch, market, and measure your program. This process is also called "change management."

2. Your program schedule will drive the program management process. Make sure you have a clear, graphic schedule that gives you time to plan each step in the program management process.

3. Make sure you have executive support from the earliest phase of the project: during the budget cycle, during the design cycle, and during the launch and rollout process. You will need executive support continuously to drive participation in the line of business organizations.

4. Do not assume that "if you build it they will come." There are many pressures working against the use of e-learning in organizations. You must overcome these barriers through your launch, marketing, and communication processes.

5. Launch events are important to generate broad awareness and excitement.

6. Marketing must continue throughout the program. You cannot assume that people understand the program goals, value, and details, and you must communicate this information continuously.

7. Prepare support and operations plans. Support needs will include general "how to" support as well as IT and other technical areas.

8. Consider using temporary field coordinators to facilitate, support, and drive your program from the line organization itself. This approach enlists support from your learning audience and is one of the most effective ways to drive rapid adoption.

9. Set up one or more learning labs to make it easy for learners to attend and complete. Do not assume that everyone can work at his or her desk.

10. Set up a measurement plan before you start content development. Decide what you want to measure, test the process, and then create a few important management reports that you will use.

11. Communicate aggressively and continually with upper management. You have spent a lot of time and money building an important program. Let upper management know what is working and where they can help.

Moving Forward

Why Blended Learning Is So Important

Why is blended learning such a hot topic? We are now at a point in e-learning where many viable options are available. The options can be confusing. Training organizations must learn how to select just the right approach to solve different business problems.

I also believe that e-learning is still in its infancy. We are just beginning to learn how the Internet and other new technologies can best be used to educate, inform, train, and support workers. The basic principles in this book will help us take advantage of new technologies and tools to come.

An interesting thing to consider: in the next twenty years the workforce will be transformed. The "Generation Y" children who are growing up with cell phones and instant messaging will be running our corporations. These workers are comfortable and adept with technology. They welcome the use of the Internet for chat, meetings, and training. But they have high expectations—and will drive us to improve the learning experience more and more.

As training professionals, we should remember a few truisms:

- *The core of training is instructional design.* The instructor and SME are still the most important people in program design and delivery, not the developer or technologist.
- *People learn by doing.* No amount of reading, video, or animation can substitute for learning by practice. We must constantly find ways to deliver experiential learning.

- *People learn differently.* No medium is perfect for everyone. By mixing media we appeal to the broadest number of learners.
- *Management is paramount.* The first-line manager will make or break any training program. They know best how to improve business performance through people.

Blended learning concepts give us the flexibility to use these principles and apply them when and where they are needed.

Where Blended Learning Is Going

By the time this book is published, new tools will be available. During the period I was writing, new tool vendors have entered the scene with new ways to create simulations, scenarios, interactivities, and online events. This innovation will continue, and as bandwidth gets higher the quality of our online learning will be higher.

Today we are at a point where every significant training program should use a blended approach. Traditional page-turning courseware is no longer sufficient. Training professionals should always think about providing two or three ways for learners to obtain the information and skills they need.

One of the exciting things coming is an emergence of blended learning "platforms." Today if you want to deliver a class, a series of webinars, and a set of online courses, you have to manage these different events and media in a wide variety of platforms. New platforms, either from LMS companies or others, will have all the elements you need in a single package—making it easy to blend programs and monitor, measure, and assess learning easily across all the different media.

The role of the program manager will never change. Your role will always be to select the right media, manage the program roll-out, and accept continuous feedback from your audience. You are the one who assesses the audience's specific needs and decides which particular blend of materials makes sense for them.

The process of education and training is a fascinating and constantly changing journey. It requires an understanding of people, processes, technology, and culture. I hope that this book has helped you, the program manager, instructional designer, teacher, or manager, learn how to take advantage of the power of blended learning to make your programs the most successful ever!

Appendix A

Case Studies and Solutions

Many of the case studies used to develop the materials in this book were published in *Blended Learning: What Works™*, a major industry study conducted in 2002 and 2003. This study is being updated in 2004. Some of the companies contacted are listed below. Many other companies were consulted for development of this book.

Accenture/Siemens

Siemens developed a global blended learning program in 2001 to train 10,000 financial professionals on a major change in accounting. The company switched from German to U.S. General Accounting Principles in order to become listed on the NYSE. This change required rapid training of business professionals in every global business unit.

Bell Canada

Bell Canada replaced a distributed, decentralized set of training programs with a set of online and blended programs for a wide variety of topics. This blended learning strategy resulted in tremendous savings by reducing overlap and reducing the number of suppliers needed to train IT, project managers, field personnel, and executives.

BT

BT rolled out a major new product for mobile professionals called M-Commerce. Sales and service personnel needed to understand many new technologies, concepts, and sales approaches to be effective. A blended program of e-learning and traditional training reduced the amount of time to train so that this important program could fit into the salespeople's already busy schedule.

Call Centers at a Major Bank

A large U.S. bank has more than 2,000 employees in five different call centers. To reduce the time it takes to train new employees, the company revamped its new hire training into a blended program that teaches call center agents how to handle complex online computer systems and many different types of inquiries in less time than ever before. The program blends ILT and e-learning and simulations into a complete curriculum.

Cisco

Cisco uses a blend of e-learning, certification programs, and online support to train thousands of certified resellers in a wide range of curricula. Their programs require passing scores and include online laboratories to create proficiency in sales, service, and a wide range of specialized technical skills.

CNA Insurance

CNA has developed an innovative blended learning solution and platform that was used to roll out a new performance management system to 2,000 managers in only a few months. This solution integrates e-learning from multiple sources, chat, collaboration, and a unique team approach and generates dramatic results.

Enterprise Software Company

An enterprise software company needed to train new and existing employees on its wide range of products. To reduce time spent away from the customer the company developed a set of tiered offerings that use both e-learning and instructor-led training. This program creates certified professionals in a wide range of their products and gives employees incentives to learn more, while saving money and time.

Flag University—U.S. Navy

The U.S. Navy Flag University is responsible for supporting and developing three hundred admirals and three hundred civilian executives in the Navy. Their program is more than seven years in length and includes a wide combination of electronic content, on-the-job study, self-assessments, and field visits to many internal and external locations.

Grant Thornton

Grant Thornton, a major accounting firm focused on mid-sized businesses, uses IP-based voice, webinars, self-study, and online interactions in a powerful and integrated way through their Grant Thornton University portal. They have pioneered the use of webcasting as an enterprise training solution for a broad range of topics and applications.

IBM

IBM uses blended learning consisting of self-study e-learning and on-the-job discussions to sensitize managers and work groups about the special needs of younger "GENx" professionals in the workplace.

FedEx Kinko's Office & Print Services

FedEx Kinko's Office & Print Services adopted e-learning as its primary learning tool in 2002. The company has developed an innovative approach to selecting the right media and uses a wide variety of e-learning, job aids, virtual classroom, and other tools to roll out new products and train new employees throughout its network of stores.

A Major Distributor of Industrial Products

A major distributor of industrial products (Company W) is a very large provider of industrial products and is one of SAP's largest customers. Their online order processing system processes millions of dollars worth of small orders every day. When they switched over to a new version of SAP, they only had a period of months to get all sales agents trained and could not afford any loss of productivity or sales after the switchover. A blended learning program was used to solve this problem.

A Major U.S. Consumer Electronics Retailer

A major U.S. consumer electronics retailer (Company C) uses e-learning extensively to improve sales, roll out new products, and increase the confidence of in-store workers at more than six hundred retail locations. Their innovative blend of e-learning and on-the-job training has delivered dramatic results.

NCR Field Service Certification

NCR uses e-learning, online labs, and instructor-led training to train their global field force on a wide range of networking topics. These individuals are located throughout the globe and use online learning, CD-ROM, and laboratories to learn about and stay current on many networking projects.

Ninth House, Inc.

Ninth House, Inc., a leading provider of executive and management skills training, uses a flexible blended learning curriculum mixed with online video exercises to train managers and executives at more than one hundred companies. Each company can mix the blended elements to meet its own needs. The elements include instructor-led training, discussion groups, exercises, and a wide variety of assessments. This approach has been widely acclaimed in many companies.

Novell

Novell introduces new products and services more than twenty times per year. Their global channel of 6,000 plus resellers needs to be trained rapidly on these products when they are introduced. Novell uses a Rapid e-Learning form of blended learning to develop and launch these programs in weeks instead of months that would be required by traditional approaches.

Royal & Sun Alliance Insurance Group

Royal & Sun Alliance Insurance Group is one of the world's largest insurers, with operations in more than thirty-five countries. To meet the needs of the Australian Financial Services Reform Act of 2001, and to improve the overall compliance and efficiency of its people, the company developed complete blended learning programs consisting of e-learning and classroom instruction with a goal of reducing risk and reducing overall training time.

Roche Pharmaceuticals

Roche used a complete and integrated blended learning approach to roll out a major new ERP upgrade across 1,800 users in a wide range of jobs. They developed a complete process for content development and blended learning that involved simulations, job aids, instructor-led training, and self-study e-learning. The program was very successful and saved thousands of hours of traditional training time.

Semiconductor Manufacturer

A major semiconductor manufacturer uses blended learning to train new and experienced engineers on the processing steps needed to operate complex chip manufacturing equipment. The blended learning program dramatically improved yields and created a low-cost, high-value process to improve quality and job satisfaction.

Verizon

Verizon needed a revamp of its new hire program for its 100,000+ field service technicians. By moving to an innovative blended learning approach, the company saved millions in training time and reduced the tremendous backlog they had for new hire training.

Blended Learning Study: Financial Overview

During 2002 and 2003 we studied approximately eighteen high-impact blended learning programs in detail, including their total costs. Table B.1 summarizes these programs and their costs and cost per learner by program size. It serves as a benchmarking tool to help you budget and benchmark your own program costs.

This chart is valuable for understanding the total investments needed to accomplish an effective blended learning program. These programs are expensive to develop: even the smallest blended learning program (which touched fewer than three hundred people) cost the organization $130,000. The average cost of a program was more than $1 million, which demonstrates the level of executive commitment needed to embark on a major blended learning program.

Cost per learner is shown in more detail in Figure B.1. It is important to note that there is a clear difference in costs for programs with more than 10,000 learners. For these larger programs, the cost per learner consistently drops below $100 per learner and can be estimated at $30 to $50 per learner. For smaller programs, the cost varies much more widely—ranging from around $250 per learner up to $1,400. *Note: the company that spent $1,400 per learner used a very complex curriculum of vendor courses and also used third-party certification programs, so this program would fall into the category of a "highly managed, highly assessed, outsourced" program.*

Table B.1. Financial Summary

Total Program Costs	
Highest Program Cost	$5,800,000
Lowest Program Cost	$ 130,000
Average Program Cost	$1,308,571
Cost Per Learner	
Total # of learners in study	1,072,000
Highest cost per learner	$ 1,400
Lowest cost per learner	$ 3.14
Average cost per learner	$ 79
Standard deviation of cost per learner	$ 340
For companies with >10,000 learners	$ 58
Standard deviation of this number	$ 32
For companies with <10,000 learners	$ 257
Standard deviation of this number	$ 400

Figure B.1. Cost per Learner

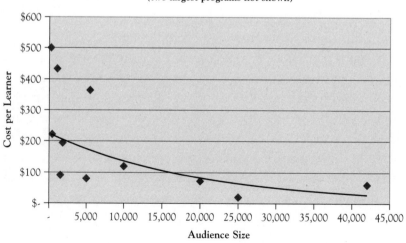

Cost per Learner vs. Audience Size
(two largest programs not shown)

As Figure B.1 shows, the programs ranged widely in size of audience. We do not imply that audience size has anything to do with the true business impact of the program, however. Programs with a smaller audience (Siemens, Company W) had huge impacts and were in fact "business critical" solutions. As shown, the cost per learner consistently drops as the program size grows, because the development and infrastructure costs are amortized over a larger audience.

Appendix C

Case Study Business Strategies

Company	Business Challenge	Cost of Failure
Siemens	Need to change accounting practices worldwide to be listed on NYSE	Billions in lost market cap. All businesses were affected.
Tellabs	Need to roll out new version of SAP project management to all field personnel	Significant loss in sales productivity and customer satisfaction. All field personnel use this system.
Roche	ERP application rollout, new version of SAP	Significant loss of productivity in sales and service operations.
A Major Distributor of Industrial Products	ERP application rollout, new version of SAP, touching every sales transaction in the company	Risk of tremendous loss of revenue because all sales transactions use SAP and A Major Distributor of Industrial Products is SAP's largest transactional customer. Many millions of dollars.
Engineering Software Co.	Need to increase productivity of sales force as an entirely new product line was rolled out.	Lack of revenue growth and loss of market share to in-house and other competitors.
BT	Need to train all field salespeople on new Internet offerings and Internet basics	Would hamper BT's ability to break into the Internet access business and dramatically reduce sales growth for products with billions in investment.

(Continued)

Company	Business Challenge	Cost of Failure
Royal & Sun	Need to certify sales professionals worldwide and create consistent sales strategies and knowledge	Sales productivity and "time to quota" problems in global audience. Cost to train manually would cost millions.
FedEx Kinko's	Replace ILT with e-learning for all field training	Saving $20M+ by transitioning from traditional to e-learning programs across the company.
Cisco	Certify all resellers on basic Cisco product selling to increase productivity and volumes	Nearly 80 percent of Cisco's revenues come through channels, so hundreds of millions are dependent on channel sales productivity. Current team stretched too thin to reach this huge audience.
Verizon	Dramatically reduce backlog (months) and time to train for new field service personnel	Tens of millions savings in lost productivity by waiting for training and time spent in training.
NCR	Globally certify professionals in network training	Millions saved in product incentives by becoming certified; impossible to train through ILT due to broad global workforce.
Major Computer Chip Manufacturer	Reduce errors and certify employees on important manufacturing processes	Quality and productivity are dependent on these processes, which run throughout all plants.
Bell Canada Enterprises	Reduce the cost of training by 50 percent or more and outsource content development	Major savings in training costs, personnel needed, and increase in employee satisfaction by creating major new portal for all employees.
Peoplesoft	Need to rollout Peoplesoft 8 Internet edition to all employees, including sales, service, and support	The most critical new product initiative for the company ever, and sales and competitive advantage dependent on complete knowledge throughout the company.

Appendix D

Program Checklist

The following checklist is presented separately to give you a simple way to see all of the information you should review before setting your media strategy, developing a budget, and developing content.

Program Name:

Business Objective:

How can we measure the business objective?

Learning Objective:

Program Type (1, 2, 3, or 4):

Total Program Budget:

- Development:

- Infrastructure:

- Deployment:

Program Development Criteria:

- Program Type (1–4):

- Audience:

  Audience Size:

  Job Role:

  Education Level:

  Familiarity with Technology:

  Motivation to Learn:

  Time Available to Learn:

  Access to Network and PC:

  Manager Involvement in Program:

- Budget:

  Development:

  Delivery or Deployment:

- Resources:

  Access to Program Manager:

  Access to Instructional Designer(s):

  Access to Web Developers:

  Access to SMEs:

- Timing:

  Development Time:

  Time to Deploy:

  Time to Complete:

  Total Program Duration:

- Content Characteristics:

  Shelf Life:

  Complexity:

  Interactivity:

- Level of Tracking Needed (by module):

  Enrollment:

  Activity:

  Completion:

  Scores:

  Certification:

  Satisfaction:

  Business Impact:

- Technology Standards:

  Bandwidth:

  Plug-Ins:

  Tracking:

  Display:

  Security:

- Other Risk Areas:

Eight Criteria for Media Selection

Criterion	Factors to Consider	Questions to Ask
1. Program Type	Type 1: Information Broadcast Type 2: Critical Information Transfer Type 3: Skills and Competencies Type 4: Certification	
2. Culture Building Goals	Is there a culture-building goal or not?	Peer to peer? Executive education? New hire training? Sales training?
3. Audience	Audience size Job role Education level Familiarity with technology Motivation to learn Time available to learn Access to network and PCs Manager involvement	Try to characterize the audience carefully. Turn yourself into a "marketing manager." How does this audience think? What is their daily life like? How will this program best affect them?
4. Budget	Development budget, including tools, development, testing, and production readiness LMS and other infrastructure Delivery or deployment budget	How large is the business problem you are solving? How much should you spend per learner on the entire program? How much will this cost per instructional hour? What is a reasonable amount of money to spend on this program? What are the infrastructure and other shared components you need to access and are they available? How much should you spend on content development to leverage the economics of e-learning?

Criterion	Factors to Consider	Questions to Ask
5. Resources	Program manager Instructional designer Web developer(s) Subject-matter experts	Do you have the resources to develop and deploy the program you want? Will you need a consultant who has developed this type of content before? Will you need to hire or borrow instructional designers or web developers? Where are the SMEs, and how much time will they have to spend with you? How will you repurpose their content?
6. Time		How quickly does this program have to be launched?
	Development time	The amount of time you have from budget availability until launch?
	Time to deploy	The time you have to launch the program?
	Time to complete	The time you have until all learners should have completed the program?
	Total program duration	How long can the program take? Is a day too long? Is a week too long? What is the total number of student hours available to you?
7. Learning Content	Content shelf life	The time before the entire program becomes obsolete and you have to maintain, update, or discard the program?
	Content complexity	Is this content for beginners, intermediate people, or advanced learners. Given the program type, what is the level of complexity within that type?
	Content interactivity	How much interactivity do you feel is demanded? Reading only? Reading and exercises? Assessments? Projects, discussions, and labs?
8. Technology	Bandwidth required	56KB, DSL, or T-1 required? Will the media have to play offline?
	Plug-ins required	Is Real Media, Windows Media, video codecs, Shockwave, Quicktime, or Flash required? (You can consider Flash a built-in standard that is already available.)

Criterion	Factors to Consider	Questions to Ask
	Tracking standards	AICC or SCORM, and what parts of the tracking are needed (see above)?
	Display	What resolution is minimum (800 × 600), and what level of color (8-bit, 16-bit, 24-bit)?
	Security	Is HTTPS encryption needed? Are passwords required to view information?
	Other risk areas	Streaming audio or video? Content dependent on a particular LCMS or publishing tool? Plug-ins required to play? Server-side scripts required?

Appendix F

Sixteen Media Types and Descriptions

Medium	What Is It? When Should It Be Used?	Live or Self-Study
1. Instructor-Led Training	Live classroom training taught by an instructor, professor, or teacher. Clearly the most interactive and traditional approach, but also the most expensive, difficult to schedule, and resource limited for large audiences. It should be used sparingly for special topics within the context of the other media.	Live
2. Webinars (Live e-Learning)	Live Internet-based education, conducted through a browser, taught by an instructor or subject-matter expert. Typically includes slides and a small amount of animation. Companies that provide this technology include Centra, Placeware, Interwise, and Webex, as well as dozens of others. This medium works very well for special topics, online demonstrations, guest lectures, and other less interactive training events that are two hours in length or shorter. It is not a full replacement for classroom education because interactivity is far less. It is very scalable, however, and can accommodate hundreds of students. Interactivity can be improved by opening up Q&A and letting students open up the phone lines for questions and discussions. You should consider it a "tell" medium, however, not a "learn" medium.	Live

(Continued)

Table F.1   (Continued)

Medium	What Is It? When Should It Be Used?	Live or Self-Study
3. Courseware (Web-Based)	Internet-based courseware, largely consisting of graphics, text, some audio, and some interactivities and assessments. Self-paced and run from a PC or other browser. There are many different types of web-based courseware, but for the purposes of this book we group courseware into basic courseware, simulations, CD-ROM courseware, and Rapid e-Learning courseware. Courseware is the most traditional of e-learning, and has traditionally been built in "chapters" with various amounts of interactivity possible. We will discuss video below. The term "interactivity" refers to exercises and tests that force the learners to try what they have learned and see the effect of their actions. The "tell" and "try" approaches both work here. The downside of courseware is that it can be very expensive to build, expensive to maintain, and alone does not give enough interactivity to hold learners' interest for new topics and in-depth type 3 and type 4 training.	Self-Study
4. Simulations (Application, Business, Process)	Scenario-based courseware, typically run on a PC or through the Internet, providing the learner with a real world to play in. Simulations fall into three categories: application, business, and process. The purpose of simulations is to give the learners a self-study approach where they can directly try the material and experience what happens. An application simulation, for example, enables learners to use a piece of software and see how it behaves, so they learn how to execute certain functions. A business simulation enables learners to change a business or personal scenario in some way and see what happens. And process simulations enable the same in either technical or business processes.	Self-Study

Table F.1   (Continued)

Medium	What Is It? When Should It Be Used?	Live or Self-Study
	Simulations are widely used for IT training, SAP training, and other forms of software application training. They are also often used for highly technical training (for example, flight training, military scenario training) but suffer from high costs to develop, so they must have large audiences or very demanding training conditions to be cost-justified.	
5. CD-ROM-Based Courseware	CD-ROM-based courseware is very different from web-based courseware. It fulfills many of the same goals, but it is often developed to take advantage of video and other local capabilities on users' PCs. The main difference is that it runs "offline" whenever a user wants, without needing access to the Internet.	Self-Study
	The primary difference between this item and courseware (item 3), is that CD-ROM-based content typically assumes that the student will run all the content on a local PC—and therefore has much more bandwidth to use. You can easily take courseware designed for the Internet and run it on a PC, and this eliminates the need for the network. But true CD-ROM-designed content (typically older titles) have more video, interactivity, and rich media (audio) built in.	
	These media-rich CD-ROMs are very expensive to build and are very useful for video-based training where audiences are either young, new to the company, or not highly educated—and you need to give them a lot of images and very little text. Chick-fil-A, for example, has an excellent CD-ROM-based video program for certifying all food preparation users in cleanliness. These types of titles can be used for types 1, 2, and 3 training, but typically do not have high levels of interactivity or assessment, since they often run disconnected from a network.	

(Continued)

Table F.1   (*Continued*)

Medium	What Is It? When Should It Be Used?	Live or Self-Study
	CD-ROM technology requires some kind of PC player and a PC with a minimum amount of memory and speed to run correctly, so when you develop this type of content you must determine the minimum PC configuration you will support to ease deployment.	
6. Rapid e-Learning Courseware (PowerPoint-Based)	This is a special form of courseware built on PowerPoint. We are identifying this separately because it is a big growth area and this type of medium has very different characteristics and applications than traditional courseware.	Self-Study
	It is very new. This medium takes PowerPoint-based content and publishes the slides, animations, and usually audio into a web-based format that can be delivered on the Internet. In most cases the content is converted to Flash, a technology that runs on virtually every PC without the need for any plug-in. These tools are excellent for type 1 and type 2 training, and they have the added benefit of letting subject-matter experts author their own content. They remove the web developer from the middle of the content development process, which is a huge time and financial saving.	
	With some tools, you can also add assessments and standard tracking technology to the courseware, so you can actually create a true type 3 course. However, these programs are limited in their interactivity and levels of assessment, so we consider them appropriate for type 1 and type 2 courseware, not as a replacement for true web-based training per se.	
	Novell has developed an extensive channel training curriculum using this format, and they can create 20+ courses per year for less than $15,000 per course and turn around new topics in four weeks or less. Products that are useful in this category include Macromedia Breeze, Impatica, and many others.	

Table F.1 (*Continued*)

Medium	What Is It? When Should It Be Used?	Live or Self-Study
7. Internet-Delivered Video	This is video replays delivered through the Internet, typically played through Real Player or Windows Media Player. This medium drives high bandwidth and is growing in usage but is often limited by deployment efficiencies. Early e-learning consisted of instructor-led training delivered through this medium, which proved to be an ineffective solution. My research has found less than excellent returns on Internet-based video. Despite the potential for this solution, most learners do not have a consistent high-bandwidth connection that can be relied on for this medium. If you believe you have a demonstration or physical image that should be shown by Internet-based video, create it as an optional "module" or hint or special exercise learners can choose to skip if they are working from a low-bandwidth location. You will dramatically lower completion rates if you force learners to watch a painfully slow video that may not run correctly. Remember that plug-ins are required for video, and you must specify in advance which formats you will support. Typical formats include Real Audio/Video, Windows Media, and streaming technologies like Akamai, which can improve delivery speed. A warning here: do not try to use "talking heads" as video on the web. The talking head instructor video (see item 9 below) was an early attempt to put existing content onto the web. It largely fails because the low bandwidth, small screen size, and small images (usually faces are small and the screen shows a lot of background) make for a very unappealing experience.	Self-Study

(*Continued*)

Table F.1 (*Continued*)

Medium	What Is It? When Should It Be Used?	Live or Self-Study
8. EPSS (Electronic Performance Support Systems)	EPSS represents a category of technology often referred to as "online help." These systems are designed to help individuals complete a certain task by giving them electronic performance support. These systems are very expensive to build but have huge returns on investment for large audiences in applications like call centers, order processing, and technical support. They are not "training" per se, but rather performance support or on-the-job assistance. EPSS systems are not covered in detail in this book but are presented here because some online courseware evolves into EPSS solutions. An EPSS system serves a different need than traditional blended learning; it is designed as a performance support tool to help someone complete a task at the time needed. Training, by contrast, is typically used to teach someone how to do something before needed. If you are building content that is starting to look like an online help system, then you may be building an EPSS system and not even know it. EPSS systems are very powerful, expensive to build, and can be justified for large production environments as a support tool to complement training. They do not replace training, however, because they do not give learners any context, theory, or business process education in the task or topics they need to understand.	Self-Study

Table F.1 (*Continued*)

Medium	What Is It? When Should It Be Used?	Live or Self-Study
9. Offline Video (Videotapes)	In my early career, I used to come home from work with three or four VCR tapes to watch at home. These were videos of actual instructor-led classes. This medium is still widely used and fits into certain applications. In retrospect, videotapes are the first attempt to turn classroom training into self-study training. They are typically recordings of actual classes, with the video shot to include the instructor's face, blackboard, flip chart, and often other materials. They do not work on small computer screens, but on a TV set the experience can be useful. We have found few companies can successfully leverage these libraries widely, largely because the video is not shot for use in a self-study format. Video for the web must be very close to a person's face, large, and surrounded with interesting visual images to be useful. Shooting video for the web is a different video shoot and can be useful for small topics and demonstrations, but requires specialized skills. This is covered in item 7 above.	Self-Study
10. Video Conferencing	Video conferencing has slowly been replaced by Internet-based video, but in many organizations continues to be one of the best ways to extend the classroom experience.	Self-Study
11. Collaboration Systems	Collaboration systems typically refer to chat rooms, discussion rooms, and messaging systems. Most are not considered training per se, but are often used as supplemental tools to help learners interact with instructors and other learners. They are used widely in the higher education market to let students interact with teaching assistants and let professors hold online office hours to answer questions.	Self-Study and Live

(*Continued*)

Table F.1 (Continued)

Medium	What Is It? When Should It Be Used?	Live or Self-Study
	They are also used in corporate applications to house FAQ databases where people can go to find the answers to frequently asked questions and ask general questions. In our research, we have not found collaboration software to be widely used in training applications per se. They are widely used for performance support and knowledge management, where a FAQ database or "ask the experts" database can connect "knowledge seekers" with "knowledge experts." We see this as a big field, but not covered in detail in this book. If you see a need to link learners to subject-matter experts and you can force SMEs to answer questions, then this medium can become an excellent surrounding media to help learners. We consider it a "resource" or "assistant" in the core-and-spoke model, not a core component. Example: one of our clients tried to use discussion groups as a mandatory way for learners to interact with instructors. This failed as the interactivity is too weak and the time between interactions is too long. As a support tool, however, it can be very powerful because questions asked before can quickly be searched for quick responses and reading.	
12. Conference Calls	Yes, believe it or not, conference calls are a training medium. You can teach a lot through conference calls, as you will see. A Major Distributor of Industrial Products, Roche, Siemens, and many other programs we researched use conference calls to kick off events, level-set programs, provide checkpoints, and gain quick feedback. You should use conference calls whenever possible; they are inexpensive to set up and deliver and give you quick feedback if they are organized carefully.	Live

Table F.1 (Continued)

Medium	What Is It? When Should It Be Used?	Live or Self-Study
13. Job Aids	Job aids refer to checklists, booklets, tent cards, and other physical documents you send to learners to help them with their learning activities. We believe that job aids must be considered as a medium for every training program. A physical card, booklet, instruction card, or even wallet card gives learners something to look at every day to remind them of critical topics, learnings, techniques, and hints from a training program. When the budget is low and the audience is large or when you want to reinforce elements from a more complex blended learning program, you should always invest the time in a job aid learners can take back to the job.	Self-Study
14. Workbooks	A workbook is a particular type of job aid designed to facilitate a learning or implementation process. It typically includes checklists, blanks to be filled in, and narrative to help someone step through a learning process. It is also used post-training to help someone perform a process or task and make sure he or she does not miss anything critical. Workbooks are excellent tools to assist in either online or instructor-led programs. They give learners a place to see the "whole picture"—to look at all the chapters at once, take notes on each chapter during a program, and then refer back to the materials at a later date. The workbook also gives you an excellent tool to organize your program into small, discrete chapters. The workbook could include instructions on how to start a web-based program, when to attend a webinar or physical course, and a list of resources, glossary, and other tools to help learners become successful. We highly recommend that you build a workbook for any blended learning program.	Self-Study

(Continued)

Table F.1   (Continued)

Medium	What Is It? When Should It Be Used?	Live or Self-Study
15. Books	Obviously, books are a great training and educational medium and should be considered in every program. In higher education the book becomes the syllabus for a class. In corporate training, learners consider books as a great supplementary resource to be used in the core-and-spoke model. If you want learners to read the book, you must make that mandate very clear and include assessments or quizzes to test reading. If your audience is highly educated, you will find the learner more interested in reading a book. If you are training line workers, production workers, or other individual contributors, it is difficult to expect them to complete a book unless it is fifty pages or less. Use books as supplementary resources or as a way to highlight certain important topics by copying selected chapters. Learners consider a book a "perk" and also give more credence to a course that includes a book.	Self-Study
16. On-the-Job Exercises	On-the-job coaching, testing, and assessment are critical. We consider this a critical component of many blended learning programs. Manager involvement is critical to any large corporate program. One of the unique ways that on-the-job coaching is used is as a definitive step in the program flow model. Example: one large retailer delivers dozens of e-learning courses to their local sales representatives. The courseware has a required step called a "learning check," which requires the learner to print out a checklist, walk through the store with a manager, and answer certain questions. The questions are randomly selected to prevent learners from cheating. The manager then enters the results in a manager-only interface to assess the learner. This forces on-the-job coaching through e-learning and also gives upper managers direct assessment data to identify how well the program is being received and its impact.	Live

Glossary

AICC *(Aviation Industry CBT Committee)*. The industry standard and standards body that developed a complete standard for launching, tracking, and measuring student progress through electronic content. This standard, which is implemented in levels, is the most widely used way in which learning management systems (LMS) launch and track electronic content. Although it is a clearly defined standard, each vendor implements it in its own way so buyers must still test their content to make sure it interacts effectively. It allows the LMS to track student progress, scores, time in a course, time in a module, mastery level (by score on assessments), and many other important learning measurements.

Assessment. A test, certification, exam, or series of questions of some kind that measure a learner's understanding or learning or mastery of a topic.

Asynchronous. Refers to media and program types where the learners work on their own time, unsynchronized with any instructor. This is also called "self-study" training.

CD-ROM. A media type in e-learning. CD-ROM disks are the physical medium that stores electronic content. CD-ROM-authored content is designed to run while the disk is inserted into a PC, meaning that the content requires files, drivers, and media on the disk. This approach was very popular in the 1980s and

1990s before the widespread availability of the Internet. Today it is still widely used to distribute courseware to locations with low bandwidth. Content designed specifically for CD-ROM delivery is usually too large and slow to run in a pure web-based environment. Therefore, when developing a course, it is important to decide whether the course will run exclusively on a CD format or also must run in a web-based architecture.

Certification. To attest as being true or as represented or as meeting a standard. Certification programs are characterized as those that demand strict measurement and reporting of completion, score, or mastery. Typically, these programs have expiration dates and require regular refreshing (typically annually). The key characteristic of certification programs is the level of tracking and reporting required, and they are "type 4" programs in our taxonomy.

Courseware. Refers to learning material that runs on a PC using software.

EPSS (Electronic Performance Support Systems). A category of system and solution that provides online help, job aids, and support to workers on the job—usually providing reference and "how to" material.

ERP (Enterprise Resource Planning). Refers to the enterprise software solutions that manage human resources, financials, inventory, manufacturing, supply chain integration, and other back-office company functions. Typical ERP software providers are Oracle, Peoplesoft, and SAP.

Flash. From Macromedia, one of the most important new technologies in e-learning today. It is both a tool and a deployment solution. The Flash Player is embedded in nearly every Internet browser in the world, making it easy to deploy Flash-based content to thousands of people with little or no technical support. The

Flash development environment includes tools from Macromedia and hundreds of other companies that can develop "flash-based" output. Flash can display graphics, movies, sound, and animation in a very efficient low-bandwidth format. Most online advertisements on the web are built in Flash.

Interactivity. A term used in e-learning for a technology or activity that requires the learner to practice something or interact with the content. There are many types of interactivities (fill in the blanks, match boxes, slide a slider bar, and so forth) used to illustrate a concept. They also are used to practice an application rollout.

Instructional Plan. A detailed plan for a blended learning or e-learning course that specifies the learning objectives, media, exercises, and approach for each module or chapter.

Job Aid. A document, printed card, poster, workbook, or other type of learning material that serves as a quick reference for employees to help them with processes, techniques, or procedures while on the job.

Knowledge Management. A broad word referring to the various approaches and technologies that store, distribute, index, and manage tacit and explicit knowledge in organizations.

LCMS (Learning Content Management System). A software system and database that houses learning content and enables multiple developers to check-in/check-out components, share components, test integrated courses, and publish courses for delivery.

Mastery. The ultimate goal of a training program. In this book it refers to the pinnacle of learning, which occurs when a person becomes an expert. Mastery is defined as "proficiency plus retention."

Metadata. Words or information that describe something else. In e-learning, course "metadata" includes the course title, its learning objectives, and other descriptive information about the course or its chapters. Standards for metadata are included in SCORM. The reason that metadata is so important in e-learning is that it allows systems to search, sequence, and track content easily.

Plug-In. A small piece of software required to run certain content. Plug-ins typically download with content and run in the learner's browser. Proprietary plug-ins are often unsupported and blocked by IT departments.

Rapid e-Learning. A technique for developing content that enables a subject-matter expert to "self-author" courseware for the web. It typically uses tools built on PowerPoint which then can be used to create Flash or live e-learning content without any special training.

Reusability. A concept (rarely used, but often discussed) in e-learning that refers to using a single course object or chapter multiple times in multiple courses. The theory is excellent; for example, if you build an exercise in Excel and it is used in many courses, you can update the courses by updating the exercise in one place. This concept is difficult to implement because of the need to carefully decide which parts of the content will be reused in advance. SCORM was designed to promote and assist in reusability of content.

Scenario. A method of developing content that presents the learner with a real-life situation (typically involving people) and asks him or her to make decisions. The scenario typically has multiple branches so the learner sees the positive or negative consequences of his or her decisions.

SCORM (Sharable Content Object Reference Model). A set of industry specifications on how electronic content is packaged, tracked, sequenced, and tagged with metadata for searching. It is not as widely implemented as AICC, but growing in adoption.

Simulation. In blended learning, a software-based activity that simulates the real world in some way, giving the learner the ability to attempt actions and see real-world results. There are different forms of simulations: application simulations, character simulations, business simulations, and process simulations.

SME. A subject-matter expert. An SME is someone who is an expert in a task, field, process, or operation. SMEs are consulted to help build courses, but usually they are too busy to conduct training themselves.

Synchronous. Refers to media and program types where the learner interacts in real time with the instructor. The people are "synchronized" together. Classroom training, conference calls, webcasts, and chat sessions are all synchronous.

Types 1, 2, 3, and 4. The different categories of training, characterized by business application, (1) Information Broadcast, (2) Critical Knowledge Transfer, (3) Skills and Competency Development, and (4) Certification Programs.

Appendix H

Selected Samples of Courseware and Media

Figure H.1. Web-Based Courseware

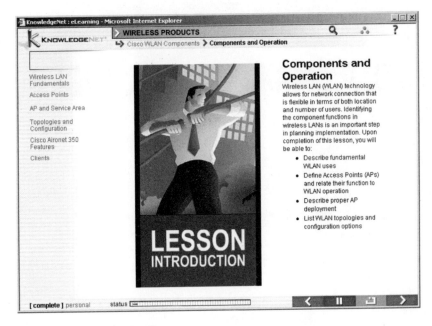

Courtesy of KnowledgeNet-Cisco.

Figure H.2.   Web-Based Courseware (BT)

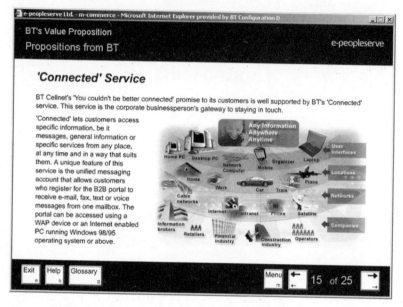

Courtesy of BT.

Figure H.3.   Web-Based Assessments and Interactivities

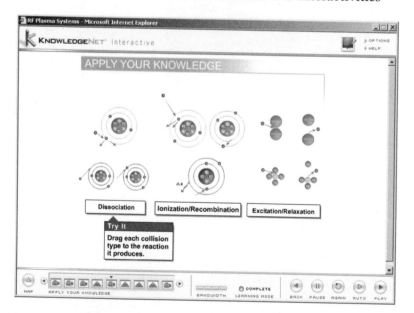

Figure H.4.   Web-Based Courseware

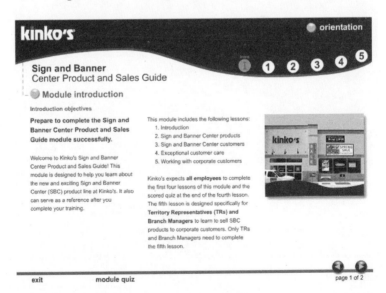

Courtesy of FedEx Kinko's Office & Print Services.

Figure H.5.   Sample Mid-Course Assessment

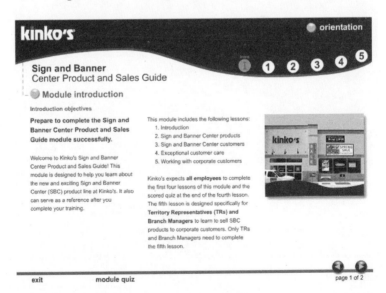

Courtesy of FedEx Kinko's Office & Print Services.

Figure H.6.   Scenario-Based Interactivity

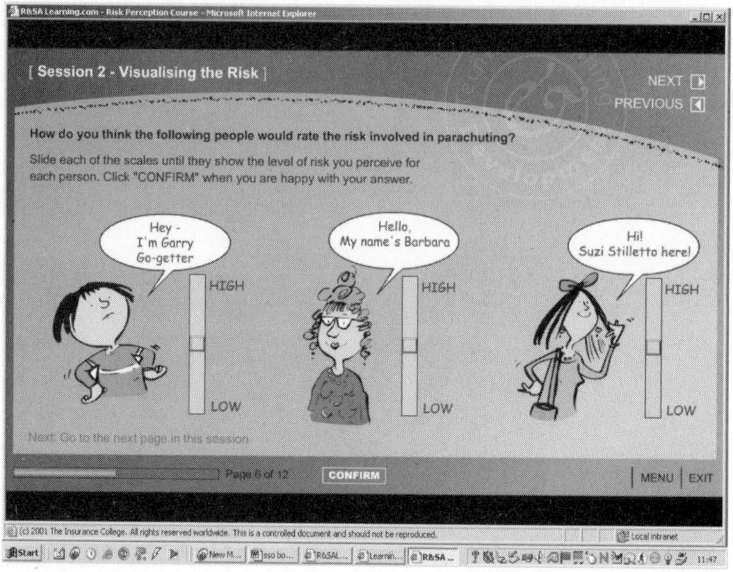

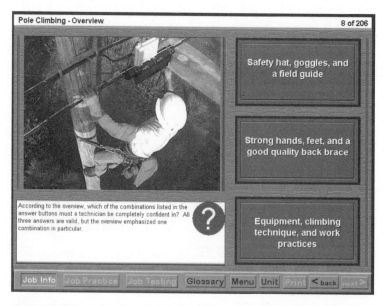

Courtesy of Royal & Sun Alliance Insurance Group

Figure H.7.   Video-Based Self-Study Courseware

Courtesy of Verizon.

Figure H.8.   Online Assessment and Practice

Ladder Safety Introduction	4 of 109

24'   28'   32'

The company provides standard ladders in three sizes :
• 24 feet
• 28 feet
• 32 feet.

| Job Info | Job Practice | Job Testing | Glossary | Menu | Unit | Print | ◄ back | next ► |

Courtesy of Verizon.

Figure H.9.   Macromedia Breeze Rapid e-Learning

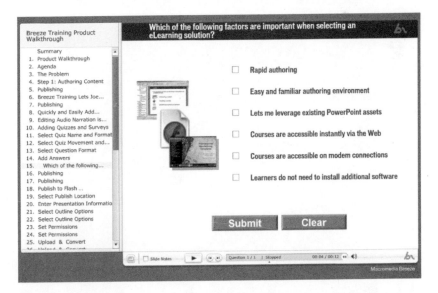

Figure H.10.   Live e-Learning with Chat and Video

Figure H.11.   Live Webinar Using IP Telephony

Sample Detailed Instructional Plan*

DIGITALTHINK CATALOG: PROJECT MANAGEMENT CURRICULUM

August 13, 2001

Project Summary

The Project Management curriculum, as a new addition to the DigitalThink catalog, is intended to provide the competencies required of any professional project manager in a professional situation. In addition to gaining these skills, learners will become familiar with the processes and knowledge areas (and their different components) laid out in the PMBOK® Guide published by the Project Management Institute. By aligning the course with the contents of the PMBOK® Guide, we are ensuring that students are familiar with the concepts and skills covered on PMI's Project Management Professional Certification exam; note, however, that this series is not an "exam prep" series, as it is designed to teach newer project managers skills and principles, as opposed to refreshing experienced PMs' knowledge of PMBOK content.

According to the initial DigitalThink strategy document, these courses are designed for people who have or will be assigned project management responsibilities, as well as anyone who works on a

---

*This instructional plan was provided compliments of DigitalThink. It illustrates the type of information and thinking that should go into the content development process (described in Chapters 3, 4, 7, and 8) for any major blended learning program.

project team and would like a better understanding of the project management discipline.

It should also be appropriate for students with the above qualifications who are also interested in PMI's Project Management Professional Certification, as this series will be aligned with the content of the Project Management Body of Knowledge®.

The Project Management curriculum represents a departure in type of content area from the traditional IT courses in the existing catalog and special considerations have been taken in the initial design to ensure that we are applying the best and most appropriate learning strategies for these types of skills and that the courses will stand out from their competitors.

One of these considerations is to structure the content based on actual tasks rather than the more typical PMI knowledge areas. While most competing project management courses are arranged according to knowledge areas, this is counter-intuitive to a skills application approach since the structure of the knowledge areas (such as communication, risk, time, and cost) does not reflect the actual application of these skills in the work of project management. The Curriculum Map portion of this document will describe the approach to this structure in more depth.

The courses will all revolve around a common scenario and require the learner to apply new skills and knowledge to the completion of various small projects associated with the scenario, such as a work breakdown structure, a schedule, a budget, etc.

Guiding Principles

Overview

The following are the guiding principles we believe will create the most effective and engaging e-learning experience for learning to apply project management skills. These are based on extensions of the principles for effective e-learning that all DigitalThink courses adhere to and are also based on an analysis of the competencies in project management and the characteristics of our intended audience.

Audience Profile

There is wide variety among the people who fill the project manager role in organizations—variety in terms of different industries, backgrounds, work style, skill sets, just to name a few. However, those people who are drawn to the field of project management usually share some common characteristics. By and large, they:

- Are highly focused
- Like to be challenged, intrigued
- Value reliability
- Value tangible results, are action-oriented
- Don't like to waste time
- Are structured, analytical
- Need a sense of progress, milestones

But within project managers, there are two sets that have somewhat different characteristics (Table I.1). Project managers in traditional organizations or industries, or those who have been in the field many years, may have a slightly different style than their counterparts who work in non-traditional organizations or who are newer to the field.

Table I.1

Traditional Project Managers	Non-Traditional Project Managers
Concerned with right and wrong	Focused on outcomes, completing projects
Serious, value adherence to structures	Do what yields results
Somewhat conservative, introverted	Extroverted, politically savvy, well-connected
Rule-governed	Flexible, adaptable
Rely heavily on established processes	See process as means to an end, not as reliant on established processes and conventions
Authoritative	Consultative, collective approach

Our design strategies will focus on ways to shape the learning experience to meet the needs of the widest variety of individuals, particularly keeping in mind the set of common characteristics, but trying to account, whenever possible, for the two different types of project managers.

Emphasis on Valuable Skills

To ensure that the courses focus on skill development rather than just on knowledge transfer, each course is arranged to support the creation of a valuable deliverable that is part of the project management life cycle, such as a work breakdown structure (WBS) or a responsibility assignment matrix (RASIC) chart. The learners, who we know are busy professionals, will come away from each course, and in fact, each module, with information they can immediately apply, rather than just more knowledge and terminology.

Scenario-Based Learning

The major learning activities will be based on a scenario, or case study project, having to do with a home construction project. This project will allow the learner to practice on actual project deliverables, analyze data, make decisions, and work with a "virtual" project team. Most importantly, the case study provides meaningful context for the application of new knowledge and skills. The documents associated with this project will be available from the Resource page as downloads or PDF files. Since outputs of one phase of a project serve as inputs for the next, the downloads will comprise a "Project Portfolio" that builds as the curriculum builds. For example, a project schedule will be available to all courses that follow the course where the project schedule is completed. Thus, learners who choose to sample courses out of sequence can reference these resources even though they may not have created their own or completed the activities associated with them.

Value-Added Resources: Templates and Other Job Aids

In addition to providing rich, complex examples for the scenario, the Resources page can include templates, checklists, job aids, URLs, and other valuable materials that learners can actually use on the job. By the time learners complete all of the courses, they should have a project management toolkit they can continue to use and benefit from.

The Resources page will also provide links to useful publications such as *The Principles of Project Management* from the PMI bookstore.

Inclusion of Multiple Perspectives: The Practitioner Panel

Many of the key skills in the project management domain involve applying judgment to a situation and making tough decisions and tradeoffs. Teaching skills like these is a challenge since there is no right or wrong answer and the variables are almost infinitely complex. In this case, the best approach is to model the kinds of analytical thinking that are required in these situations and then provide learners an opportunity to practice making decisions and getting feedback. Certainly, tutors can help provide this type of feedback in some cases. But in order to highlight this important aspect of project management, we've chosen to create a "Practitioner Panel" that appears frequently in each course. The Practitioner Panel consists of three personas—all project managers in different fields, with different strengths and areas of focus. These three characters comment on the information from multiple perspectives, sharing their own best practices and their own modes of analysis for different situations. The discussion area could even be seeded with comments from these three "virtual peers" that accompany the learner throughout the curriculum.

We hope this technique will allow us to model the techniques used by seasoned project managers in a variety of contexts, especially those that involve judgment based on experience.

A Layered Learning Environment: The Iceberg Principle

We seek to create a learner experience that feels direct and to the point, is highly modular, and addresses the needs of busy professionals who want new and valuable information quickly. One of the ways to meet this goal is to shift our information design approach from a scrolling page to a layered or stacked page.

By this, we mean that only the most salient points would be illustrated on the "base page" of each lesson and that this base page would contain a number of links to drill down to more detail and complexity. Like an iceberg, only a portion is visible from the highest point, and much more is revealed the deeper one goes.

Typically, the convention of sidebars has been used in catalog courses to convey "ancillary" information that is considered supplemental. In this case, these deeper layers would be positioned as part of the lesson, and the environment would be set up to encourage the learner to delve deeper and discover more. This gives the impression of a more non-linear learning environment without having to make more extensive structural changes usually necessary to do that. It also creates more opportunity for user choice and moves further away from the "book" metaphor that has continued to be the norm in most web-based training.

Figure H.1 shows the structure of the curriculum and how the courses map to PMI topic areas. All titles are working titles at this point.

Curriculum Breakdown

The following outlines the high-level performance objectives addressed by each course (all titles are working titles):

Project Management Framework

Project Management Within an Organization

- Recognize the PM function across/throughout an organization
- Recognize PM practices as the backbone of an organization

Figure I.1

Project Management Foundations
A Practitioner's Guide to the Art and Science of Project Management

curriculum map

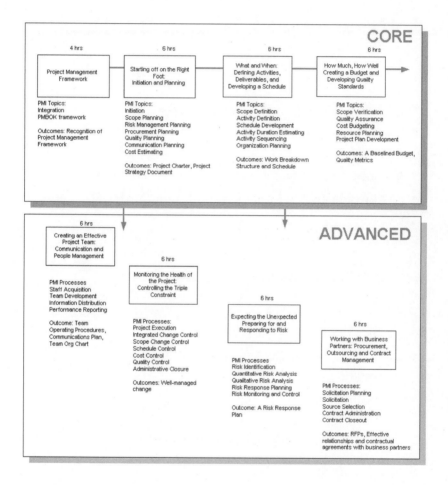

- Recognize significant changes in the workplace that make PM relevant, useful

Overview of Project Management and Key Project Management Definitions

- Identify a project
- Identify a program

- Identify project stakeholders
- Identify the triple constraint (function and significance)
- Define the project management life cycle/phases
- Define knowledge areas (note: this includes integration)
- Describe the role of the PMBOK in project management practice

Project Management as a Profession

- Identify key profiles/roles within a project
- Identify key management skills required to manage projects
- Describe project management certification/designation
- Describe project management profession in the 21st Century

Starting Off on the Right Foot: Initiation

Requirements Definition

- Conduct requirements session with client—understanding objectives
- Define and validate assumptions

A Project's Strategic Alignment Within the Organization

- Develop the project's business case
- Perform cost/benefit analysis
- Map strategic objectives of the project to those of the organization
- Project's alignment within the current corporate portfolio of projects

The Project Charter

- Define elements of a solid project charter; question assumptions
- Create project plan approach (PMBOK knowledge planning areas)
- Advise sponsor of the project's feasibility—serve as subject-matter expert
- Act as an advocate for project management practices at the outset of a project

Plan the Work and Work the Plan—Part I

What and When: Defining the Deliverables and Developing a Schedule

Develop a Work Breakdown Structure (WBS)

- Identify tangible deliverables
- Break deliverables down to the appropriate work package level

Develop the Project's Schedule

- Incorporate the WBS into the schedule
- Define activities required to complete work package
- Sequence activities (create the relationships among the activities)
- Assign duration to each activity
- Assign resources to each activity
- Determine critical path
- Evaluate schedule feasibility and make appropriate adjustments
- Baseline project schedule

Plan the Work and Work the Plan—Part II

How Much, How Well: Creating a Budget and Developing Quality Standards

The Project Scope and Quality Setting

- Utilize the WBS and verify that it meets the requirements
- Set quality parameters and standards
- Compare quality tradeoffs using triple constraint

Develop the Project's Budget

- Utilize the WBS and conduct bottom-up estimating technique
- Define the resource costs for each work package
- Assign costs to each work package
- Develop operational project budget

Controlling Project Outcomes: Attaining the Triple Constraint and Fitness for Use

Conduct Variance Analysis

- Compare actuals to baseline (schedule and cost)
- Calculate earned value
- Evaluate quality metrics of project outcomes
- Evaluate corrective measures, and choose the best action

Utilize the Change Management Process

- Manage stakeholder expectations
- Evaluate change requests
- Recognize deviation and change and its magnitude within set parameters

- Evaluate the impact of potential changes
- Re-baseline approved change items

Ensure Project Quality Standards

- Perform quality tests
- Get sign-off on deliverables
- Perform closure; capture lessons learned

Working with Business Partners: Procurement, Outsourcing, and Contract Management

Define Procurement and Outsourcing Requirements

- Determine "make or buy" and *who* can accomplish this (products and services)
- Solicit quotes, bids
- Evaluate and select a source
- Distinguish between cost plus and fixed price (flexibility and risk)
- Develop negotiating strategy
- Conduct negotiations

Manage Quality and Responsiveness of Subcontractors

- Manage outsourcer expectations and relationships
- Establish quality parameters
- Manage the delivery of the product/service
- Closeout contract (legal, issue last payment, close project account)
- Evaluate vendor's performance

Expecting the Unexpected: Preparing for and Responding to Risk

Recognizing Risks

- Understand the value of proactively managing risk
- Identify potential risks
- Identify known unknowns versus unknown unknowns
- Quantify risk probability and impact
- Employ the quadrant analysis, the decision tree, and expected value
- Proactively plan for those risks that are high probability and high severity of consequences
- Respond effectively to challenging situations
- Prepare team for risk readiness and to anticipate change

Creating an Effective Project Team: Communication and People Management

Developing the Team and Creating Synergy

- Define roles and responsibilities, skills level
- Ensure diverse team compositions (process, people, technology)
- Negotiate and balance tradeoffs to acquire team members
- Compensate for team deficiencies
- Create team operating procedures
- Define resource responsibilities with the RASIC Chart
- Develop the team, motivate, recognize, perform evaluations

Facilitating Proactive Communications

- Develop stakeholder analysis
- Manage stakeholder expectations

- Communicate project status to team and stakeholders using appropriate vehicles
- Define issues management process (identification, resolution, escalation)
- Manage conflicts and decisions

Learner Experience Strategy

Overall Learning Experience

The learning experience for these courses should address the needs of project managers to achieve tangible results and get practical information in a short amount of time. These needs should also be balanced with a strategy that provides learning of significant depth and complexity to actually be useful and applicable in the real world.

In making design choices about specific lessons and topics, the rule should be to favor depth over breadth. Project management is a huge domain, and we cannot hope to address every subtlety of the subject. The learning experience will be a much more effective one if we carefully choose the most valuable topics or learning objectives and treat those with adequate depth rather than trying to cover all the content.

The courses will include frequent opportunities to respond and interact with the learning environment—both for the presentation of new concepts and for practice of new skills. The majority (roughly 75 percent) of all lessons should contain an interactive presentation element and nearly half of all lessons (roughly 40 percent) should use an interactive element for practice or assessment.

Project management is both an art and a science. In some cases, practitioners need to follow specific processes and make clear-cut decisions; in other cases, there is no "right" answer and it is more important to know how to analyze complex variables, predict the implications of choices, and make decisions. The courses will attempt to model this kind of analytic skill by emphasizing multiple perspectives on some topics and allowing students to "hear" multiple ways of approaching a problem.

Most of all, the course will focus on supporting *the acquisition of skills* in the field of project management.

Practice and Assessment Methodology

Try It and Apply It

Course activities will be categorized in two ways. Within lessons, learners will have an opportunity to interact with the material and practice skills in ways that are somewhat exploratory rather than assessment-driven. They should be able to manipulate variables, see the outcome, and practice applying new terminology and concepts in a safe, risk-free environment. These are referred to as "Try It" activities.

Each module should also contain corresponding "Apply It" activities. These are more complex exercises that require the learner to apply a set of new skills to a project deliverable that is connected to the central scenario. An example would be to build a portion of a Work Breakdown Structure or a Communication Plan.

Quizzes

Conventional multiple-choice quizzes will be used at the end of each module as well as throughout a module as appropriate. Whenever possible, quiz questions should be based on scenarios and should require the learner to synthesize, interpret, or generalize in addition to simply recalling information.

Tutors

Each course will have no more than three tutor-supported exercises (TSEs). The TSEs will focus on activities that could have multiple approaches, that require problem solving, and that generally require a student to accomplish a specific goal without using a specific method. This will allow the tutors to give value-added feedback about the merits of a learner's analytic abilities in addition to focusing on "grading" right or wrong answers.

Content-Specific Learning Strategies

Several recurring types of learning objectives within this curriculum should be treated consistently throughout the courses. The Design Guidelines (presented in Table I.2) elaborate further on these treatments and provide examples. The following design "toolkit" should be added to and expanded as the team discovers other instructional patterns within the material.

Use of Interactivity/Modalities

See Design Guidelines

Course Environment Look and Feel

See Design Guidelines

Course Navigation

See Design Guidelines

Consistent Course Elements

PMI Matrix

A PDF or graphic will be available on the resource page for each course that shows the courses in relation to the PMI knowledge areas and processes.

New Approach to Module One

Rather than starting each course with the typical first module that describes the course and how to use the e-learning environment, we will create a link to a standard module, one from each course, that learners can access only if they feel they need this extra help. The design of the courses should be intuitive enough and contain contextual instructions (i.e., tutors) to make the courses easy to navigate without requiring learners to complete a series of introductory lessons before getting to the course content.

Table I.2

Instructional Requirement, Content Type, or Learning Objective	Toolkit Element	Description, Example
Evaluate deliverables: Review a document and apply a set of criteria		Review excerpt of a project charter and find faulty assumptions.
Predict the impact of change within a system	Manipulate and observe variables	Observe how changes to one part of the triple constraint (scope) affect the other aspects (cost, time, and quality).
Make decisions and tradeoffs	Goal-based choice	Given a goal or priority (time to market is most important), make a choice and predict the implications it will have for the rest of the system (cost goes up or quality may go down). Feedback lets you observe the results of your choice and see if you were correct in your prediction.
Respond to a chain of events	Branching scenarios	
Compare multiple problem-solving methods, multiple perspectives on an issue	Practitioner panel	The panel members each share how they approach team building in their organizations.
Compare multiple approaches and identify the best for a given situation	Practitioner panel (w/choice)	The panel members each share their estimating technique (parametric modeling vs. historical data) for getting to a cost estimate. Learner selects the most appropriate for the situation.
Identify a type within category (i.e., "What kind of ( ) is this?")	Scenario categorization	Given a scenario, learner is asked to select the type of risk analysis depicted in the scenario.

Table I.2   (Continued)

Instructional Requirement, Content Type, or Learning Objective	Toolkit Element	Description, Example
Analyze multiple sources of information and make a judgment	Case file	Review the WBS and the activity list and look for discrepancies. Review "dossiers" of potential team members and select the best candidates.
Work outside the learning environment	On-your-own exercise	Use an optional tool (such as MS Project® or Excel) to complete an activity. Apply principles to actual project in the real world.
Express relationships	Drag-and-drop diagram creator	Drag work packages into the proper relationships to create a work breakdown structure. Drag team members into an organizational chart. Drag risks into the severity/ likelihood matrix.

First and Final Lessons—Consistent Approach

The first and final lessons in each module will follow a consistent framework and include the following elements:

- An intriguing question (for example, "Do you know the most common cause of scope creep on a project?").
- A summary of the skills taught in the module, described simply and in the context of the scenario (for example, "Now it's time to create a baseline budget for this project. You've already estimated the resources you need, so it's time to attach actual dollars. When you complete the module, you should have budget for XYZ project.").

- The perspective of the Practitioner Panel on the subject (for example, "In my field, I have to make sure that my budget reflects . . .").
- A PMI icon that pops up a window showing the PMI knowledge areas and process groups addressed by the module (This module addresses activity duration, estimating, and activity sequencing in the Planning Phase of a project.).
- An icon that indicates where the learner is in the context of the course, that is, a visual progress marker.

The final lesson of a module will include the following components:

- The answer to the initial question posed in the first lesson (which should have been answered also somewhere in the module).
- A summary of key points—just a few sentences.
- A sidebar link to a list of new terms (with glossary links).
- A link to a module-end quiz.

In addition, these first and final lessons should have a modular, visual magazine-style layout with minimal scrolling and text.

Integration Icon

To address areas where different knowledge areas intersect, we will create icons that indicate the integration of multiple areas. For example, there may be a communication aspect within Control as one needs to report project health to stakeholders. These sidebars will help to emphasize the related nature of the components.

"More" Icon or link

Rather than placing all of the instructional text on the page, the paragraphs should focus on the main point and then provide a link that opens a sidebar window that goes into more depth. This will support the layered feeling of the learning environment and minimize text on the "base page."

Practitioner Panel

This virtual panel of project managers will appear in lessons and "try it" exercises to shed light on multiple approaches. The members of the panel will have distinctive profiles—varied by industry, work style, age, and organization type—that will provide vehicles for exploring the complexity of project management among a wide range of businesses.

QuickChecks

Standard QuickChecks will be used in lessons, as necessary, to confirm understanding of foundation concepts.

Use of Collaboration

Tutors and Discussion will both be used in these courses. (See Assessments for a description of tutor use.) The Discussion Area will be structured according to "issues" or "hot topics" rather than module titles or course topics. Suggestions to read and contribute to the discussion should be integrated, to the greatest extent possible, into the course activities. The discussion area will be seeded with comments from the practitioner panel characters and, if possible, tutors should be asked to continue to seed the area with these types of comments in the "voice" of the practitioners.

About the Author

Josh Bersin has spent the majority of his career in sales, marketing, product management, and product development. He developed, managed, and participated in many training programs at IBM, Sybase, and other large corporations. In the early 1980s he participated in one of the most extensive and successful blended learning programs in the world: IBM's Entry Market Education, the "sales school" for all new field sales and technical representatives. It involved a rich mix of online, in-person, and simulation-based experiences—and was tremendously effective.

In the late 1990s he entered the e-learning market as one of the early members of a pioneering company in the Learning Management Systems market, Arista Knowledge Systems. In 2000 Arista was sold to DigitalThink, a leading e-learning content development company. Bersin then spent the next eighteen months at DigitalThink running product management and marketing.

Bersin found while working with dozens of companies embarking on e-learning that quick wins are easy, but that real success was elusive. So in late 2001 he left DigitalThink to focus on research and consulting. Bersin and his group's mission is to research "What Works" in large corporate e-learning programs with the goal of identifying the best practices, lessons learned, and repeatable methodologies that others can use. He focuses on practical and proven approaches that drive cost-effective business impact. This book is the result of this work.

Index

A

Accenture, 22
Activity reports, 239fig
Activity tracking level, 50
AICC (Aviation Industry CBT Committee), 8–10, 168, 225
Aligning training/business objectives, 27–29, 28fig
Arthur Andersen, 101
Articulate, 171, 191
Assessment tools, 201
ASTD's 2003 survey, 15
Attention getting process, 43–45
Audience issues: cost per learner and audience size, 131, 132; model selection and, 101–105
Audio/video streaming tools, 201
Auditory learners, 32–33
Authorware, 7, 12, 190, 191, 230

B

Bandwidth requirements, 116
Bersin, J., 24, 217
Blended learning: What Works study: described, 119, 129–130; findings on program cost per learner, 132–134; metrics of, 131t; models used in, 130t; on wide variety of costs, 130–131
Blended learning: economics of, 123–124; example of early, 4–5; future of, 246–247; history of development, 1–12; impact on achieving mastery, 42; importance of, 245–246; savings due to transition to, 129–135, 140, 142
Blended learning business: alignment with business objectives, 27–29, 28fig;
certification programs, 26–27; creating measurable goals, 24–26; high-impact programs, 21–24; limited resources issue, 15–16; portfolio management and identifying high-impact investments, 16–18; as powerful business tool, 29–30; program portfolio allocation, 18–19fig; trap of "cost reduction" programs, 19–20
Blended learning design concepts: experiential learning, 39–40fig; four types of corporate training, 45–47; how people learn, 31–33; mastery of learning, 33–34; six modes of learning, 34–39; socialization/gaining attention cultural factors, 42–45; Thompson NETg Job Impact Study on, 37, 38fig, 40–42; tracking/reporting program characteristic, 47–52
Blended learning models: core-and-spoke, 56, 73–83t; e-learning self-study/other media model, 85t–86; five specific models of, 83–85t; instructor-led/self-study blended model, 85t, 86–88; live e-learning/other media model, 85t, 88–90; OTJ (on-the-job) model, 85t, 90–92; program flow, 55–56, 57–73, 83t; simulation/lab-centered model, 85t, 93–95; spray and pray approach, 57; used in *What Works* study, 130t
Blended learning models selection criterion: 1: program type, 97–98; 2: cultural goals, 99t–101, 100fig; 3: audience, 101–105; 4: budget, 105–106, 141t; 5: resources, 106–111; 6: time, 111–113; 7: learning content, 113–115; 8: technology, 115–117
Books (media type), 154t

British Airways, 104

British Telcom's Mobile-Commerce sales training, 50–51

British Telecom sales training, 65, 66*fig*, 67

British Telecom's M-commerce, 155

British Airways learning portal, 224*fig*

Budget: computing cost per learner, 122–123; economics of blended learning and, 123–124; five components of, 124–129; savings due to transition to blended learning, 129–135, 140, 142; as selecting model criterion, 105–106, 141*t*; sizing the, 120–122

Budget components: content development costs, 124–125; delivery costs, 106, 126–127; instrastructure costs (LMS, hardware, and software), 125–126; learner time and travel, 129; program management costs, 127–128

Budget Worksheet, 136*e*–139*e*

Budget Worksheet Application, 135, 140*fig*

Business/financial numeric simulations, 197, 199–200, 201*fig*

C

Camtasia, 230

Camtasia Producer, 195*fig*

CD-ROM based courseware: delivery costs of, 127; as media type, 147*t*

CD-ROM Era: lessons learned from, 9–10, 11*t*; overview of, 6–7

Celebrity instructors, 155

Centra, 201, 230

Certification programs/training (type 4): core-and-spoke model used in, 76–77*fig*; as corporate training type, 45–47, 46*fig*, 157–158; media salability in, 159–160; unique characteristics of, 26–27

Certification tracking level, 51–52

Cisco's Certified Network Engineer program, 103

Click2Learn, 7

CNA "Coffee Shop," 72*fig*

CNA's performance management program, 155–156

Collaboration media type, 151*t*–152*t*

Company C retail sales training, 80

Company F's new hire call-center training, 60*t*, 67–69, 68*fig*

Complete courseware development tools, 200

Completion tracking level, 50–51

Content delivery system, 220–221

Content development: business strategy for, 180*e*–181*e*; costs of, 124–125; developing a program plan stage of, 180; developing standards stage of, 181–183; development tools used during, 189–193*fig*; e-learning, 184–186, 185*fig*; instructional design team and, 178–179; instructional plan stage of, 180–181, 182*fig*; live e-learning or Webinar, 187–189*fig*, 188*fig*; making content reusable, 183–184; outsourcing, 202–204; of simulations, 193–200*fig*, 201*fig*; tips and techniques used in, 200–202; typical challenges of, 179. *See also* Development time (target launch date)

Content flow model, 77

Content mix: complexity of, 113–114*fig*; durability of, 160–161, 162*fig*, 163*fig*; interactivity (learning by doing) of, 114–115; network and PCs to access, 104–105; program type as driving, 47; shelf life of, 113; time to build vs. shelf life of, 163–165, 164*fig*

Contest marketing, 231*fig*

Core-and-spoke model: benefits of using, 74, 77–78; compared to content flow model, 77; compared to program flow model, 73, 83*t*; described, 56; lesson learned about, 82; overview of, 73–74

Core-and-spoke model examples: Company C retail sales training, 80; used in IT certification programs, 76–77*fig*; Safari Books Online, 74, 75*fig*; semiconductor manufacturing engineer training, 79*fig*; Skillsoft's Books 24X7 division, 74, 76*fig*; U.S. Navy executive education, 80–82*fig*, 81*fig*

Corporate training types: examples of, 49*t*; listed, 46*t*; overview of, 45–47

Cost reduction program, 19–20

Critical knowledge transfer program, 45–47, 46*fig*, 155–156

Culture-building goals: ILT medium appropriate for, 155; model selection criterion, 99*t*–100*fig*

D

Dean, B., 164
Delivery mode reports, 240*fig*
Delivery/deployment budget, 106, 126–127
Dell Computer, 94
"Delta training," 155
Design concepts. *See* Blended learning design concepts
Development budget, 105
Development time (target launch date): avoiding long cycles of, 165–166; described, 112. *See also* Content development
Development tools: decisions on purchasing/using, 229–230; described, 189–193*fig*; examples/types listed, 200–201; learning technology/infrastructure built with, 222; Lectora, 193*fig*; selecting tool set, 191–192; tips on using, 201; Trainersoft, 192*fig*
DigitalThink, 181
Discussion learning process, 155
Display standards, 116
Doing (experiential learning): described, 33, 37; research supporting value of, 39–40*fig*
DreamWeaver, 108, 190, 192, 229
Durability issue, 160–161, 162*fig*, 163*fig*
Dynamic animation/graphics tools, 200

E

E-learning: British Airways's facilitation of, 104; challenge of utilizing, 224*fig*; content development process for, 194–196, 195*fig*; difference between costs of of instructor-led and, 124; experiential learning in, 39; Grant Thronton live e-learning meeting room, 111*fig*; interactivity used in, 49; Rapid e-learning tools/courseware, 57, 109–111; socialization/gaining attention factors ignored in, 43. *See also* Live e-learning/other media model
E-learning self-study/other media model, 85*t*–86
ElementK, 74, 221
Enrollment reports, 238*fig*
Enrollment tracking level, 50
EPSS (Electronic Performance Support Systems), 164

Executive summary reports, 241*fig*
Experiential learning: described, 33, 37; research supporting value of, 39–40*fig*
Expert instructors, 155

F

Feedback and conclusion event, 61
Field coordinators, 234–235
Final assessment event, 60–61
Firefly, 191, 230
Fireworks, 229
Flash, 12, 108, 170, 190, 192, 230
FrontPage, 190, 229

G

GAAP (Generally Accepted Accounting Practices), 21
General Motors, 6
"Generation Y" children, 245
Giant Eagle Foods, 102–103, 233, 234
Goals: creating measurable, 24–26; cultural and motivational, 45; culture-building, 99*t*–100; culture-building vs. performance, 100*fig*–101
Grant Thornton: blended learning paradigm used by, 152, 154; live e-learning meeting room used by, 111*fig*; Webcast design/development process, 153*fig*; webcasting (live e-learning) as core training medium by, 100–101; webinars development process/use by, 187–189*fig*, 190*fig*

H

Hearing mode of learning, 36–37
High-impact programs, 21–24
HIPPAA rules, 27, 167
Hosted third-party content, 221
HTML knowledge, 108
HTML web development tools, 190, 230

I

IBM, 6, 38, 115, 158
ILT (instructor-led training): appropriate use/selection of, 143, 155–156; description of traditional, 1, 3; difference between costs of e-learning and, 124; savings from transition to blended learning from, 129–135, 140–142

Impactica, 171

InfoPack, 230

Information broadcast programs, 45–47, 46*fig*, 154–155

Infrastructure. *See* Learning technology/infrastructure

Initial Learning Activity, 59

Instructional design team: content development and, 178–179; program manager, 106, 168; project manager, 106–107, 168; SMEs (subject-matter experts), 108–111, 168, 184–187, 200–201; Web developer, 108, 178

Instructional design tools, 201

Instructional designer: content development and, 168; model selection and, 107–108

Instructional plan, 180–181, 182*fig*

Instructor-led training tools, 190

Instructor-led/self-study blended model, 85*t*, 86–88

Intel, 34

Interactivities: CNA blended learning use of, 70–73; content (learning by doing), 114–115; defining, 39, 114; e-learning, 49

Internet access, 104–105

Interwise, 201, 230

J

Java script, 108

K

Kelly, T., 217

Kickoff event, 58–59

Kinesthetic learners, 33

Kinko's, 113–114*fig*

Knowledgeware, 230

L

LCMS (learning content management system), 220–221, 222, 229–230

Learner satisfaction tracking level, 52

Learners: audience size and cost per, 131, 132; computing cost per, 122–123, 130–131*t*; infrastructure for supporting, 232–233; time and travel costs to, 129, 133–134; *What Works* study findings on cost per, 132–134

Learning: audience motivation for, 103; content plus context requirement of, 9; experiential, 33; research on process of, 31–33; six modes of, 34–39, 35*fig*; visual, auditory, and kinesthetic, 32–33

Learning by teaching, 38–39

Learning Delivery Continuum, 190*fig*

Learning labs, 233–234

Learning portal, 223–224*fig*

Learning technology/infrastructure: content delivery system, 220–221; development tools, 222, 229–230; hosted third-party content, 221; LCMS (learning content management system), 220–221, 222; for learner support and operations, 232–233; learning portal, 223–224*fig*; media selection and; model selection and, 115–117; network, 222–223; purchasing decisions on, 226–227; review of blended, 217–218*fig*. *See also* LMS (learning management systems); Technology-based training

Lectora, 190, 193*fig*, 230

Line management communication, 238*fig*–241*fig*

Live e-learning meeting room, 111*fig*

Live e-learning tools, 201

Live e-learning/other media model: blending of self-study and, 150–151*t*, 152, 154; content development of, 187–189*fig*, 190*fig*; description of, 85*t*; examples of best practices in, 150, 152, 154; when to use, challenges and examples of, 88–90. *See also* E-learning; Synchronous events

LMS (learning management systems): budget costs of, 125–126; budget issues of providing, 106; certification criteria found in, 52; completion information stored in, 50; decisions on using, 227–228; described, 8–10; using industry standards of tracking in, 168–169; low-cost approaches to, 228–229; Macromedia Breeze Rapid e-learning solution with embedded, 229*fig*; measuring/reporting progress and role of, 236–237; review of, 219; testing interoperability with, 221. *See also* Learning technology/infrastructure

M

Macromedia, 7
Macromedia Breeze, 110–111, 171, 191, 229*fig*
Mainframe-based training, 3–5
Managers: motivating first-line, 104; program role of, 105
Marketing program, 230–232*fig*, 231*fig*
Mastery: blending impact on achieving, 42; defining, 33–34; learning by doing required for, 114
Media selection: applying four types of training to, 47; avoiding long development cycles issue of, 165–166; content durability issue of, 160–161, 162*fig*, 163*fig*; keeping the process simple, 172, 184; matrix summary of, 173*t*; program cost and, 132; Rapid e-learning issue of, 169–172; scalability issue of, 159–160*fig*; time to build vs. shelf life, 163–165, 164*fig*; tracking and reporting issues and, 166–169; tracking standard issue and, 168–169; urgency issue of, 161–163*fig*
Media types: live vs. self-study, 150–151*t*, 152, 154; OTJ (on-the-job) exercises, 146–148
Motivation: of audience to learn, 103; encouraging first-line manager, 104

N

"National Conference" training activity (Grant Thornton), 101
National Training Laboratory, 39
NCR's global network certification program, 104, 159–160
NETg, 74, 221, 233
Network, 222–223
Newsletter marketing, 231*fig*
Ninth House, Inc.: business scenario simulation features used by, 200*fig*; leadership training program, 64*fig*
Novell, 34, 110*fig*, 115, 161
Novell's Rapid e-learning, 171*fig*–172

O

Ongoing marketing, 230–232*fig*, 231*fig*
OTJ (on-the-job) exercises: benefits of using, 158–159; diversity training

using, 148; overview of, 154*t*; retail sales training using, 147; when to use, 146–147
OTJ (on-the-job) model, 85*t*, 90–92
Outsourcing: content development, 202–204; simulation development, 201–202

P

PC CD-ROM Era: lessons learned from, 9–10, 11*t*; overview of, 6–7
PC deployment standards, 225–226
Photoshop, 190, 229
Placeware, 201, 230
Plug-in requirements, 116
PowerPoint, 109, 110, 170–171, 190
PowerSim, 201*fig*
Program design: blended learning design concepts used in, 31–52, 38*fig*, 40*fig*; characteristics for each type, 48*t*; program type as driving, 47
Program flow model: benefits of, 61–62; compared to core-and-spoke model, 73, 83*t*; described, 55–56; overview of, 57–61
Program flow model examples: British Telecom sales training, 65, 66*fig*, 67; CNA Insurance leadership and executive training, 69–73; Company F's new hire call-center training, 60*t*, 67–69, 68*fig*; Ninth House leadership training, 64*fig*–65; process steps illustrated, 58*fig*; Roche Pharmaceuticals SAP rollout, 62*fig*–63
Program flow model steps: feedback and conclusion event, 61; final assessment event, 60–61; Initial Learning Activity, 59; kickoff event, 58–59
Program lifecycle, 112*fig*, 225*fig*, 235*fig*–236. *See also* Time issues
Program management: challenge of utilizing e-learning and, 233–234*fig*; communicating with line management, 238*fig*–241*fig*; communicating with upper management, 237–238; costs of, 127–128; executive/management support of, 227–229; field coordinators role in, 234–235; learning labs technique for, 233–234; measuring/reporting progress as part of, 235*fig*–237;

Program management (*Continued*)
ongoing marketing, 230–232*fig*,
231*fig*; program launch, 226–227;
reviewing program schedule, 225–226;
specific launch events, 229–230; support and operations infrastructure,
232–233
Program manager: content development
and, 168; model selection and, 106
Program plan, 180
Program schedule, 225–226
Program types: 1: information broadcast
programs, 45–47, 46*fig*, 154–155; 2:
critical knowledge transfer programs,
45–47, 46*fig*, 155–156; 3: skills and
competency programs, 45–47, 46*fig*,
156–157; as model selection criterion,
97–98. *See also* Certification programs/
training (type 4)
Project manager: content development
and, 168; model selection and,
106–107

Q

Questionmark, 191, 230

R

Rapid e-learning: Macromedia Breeze
Rapid e-learning solution with
embedded LMS, 229*fig*; media
selection and, 169–172; Novell's,
171*fig*–172; tools used in, 57,
109–111
Reading mode of learning, 35
Resource issues: instructional designer,
107–108; as model selection criterion,
106–111; program manager, 106; project manager, 106–107; SMEs (subject-matter experts), 108–111; web
developer, 108
Retention: experiential learning driving,
40*fig*; Thompson NETg Job Impact
Study on, 40–42
RoboDemo, 191, 230
Roche Pharmaceuticals, 115, 184
Roche Pharmaceuticals SAP rollout,
62*fig*–63
ROI (return on investment) of training,
129
RWD Technologies, 115

S

Sabre learning portal, 224*fig*
Safari Books Online, 74, 75*fig*
Sarbanes Oxley compliance, 167
Sarbanes-Oxley Bill, 27
Satellite-based live video, 5–6
Scalability issues, 159–160*fig*
Scenario-based simulations, 197, 198*fig*,
199*fig*, 200*fig*
Score tracking level, 51
Score/learning results reports, 241*fig*
SCROM (Sharable Content Object
Reference Model), 8–9, 168, 225
Security standards, 116
Seeing mode of learning, 35–36
Self-study media: blending of live and,
150–151*t*, 152, 154; described,
159–160; pros/cons of live vs., 151*t*;
typical learning activity in, 226*fig*
Semiconductor manufacturing engineer
training, 79*fig*
Siemens, 21, 22, 94, 121–122, 199,
236–237
Simulation content development: busi-
ness/financial numeric simulations,
197, 199–200, 201*fig*; overview of,
193–194; scenario-based simulations,
197, 198*fig*, 199*fig*, 200*fig*; software
application simulations, 194–196,
195*fig*
Simulation/lab-centered model, 85*t*,
93–95
Simulations: benefits of using, 194*fig*;
content development of, 193–200*fig*,
201*fig*; deployment risks of, 117;
described, 39; outsourcing specialized
skills for, 201–202
Skills/competency development program,
45–47, 46*fig*, 156–157
Skillsoft, 221
Skillsoft's Books 24X7 division, 74, 76*fig*
SMEs (subject-matter experts): content
development and, 168–169; e-learning content development process and
role of, 184–185; Grant Thornton's
approach to using, 187–188; learner
questions addressed by, 233; model
selection and, 108–111; working with,
186–187, 200–201
Socialization process, 42–45
Spray and pray approach, 57

SQL, 108

Standards: AICC (Aviation Industry CBT Committee), 8–10, 168, 225; content development and, 181–183; PC deployment, 225–226; SCROM (Sharable Content Object Reference Model), 8–9, 168, 225; using and setting technology, 225–226. *See also* Tracking standards

Stanford University Interactive TV network, 6

Static graphics tools, 190

Survey tools, 201

Survey/satisfaction reports, 240*fig*

Synchronous events, 159. *See also* Live e-learning/other media model

T

Target end date, 113

Technology-based training: evolution of, 1, 2*fig*; learning management systems/AICC, 8–10; mainframe-based training as first, 3–5; PC CD-ROM Era of, 6–7, 9–10, 11*t*; Web-based training, 10, 12. *See also* Learning technology/infrastructure

Thompson NETg Job Impact Study, 37, 38*fig*, 40–42

Time issues: development time (target launch date), 112, 165–166; model selection and, 111–113; program costs and, 133–134; time to build vs. shelf life, 163–165, 164*fig*; urgency as, 161–163*fig*. *See also* Program lifecycle

Toolbook, 7

Tracking and reporting: activity reports, 239*fig*; delivery mode reports, 240*fig*; enrollment reports, 238*fig*; executive summary reports, 241*fig*; five levels of, 50–52; issue of, 47, 50; media selection and issue of, 166–168; score/learning results reports, 241*fig*; survey/satisfaction reports, 240*fig*

Tracking standards: AICC (Aviation Industry CBT Committee), 8–10, 168; media selection and, 168–169; model selection and, 116; SCROM (Sharable Content Object Reference Model), 8–9, 168. *See also* Standards

Trainersoft, 190, 192*fig*, 230

Training: aligning business objectives with, 27–29, 28*fig*; certification, 26–27, 45–47, 46*fig*; creating measurable goals for, 24–26; evolution of technology-based, 1, 2*fig*; four types of corporate, 45–47, 46*fig*; instructor-led, 1, 3; mainframe-based, 3–5; ROI (return on investment) of, 129; satellite-based live video, 5–6; trap of "cost reduction" program, 19–20; Web-based, 10, 12

Training Investment Model: overview of, 16–18, 17*fig*; program portfolio allocation under, 18–19*fig*

Trivantis, 181

Types of corporate training. *See* Corporate training types

U

United Airlines, 233–234

Upper management communication, 237–238

Urgency issue, 161–163*fig*

U.S. Navy executive education, 80–82*fig*, 81*fig*

U.S. Navy Flag Executive Education, 102

V

Verizon, 91–92, 160, 226, 227*fig*

Visual learners, 32

W

Watching mode of learning, 36–37

Web developer: content development and, 168; model selection and, 108

Web development, program cost and in-house vs. outsourced, 132

Web-based application simulation tools, 201

Web-based courseware, 36*fig*

Web-based training, 10, 12

Webex, 201, 230

Webinars (live e-learning): content development of, 187–189*fig*, 190*fig*; description of, 85*t*, 88–90; live vs. self-study media used in, 151*t*

Wells Fargo, 94

Pfeiffer Publications Guide

This guide is designed to familiarize you with the various types of Pfeiffer publications. The formats section describes the various types of products that we publish; the methodologies section describes the many different ways that content might be provided within a product. We also provide a list of the topic areas in which we publish.

FORMATS

In addition to its extensive book-publishing program, Pfeiffer offers content in an array of formats, from fieldbooks for the practitioner to complete, ready-to-use training packages that support group learning.

FIELDBOOK Designed to provide information and guidance to practitioners in the midst of action. Most fieldbooks are companions to another, sometimes earlier, work, from which its ideas are derived; the fieldbook makes practical what was theoretical in the original text. Fieldbooks can certainly be read from cover to cover. More likely, though, you'll find yourself bouncing around following a particular theme, or dipping in as the mood, and the situation, dictate.

HANDBOOK A contributed volume of work on a single topic, comprising an eclectic mix of ideas, case studies, and best practices sourced by practitioners and experts in the field.

An editor or team of editors usually is appointed to seek out contributors and to evaluate content for relevance to the topic. Think of a handbook not as a ready-to-eat meal, but as a cookbook of ingredients that enables you to create the most fitting experience for the occasion.

RESOURCE Materials designed to support group learning. They come in many forms: a complete, ready-to-use exercise (such as a game); a comprehensive resource on one topic (such as conflict management) containing a variety of methods and approaches; or a collection of like-minded activities (such as icebreakers) on multiple subjects and situations.

TRAINING PACKAGE An entire, ready-to-use learning program that focuses on a particular topic or skill. All packages comprise a guide for the facilitator/trainer and a workbook for the participants. Some packages are supported with additional media—such as video—or learning aids, instruments, or other devices to help participants understand concepts or practice and develop skills.

- *Facilitator/trainer's guide* Contains an introduction to the program, advice on how to organize and facilitate the learning event, and step-by-step instructor notes. The guide also contains copies of presentation materials—handouts, presentations, and overhead designs, for example—used in the program.

- *Participant's workbook* Contains exercises and reading materials that support the learning goal and serves as a valuable reference and support guide for participants in the weeks and months that follow the learning event. Typically, each participant will require his or her own workbook.

ELECTRONIC CD-ROMs and web-based products transform static Pfeiffer content into dynamic, interactive experiences. Designed to take advantage of the searchability, automation, and ease-of-use that technology provides, our e-products bring convenience and immediate accessibility to your workspace.

METHODOLOGIES

CASE STUDY A presentation, in narrative form, of an actual event that has occurred inside an organization. Case studies are not prescriptive, nor are they used to prove a point; they are designed to develop critical analysis and decision-making skills. A case study has a specific time frame, specifies a sequence of events, is narrative in structure, and contains a plot structure—an issue (what should be/have been done?). Use case studies when the goal is to enable participants to apply previously learned theories to the circumstances in the case, decide what is pertinent, identify the real issues, decide what should have been done, and develop a plan of action.

ENERGIZER A short activity that develops readiness for the next session or learning event. Energizers are most commonly used after a break or lunch to stimulate or refocus the group. Many involve some form of physical activity, so they are a useful way to counter post-lunch lethargy. Other uses include transitioning from one topic to another, where "mental" distancing is important.

EXPERIENTIAL LEARNING ACTIVITY (ELA) A facilitator-led intervention that moves participants through the learning cycle from experience to application (also known as a Structured Experience). ELAs are carefully thought-out designs in which there is a definite learning purpose and intended outcome. Each step—everything that participants do during the activity—facilitates the accomplishment of the stated goal. Each ELA includes complete instructions for facilitating the intervention and a clear statement of goals, suggested group size and timing, materials required, an explanation of the process, and, where appropriate, possible variations to the activity. (For more detail on Experiential Learning Activities, see the Introduction to the *Reference Guide to Handbooks and Annuals*, 1999 edition, Pfeiffer, San Francisco.)

GAME A group activity that has the purpose of fostering team spirit and togetherness in addition to the achievement of a pre-stated goal. Usually contrived—undertaking a desert expedition, for example—this type of learning method offers an engaging means for participants to demonstrate and practice business and interpersonal skills. Games are effective for team building and personal development mainly because the goal is subordinate to the process—the means through which participants reach decisions, collaborate, communicate, and generate trust and understanding. Games often engage teams in "friendly" competition.

ICEBREAKER A (usually) short activity designed to help participants overcome initial anxiety in a training session and/or to acquaint the participants with one another. An icebreaker can be a fun activity or can be tied to specific topics or training goals. While a useful tool in itself, the icebreaker comes into its own in situations where tension or resistance exists within a group.

INSTRUMENT A device used to assess, appraise, evaluate, describe, classify, and summarize various aspects of human behavior. The term used to describe an instrument depends primarily on its format and purpose. These terms include survey, questionnaire, inventory, diagnostic, survey, and poll. Some uses of instruments include providing instrumental feedback to group members, studying here-and-now processes or functioning within a group, manipulating group composition, and evaluating outcomes of training and other interventions.

Instruments are popular in the training and HR field because, in general, more growth can occur if an individual is provided with a method for focusing specifically on his or her own behavior. Instruments also are used to obtain information that will serve as a basis for change and to assist in workforce planning efforts.

Paper-and-pencil tests still dominate the instrument landscape with a typical package comprising a facilitator's guide, which offers advice on administering the instrument and interpreting the collected data, and an initial set of instruments. Additional instruments are available separately. Pfeiffer, though, is investing heavily in e-instruments. Electronic instrumentation provides effortless distribution and, for larger groups particularly, offers advantages over paper-and-pencil tests in the time it takes to analyze data and provide feedback.

LECTURETTE A short talk that provides an explanation of a principle, model, or process that is pertinent to the participants' current learning needs. A lecturette is intended to establish a common language bond between the trainer and the participants by providing a mutual frame of reference. Use a lecturette as an introduction to a group activity or event, as an interjection during an event, or as a handout.

MODEL A graphic depiction of a system or process and the relationship among its elements. Models provide a frame of reference and something more tangible, and more easily remembered, than a verbal explanation. They also give participants something to "go on," enabling them to track their own progress as they experience the dynamics, processes, and relationships being depicted in the model.

ROLE PLAY A technique in which people assume a role in a situation/ scenario: a customer service rep in an angry-customer exchange, for example. The way in which the role is approached is then discussed and feedback is offered. The role play is often repeated using a different approach and/or incorporating changes made based on feedback received. In other words, role playing is a spontaneous interaction involving realistic behavior under artificial (and safe) conditions.

SIMULATION A methodology for understanding the interrelationships among components of a system or process. Simulations differ from games in that they test or use a model that depicts or mirrors some aspect of reality in form, if not necessarily in content. Learning occurs by studying the effects of change on one or more factors of the model. Simulations are commonly used to test hypotheses about what happens in a system—often referred to as "what if?" analysis—or to examine best-case/worst-case scenarios.

THEORY A presentation of an idea from a conjectural perspective. Theories are useful because they encourage us to examine behavior and phenomena through a different lens.

TOPICS

The twin goals of providing effective and practical solutions for workforce training and organization development and meeting the educational needs of training and human resource professionals shape Pfeiffer's publishing program. Core topics include the following:

Leadership & Management

Communication & Presentation

Coaching & Mentoring

Training & Development

E-Learning

Teams & Collaboration

OD & Strategic Planning

Human Resources

Consulting

What will you find on pfeiffer.com?

- The best in workplace performance solutions for training and HR professionals

- Downloadable training tools, exercises, and content

- Web-exclusive offers

- Training tips, articles, and news

- Seamless on-line ordering

- Author guidelines, information on becoming a Pfeiffer Affiliate, and much more

Discover more at www.pfeiffer.com

Customer Care

Have a question, comment, or suggestion? Contact us! We value your feedback and we want to hear from you.

For questions about this or other Pfeiffer products, you may contact us by:

E-mail: **customer@wiley.com**

Mail: **Customer Care Wiley/Pfeiffer**
10475 Crosspoint Blvd.
Indianapolis, IN 46256

Phone: **(US) 800-274-4434** (Outside the US: 317-572-3985)

Fax: **(US) 800-569-0443** (Outside the US: 317-572-4002)

To order additional copies of this title or to browse other Pfeiffer products, visit us online at **www.pfeiffer.com**.

For **Technical Support** questions call **(800) 274-4434.**

For authors guidelines, log on to www.pfeiffer.com and click on "Resources for Authors."

If you are . . .

A **college bookstore, a professor, an instructor, or work in higher education** and you'd like to place an order or request an exam copy, please contact jbreview@wiley.com.

A **general retail bookseller** and you'd like to establish an account or speak to a local sales representative, contact Melissa Grecco at 201-748-6267 or mgrecco@wiley.com.

An **exclusively on-line bookseller**, contact Amy Blanchard at 530-756-9456 or ablanchard @wiley.com or Jennifer Johnson at 206-568-3883 or jjohnson@wiley.com, both of our Online Sales department.

A **librarian or library representative**, contact John Chambers in our Library Sales department at 201-748-6291 or jchamber@wiley.com.

A **reseller, training company/consultant, or corporate trainer**, contact Charles Regan in our Special Sales department at 201-748-6553 or cregan@wiley.com.

A **specialty retail distributor** (includes specialty gift stores, museum shops, and corporate bulk sales), contact Kim Hendrickson in our Special Sales department at 201-748-6037 or khendric@wiley.com.

Purchasing for the **Federal government**, contact Ron Cunningham in our Special Sales department at 317-572-3053 or rcunning@wiley.com.

Purchasing for a **State or Local government**, contact Charles Regan in our Special Sales department at 201-748-6553 or cregan@wiley.com.